Tragic Fools

Kim Cormack

Copyright © 2020 by Kim Cormack

All rights reserved.

No part of this book may be reproduced in any form or by any electronic or mechanical means, including information storage and retrieval systems, without written permission from the author, except for the use of brief quotations in a book review.

Mythomedia Press 2754 10th Ave

V9Y2N9 Port Alberni BC

ACKNOWLEDGMENTS

To my wonderful parents, I wish we didn't have to rain check the big 50th anniversary party you deserve. The 2020 pandemic is going on, and we're responsible humans. It will make future generations proud. Your love is truly inspiring. Thank you for always loving us unconditionally.

To my awesome offspring, I love you more than words can express. I love you always and forever, Jace and Cam. Our family has evolved in many ways. Jace, you are my baby bird. Cam, you are my sweet prince. Our unconventional family, full of love and laughter, will always be my greatest accomplishment.

I don't know what I'd do without my release fun editing trio. You are so appreciated. Haley McGee, my editing goddess, thank you for always cruising me through the first round of editing like a comedy smackdown. My partner in debauchery, Dragon love xo.

Leanne Ruissen, my grammar goddess, you catch those mistakes that would have snuck through without your eye and expertise and point out places in need of clarity. You rock xo.

Thank you for being my first beta reader before putting the book out there, Tasha Lee. You are awesome xo.

My incredible series readers, you make me feel like my imagination has a greater purpose. Your emails, messages and reviews make my day. This has been a difficult year. Some of us have been sick, others have lost loved ones. I hope this series brings you laughter and joy. Be good humans. Stay strong. No judgment. No fear.

The tentacles and chess pieces were deviations from deviant art. There are links to the artist of each on my page. The dragon eye pendant on the cover can be purchased using this link. http://wwww.esty.com/shop/BlueRoseCreationsBRC

To Everyone in Essential Services

This has been a challenging year. We've been forced to see past ourselves to save our elderly and immune-compromised. Thank you for your strength. Thank you for bearing a load too heavy to carry. Thank you for every time you went to work afraid. Thank you for the heartbreak and trauma you've endured. You are the true heroes.

WARNING

The information contained within this book is not intended for mortals. Reading this may inadvertently trigger a Correction. If you survive or have shown great bravery during your demise, you may be given a second chance at life by the Guardians of the in-between. For your soul's protection, you must join one of three Clans of immortals living on Earth. Clan Ankh, Trinity or Triad will train your partially mortal brain to reboot without a shock response and attach you to your Testing Group, then you will be taken to another world and dropped into Immortal Testing to prove after dying thousands of times, you comprehend the greater good and would never leave your fallen behind. You will be returned to Earth to serve an eternity in Tri-Clan, training Correction survivours, maintaining order and protecting the mortal population from themselves. You are still reading this, aren't you? Welcome to your afterlife.

The end of her life was only the beginning of her story...

1
PSYCHIC EX ISSUES

*T*he bliss of sun-kissed skin awakened her. Twitching fingers in velvety sand as a heavenly breeze tickled her spine, Kayn peered up, grinning. *Somebody gave her an immortal time out.* Even with unlimited free passes to the in-between, a surprise trip was jarring until she recalled why she died. *Who killed her this time?* Cross-legged in pristine desert with silky granules trickling through fingers, her memory kicked in, clarifying why she was deceased. *Lexy knocked on her door and took her out of the equation. Their Oracle must have caught Kevin telepathically asking her to warn him before Ankh stole the girl he had a thing for. Her attachment to him was always getting her in trouble. She shouldn't be having conversations with an ex-boyfriend while in bed with her new one. Frost's patience had to be wearing thin. They'd just been separated as punishment for killing Kevin at a banquet. She tossed her ex off a balcony for giving her a clover. It was still funny.* Sensing a presence, Kayn got up, squinting in luminescence.

Ankh's Guardian Azariah sighed, "I'm beginning to think you enjoy being punished."

She didn't know what to say, she kind of did.

"Being part Guardian doesn't mean you can bend rules to your will," the angelic entity reprimanded.

Brushing the sand off her short ivory in-between attire, Kayn responded, "I wasn't going to say anything."

With divine angelic light attaching Clan Ankh's Guardian to the sky, Azariah wandered off, explaining, "That's just it, if he can tap into your mind, you have no say over what he knows."

Keeping pace, strolling the clean slate desert with warm silken sand underfoot, beneath an azure sky, Kayn thought of a monarch butterfly. An orange and black distraction flitted by as proof she wasn't focusing on what the Guardian was saying.

The angelic entity trailing radiant light, scolded, "I'm not talking to hear myself speak, child."

She wasn't a child. Now, a variety of vibrant butterflies were fluttering around. *She couldn't shut her feral imagination down.* Wincing, Kayn apologised, "I'm listening, I swear."

With a clap of her hands, distractions vanished. Smiling, Azariah carried on, "Here is the issue, Ankh needs a Venom before Immortal Testing. As you know, the Third-Tier sped up the timeline in response to the glitch your group used to get out. Currently, Triad is the only Clan with one. Your ex's crush means nothing. Residual mortal sentiment is clouding your judgement."

It was, she couldn't deny it.

BACK IN THE LAND OF the living, Ankh's Oracle voluntarily stayed with Zach to make sure Kayn remained deceased until their compromised job was finished. Relaxing on the queen-sized bed by Kayn's corpse, Jenna mindlessly flicked channels.

With Kayn's head on his lap, Zach gently stroked her hair, asking, "Do we have to keep killing her? Can't we lock her in a tomb?"

"The bracelet to block Kevin's connection isn't working. I need to tweak it. He's psychic, they're linked. Taking her out when we're dealing with Triad may be our only option."

"We all have ties to other Clans, I used to be Triad," Zach implored, meeting Jenna's eyes.

"Aren't you glad we stole you?" Jenna baited as Kayn's chest rose and fell. "Heads up, Handler. She's back."

"Can't we just keep her occupied? She doesn't know where they went," Zach bartered.

"Azariah needs time with her, a Guardian's word is law, take her out," Jenna instructed.

Looping an arm around her neck, he released his grasp as she went limp, muttering, "You're doing it next time."

"Suck it up Zach, you're immortal." Jenna teased with a smile.

EVERYTHING WAS UNCOMFORTABLY WHITE AS Kayn opened her eyes with a brief flash of waking up in the hospital after her Sweet Sleep. *This time, it wasn't Kevin*

by her side as she clued into where she was. She remembered this place. She'd been here before.

Radiance encompassed Ankh's Guardian Azariah as she helped Kayn up, praising, "Impressive regeneration time."

"I've been healing faster," Kayn admitted, grimacing as she took in where she was. *A blank white cell. The word nothing described this destination. She had concentration issues. Funny, well played Azariah, bravo. It felt like their Guardian was working up to an epic punishment reveal.*

Grinning, Azariah explained, "Time runs faster in a blank cell. Your soul can't escape or think up distractions. We'll stay here, so your Handler doesn't have to keep killing you each time you rise."

An immortal penalty box, so she couldn't think up butterflies or heal herself to escape the boredom, clever. Kayn had to ask. "Am I going to be punished?"

"Do you need to be punished?" Azariah probed with a knowing twinkle in her eye.

Damn it, she did. There was a lingering silence as it sunk in. *It felt like she could stop Kevin from having access to her mind if she wanted him gone. There it was...her truth. She wanted a way to keep their friendship alive, even if they were supposed to be enemies. Even if they always would be. He was her last attachment to a mortal simplicity that was no longer. She was going to lose the trust of her Clan. It felt like she was in the Testing again, being forced to see past mortal bonds engrained in her being.*

"Calm down, we don't want to sever the connection. The Clans join forces on occasion. We need to control the flow of information. Having two Guardian offspring in the same Clan, Ankh may require assistance as you did when Abaddon tried to force you to send a group through the Hall of Souls. My brother jumped the gun when he took the cap off your abilities. You are a spiritual anomaly, a Conduit who is part Guardian. The Third-Tier will be looking for a way to take you out of the equation to hold off the Daughters of Seth Prophecy."

It would be helpful if someone explained what the Daughters of Seth Prophecy was.

Grinning, Ankh's Guardian, replied, "Prophecies have a loose narrative. New moves come into play. It couldn't be worse timing to train a new group for Testing, with survivors in the middle of the evolution process. Believing they've set us up for failure by giving us an unbeatable scenario, reveals the Third-Tier's weakness. They underestimate us. We thrive in impossible situations. Knowing a Venom can put trapped souls into hibernation in a sleep chamber to await freedom with the next continent in gives us a way. When all is lost, all one needs is a faint glimmer of hope and courage to fight. If we find a Venom for the next Testing group, we have an insurance clause. It's that simple."

Sure, they'll just find a rare immortal being in a North American population of 346.3 million. "Do Guardian magic and point one out, I'm on it," Kayn saucily replied.

"Being confined to this spiritual plain has limitations. If you'll allow me, I'd like to have another look at the basis of your connection to the Triad," Azariah asked in shimmering light with open arms.

As Kayn stepped into the Guardian's divine embrace, the predatory Conduit was subdued by tranquillity in the root of her being. Beautiful memories floated through her stream of consciousness with easy smiles and magical healing kisses on wounded knees. She drifted off to sleep each night snuggling stuffed animals, feeling safe. She recalled easy laughter in carefree moments, racing siblings in the upstairs hallway to see who'd be first to slide on their tummy down carpeted stairs. Family days on the beach building sandcastles by the sea, turning over rocks to capture fleeing crabs. Salty ocean air through an open car window on the drive home and grape soda stains on her sleeping brother's face. Childhood sleepovers using hairbrushes as microphones, jumping on beds. Snuggling under blankets watching movies devouring bowls of pink elephant popcorn on the couch. Climbing to the highest branch of the apple tree where they'd perch to eat while viewing their entire world. In every scenario, Kevin was present or referenced to tug her heart back.

Maturing in visions, she reached the age of Correction. Blissfully unaware of her demise, she sprinted across a finish line as a track champion with Kevin overzealously cheering. Each moment, every action, forging an unbreakable bond, maturing into love, solidifying a link created by thousands of unforgettable moments.

Caressing her hair, Azariah summoned her out of the visions, whispering, "We can leave the connection open. I'm secure, he won't violate your trust."

Part of her wanted to remain in the beautiful lucid dream with only light in her soul, void of the darkness she often found herself lost in. "I wish I could go back," Kayn confessed, in her arms, pining for the simple bliss of childhood.

Knowing she wasn't ready to let go, Azariah assured, "Those memories will always be wherever you are."

"I'm not good at being immortal," Kayn mumbled.

"Who is?" Azariah taunted, stepping away to meet her eyes, lovingly tucking curls behind her ear.

"You kept Jenna for decades," Kayn sparred, smiling.

Intrigued by her choice, the Guardian disclosed, "Jenna sacrificed herself for someone else's misdeeds."

She hadn't heard this story.

Her luminescent relation explained, "We accepted an ill-advised deal believing Haley's Testing group was destined to survive. Alas, Oracle's predictions rarely come with a time stamp. Haley did survive twenty years later when intuition led her to you. Fortunately, Jenna was powerful enough to maintain duties through psychic connections."

Their Clan was soap opera. Curious, Kayn enquired, "Whose punishment did Jenna take?"

Azariah teased, "You'll figure it out."

Why aren't we using Haley?

"She's a talented intuitionist but decades lost in a Venom-induced dream state stunted Haley's Enlightening process. She isn't a viable Oracle yet," the angelic being responded to her thought.

Psychics advertise, they can't be that difficult to find. Fascinated, Kayn suggested, "Can't we just make an appointment with a psychic and snag one?"

"There are varying degrees of Clairvoyant. Only top tier has a shot at surviving Testing. The new girl Emma is top tier, but if her group can't connect, it won't matter," Azariah clarified with a genuine smile.

Standing in a blank slate room having a casual chat, Kayn forgot she was speaking to a heavenly being. *Her Aunt. That was still weird. If they stole the girl, Kevin would think she didn't care. She wasn't supposed to. She needed to get back to Frost so she could explain.* Feeling a tickle, Kayn looked at her hand as it began disintegrating into sand. *Well, this isn't supposed to happen.*

Unamused by her niece's ability to override commands, Azariah loudly clapped her hands, scowling. Kayn solidified, the miffed majestic being, reprimanded, "I haven't granted you permission to leave."

"I can't control this shit," Kayn lipped like an insolent teen.

"Are you insane? Have you forgotten who you're with?" Azariah fired back.

What was wrong with her? Kayn said, "I'm not doing it on purpose."

Furious, Azariah paced back and forth, towing a beam of sparkling light in the room of nothing, muttering, "Seth, you ignorant ass. Idiot."

Oh, shit. She broke a Guardian. Kayn nervously, apologised, "I'm sorry, I didn't mean to say that."

"I guess there's no point in staying here. We might as well enjoy the scenery," the luminescent being, sighed, half-assed waving her hand.

In a flash of blinding light, the pair was in a meadow of flowers, ankle-deep in lush, fragrant grass under a splotchy blue sky. *It always looked like someone tossed buckets of paint up there.* They wandered in silence. With each step into the bliss-inducing experience, fragrant flowers, gentle humming of bees and whispering butterfly's wings, reminded her of how blessed she was to be granted access to this magical world.

Out of nowhere, Azariah coyly asked, "What powers do you have?"

Her horrible excuse for a parental figure cautioned her about disclosing certain things.

Stopping, Azariah laughed, "You know I can hear your thoughts, just tell me what we're up against so we can find a way to hide it." Making herself comfortable in the grass, she prompted, "Sit, confess all, I vow to find a way to help you."

Guess there was no point in attempting to hide anything. Kayn sat by her, disclosing, "I've created orbs of light.

Blue orbs blow things up, and white ones get me in trouble, you know about that incident."

"Yes, accidentally sending forty demons through the hall of souls doesn't go unnoticed. Tri-Clan will be cleaning up that mess for years, and now, you have a target on your back. You are the magical ticket to mortality for every demon out there," Azariah chuckled, picking grass and tossed it.

Kevin always did that. Kayn's heart clenched as her thoughts travelled back to her mortal life. Steering her mind away, she confessed, "Conduit, Siren and I may have stopped a bullet or two."

"Next time, you're here we'll talk about that. I'm sensing our time is up," Azariah answered. Plucking a pink flower, the Guardian tucked it behind Kayn's ear and whispered, "Don't worry, we'll figure this out."

White light blinded her. As the glare ceased, Kayn saw Kevin's Granny in youthful form, with freckles and flowing red hair. Winnie announced, "The job is done. Kayn is free to leave."

A part of her always wanted to run into Kevin's grandmother's arms. She'd loved Granny Winnie and missed her but knew they weren't the same people. They weren't even people at all, only pawns in an immortal game. It was time to go back and deal with the fallout from her secret conversation with Kevin. If the situation were reversed, and Frost was chatting with an ex next to her in bed, she'd be hurt. Her Mother's words, sprang to mind, 'Omitting part of the truth to protect someone's feelings never works out how you think it will.' She was right. She may never have the chance to say those words, but she could honour her memory by listening to her advice.

Smiling at her inner dialogue, young Granny suggested, "Tell the truth, and let chips fall where they may. It's a long afterlife, you have nothing but time."

With that telltale glint in her eyes, she'd always know it was her, no matter what age Winnie appeared. Unable to help it, Kayn asked, "Did Ankh take the girl?" Laughing, Azariah vanished.

Used to her one-track mind, Winnie disclosed, "She was stolen by Trinity while Ankh and Triad were fighting. Kevin knows it was Trinity," Winnie replied as the scenery flashed and they were strolling through the warm, inviting desert.

This timeout was for nothing. Feeling strange, Kayn looked at her hand as she disintegrated into a cloud of golden dust and floated away on a gentle breeze.

OPENING HER EYES, WITH HER HEAD ON ZACH'S LAP IN THE land of the living. *There was panic in his eyes. Here we go.*

"Trinity may already be here. Small talk later. Get your jacket, grab your bag, we need to run," her Handler urged.

"What's going on?" Kayn said, scrambling into her boots. They sprinted down the hall, took the stairs and dashed out into the frigid Alaskan air. *Oh, sweet lord, it was cold. The RV was gone. They got left behind.*

Going back inside, Zach gave her the rundown, "Trinity snuck in and stole the Venom while Ankh and Triad were fighting at the other job. Jenna had a vision and took off. Mel came in and gave me an Aries group card, saying, if the RV is gone, don't panic, join the distractions at the pub."

Walking down the hall, Kayn vowed, "I wasn't going to tell him anything."

"I know," her Handler affirmed as they entered the pub and took off their jackets. "Game face, Brighton," he teased, as they strolled up to the counter of local riffraff. Chuckling, Zach patted down her bedhead, whispering, "You're looking recently resurrected feral this evening."

She'd been hoping it was Frost and Lily with Mel as distractions. She didn't see anyone she recognised.

Nudging her, Zach whispered, "Ten o'clock."

She glanced to her upper left and giggled. *Ten o'clock.* In an unexpected plot twist, their backup was Killian from the other continent with his massive muscular frame and wavy mane, sitting by a curvaceous black goddess so breathtaking, everyone was enamoured. With those two alluring unicorns, Mel seamlessly blended in with locals, downing shots like it was the end of the world.

Leaning in, Zach whispered in her ear, "She is insanely hot, I'm going in."

That seductive being was way out of Zach's league. He was in the minors, destined to strike out so fast, all you'd see is a blur of her blowing him off. Owing her Handler for blindly believing in her innocence, Kayn said, "Go Zach." Snickering, as they picked up their drinks and strolled over.

Killian raised his glass in greeting, "Guess we're diversion buddies, our plan to be newbie protection backup was foiled by a five-minute bathroom break. Drink up, you two. Jenna says, acting like nobody is showing up until tomorrow and looking unprepared is how we're going to buy the others enough time to get away."

"Emery," the hot stranger introduced herself, extending her perfectly manicured hand to Zach.

Awestruck, Zach shook her hand, flirting, "Your British accent is amazing."

Grinning, Amar's continent's vixen, cheekily reciprocated, "Your everything is amazing."

Wow. Zach didn't usually have girls come on this strong.

A tray of shots was placed on their table. Killian raised one, saluting, "Go hard or go home."

The table of immortals slammed three in a row, throwing caution to the wind. *Emery seemed familiar.* "Have we met?" Kayn enquired, shaking her hand.

"I was blitzed at our last banquet, it's possible. Either way, it's nice to meet you coherent," Emery toyed.

The way Mel was slamming drinks back, their play was obvious. They were expecting Thorne. Mel was the bait.

"Slow down, love. I don't want to hold your hair later while you're parking the tiger," Emery commented, coyly sipping wine, adjusting her seductively crossed legs.

Parking the tiger?

"Hurling, upchucking, technicolour yawn, ralph," Killian deciphered British slang.

"Praying to the porcelain god, barfing, boot and rally, blowing chunks, tossing your cookies," Zach commentated.

"Chilling my anxiety, it'll sting less when he ignores me. The girl Thorne was seeing made it out of Testing with the other continent. He may be over me," Mel disclosed, doing another shot.

"You're not that easy to get over, Mel," Zach affirmed, giving her hand a reassuring squeeze.

Where did she know Emery from? It was driving her crazy. All eyes darted to the door as Trinity wandered in.

Zach whispered, "Heads up."

Raking a hand through his sexy mane, Killian whispered, "Immortal lie detector in the house, get ready to pull out the big guns, Mel."

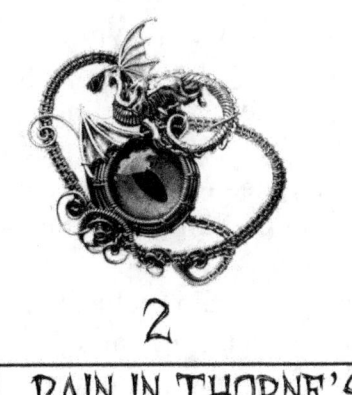

2
ROYAL PAIN IN THORNE'S ASS

*S*ome bonds can't be broken by time. Mel's eyes locked with the leader of Trinity's as he came in. *Ultimately, losing him had been a choice. She'd chosen Ankh over Trinity. It was her call.* Her time with Trinity before coming to Ankh was tumultuous. She'd been a royal pain in Thorne's ass. Guilt-ridden, she spent nearly a year trying to kill herself as penance for her family's demise. For an immortal with a healing ability, it was pointless. She lured him in with ridiculous drama. His days were devoted to convincing her she was worthy of being saved, and hers were spent proving why she wasn't. With an intense connection teetering on the edge of more, everyone knew they cared for each other. On her final night with Trinity, she was about to leap to her temporary demise when their feelings came to fruition in an explosion of passion on a cliffside beneath the stars. The next day, she ended up in Ankh.

Since becoming Ankh, whenever she found herself in the leader of Trinity's presence, either he was aggravated by the games she was playing or cautioning her to stay away during a fight so he wouldn't be forced to harm her. Tonight, Mel was plotting to use his feelings to distract him so her Clan could get away with their unsealed under eighteen Ankh. When he walked past her to the bar, she couldn't help but smile. *He wasn't stupid.*

Pulling a chair up to their table, her old friend Glory, declared, "I'll bite. Mel, Zach and Kayn, we expected. Emery and Big Sexy are a surprise. Are you here protecting Amar's kid?"

Big Sexy, that was funny.

"Go ahead, take a shot for having the balls to strut in here like you stand a chance," Killian provoked, sliding the tray over.

"They're in the hotel, aren't they?" Glory grilled, looking into Mel's eyes.

Smiling, Mel redirected their conversation, "It's nice to see you too." *She didn't have to turn around, she felt him there.* She did another shot before saying his name, "Thorne."

"Melody," Thorne responded, pulling up a chair. "Did we get here early?"

"I'm not saying a word," Mel laughed, downing another.

"You will," Thorne boldly decreed, holding her captive with piercing blue truth-seeking eyes.

She wanted him. Maybe she always would. Pretending to be carefree when she was freaking out inside was proving to be difficult.

"If you keep slamming shots, you'll tell me everything," Thorne teased, snatching a shot of whisky off their tray.

Without his fib extracting eyes leaving hers, he licked a droplet off his bottom lip, and her mind went blank. *What was she supposed to be doing?* About to match his shot, Mel put it down. *He was right. She needed to buy time, good thing she had a million things to confess. If it wasn't what he was here for, why not*? Shaking her head, Mel switched topics, "I'm glad the girl you were seeing made it out with the other continent."

"That was nothing," Thorne confessed, sliding his hand over hers like they were alone in the room. "I was just trying to stop myself from doing something reckless at a banquet."

"Me?" Mel baited with a charming, dimpled grin.

"You," Thorne disclosed. "In retrospect, we should have spent the night together for closure." Caressing her palm, he whispered, "I still miss you." Getting back on task, Trinity's leader compelled, "Is it just the five of you at the bar?"

Checking for witnesses, Mel said, "Yes." Bringing up the elephant in the room, she whispered, "You're here to steal our unsealed Ankh."

Tucking her shoulder-length brown hair behind her ears, like she usually wore it, Thorne answered, "Obviously."

He thought her nervous tick was a style choice, cute. "You won't," Mel confidently stated, sliding him another whisky.

"Trinity doesn't participate in drunk fight club," Thorne teased, downing the drink.

Grinning, Mel provoked, "What about pillow fight club? You used to love pillow fight club."

He mic dropped reality, "There were no pillows on our cliff."

Our cliff. Tears filled her eyes as the passionate encounter on a cliff beneath the stars surfaced. She whispered, "I spent a year trying to kill myself, knowing it wouldn't work because I'm immortal. How did you have the patience to deal with me? How are you so optimistic and understanding when our afterlives are this hard?"

"Because there were people like you, along the way," he admitted with a sheen of tears.

She was going to have to confess everything else to stop herself from telling him what she wasn't supposed to say. Pulling it together, Mel said, "I tuck my hair behind my ears when I'm nervous."

Playing with her hair, Thorne probed, "Do I still make you nervous?"

Mel nodded, lost in his steel blue lie extracting eyes. *No matter what she did, her heart wouldn't let go of that beautiful night. They had to get over each other this wasn't healthy.*

Tenderly kissing her hand, he admitted, "You make me nervous too. Whenever we run into each other, it aches like we lost each other yesterday. I try to stay away. I'll be arguing with myself, then you smile with those dimples and I can't."

"Thorne," she whispered as he slid a hand onto her knee.

Caressing it, he whispered, "Mel."

She wanted to tear his clothes off.

Making it clear he caught her thought, Thorne leaned in and whispered, "Right here?"

"Come to my room, so we can be alone. You foiled the job and stole the girl. You know where our backup is," Mel persuaded. *She needed to prove her heart wrong.*

Thorne suggested, "Let's go to my room where we won't be interrupted."

Worrying she was the one being played, she put it to rest knowing who he was. In this scenario, she was the bad guy. Leaving their coats on the rack, they slipped out, speed-walked down the hall, hitting nearly a jog as they scooted into the elevator, laughing. As the elevator door slid shut, their mouths met in passionate persuasion.

Breathless as their lips parted, Thorne gazed into her eyes, confessing, "I do love you."

"I've never stopped. I wish…" Her declaration of love was interrupted as the elevator door slid open, revealing a Trinity poised with bow drawn. *He'd set her up.* An arrow whooshed into her heart. Stunned, Melody dropped. Thorne cradled her in his arms as the light flickered and went out.

3
BIG SEXY SNACKS

The rest of Ankh's distractions were three sheets to the wind dancing when Ankh symbols heated beneath their fingerless gloves, letting them know one of their own was dead. They sprinted out of the pub into the hall. The elevator opened as they approached. Mel's body was on the floor with a gaping chest wound and blood pooling behind her.

Killian commented, "Taking out our only Healer, smart. Emery, there's a camera. If the footage is stored online, we'll need to call the Aries group. Zach, go with her, watch her back." They slipped out as the door closed.

"An arrow to the heart?" Killian questioned as he broke the camera and pressed garage.

Focused on willing energy into Mel, Kayn didn't reply. Mel gasped as her eyes opened.

"Impressive, you're a Healer too," Killian remarked, as he held out a hand to help her up.

Dizzy, Kayn held his gaze and said, "Trust me," as she siphoned enough energy to stay on her feet through their joined hands. Confused, the burly Adonis swayed, quickly regaining his bearings. While helping Mel up, Kayn looked at her snack and asked, "You good?"

"All good, energy thief," he chuckled, shaking his head.

His energy made her feel like she could bench press a Buick. Kayn directed, "Mel, take off your shirt and sop up as much blood as you can. Killian, give Mel your shirt so she isn't topless." They dressed, and cleaned with the elevator open, thankful for the heated landing.

Reading a text, Killian announced, "They have our bags and jackets from the bar. Trinity's coats were still in the pub. I bet they're searching the hotel. We'll have to run out to the truck without jackets. Let's go!"

Darting out into frigid two am Alaskan air through icy crackling snow, they got into the truck. Emery casually drove away from the hotel with the biggest grin as they put coats on and noticed there were too many.

Killian chuckled, "Did you take everyone's jackets?"

"I did," Emery laughed. "Zach also may have flattened the tires of every vehicle in the parking lot."

Everyone was celebrating their escape. Kayn dug through her bag praying her cell was in there. The light was blinking. *There was a message.* Afraid to read it, she stared at the flashing light. *Reality was a buzz kill. She'd been the cause of their separation again. He had to be getting sick and tired of her shit. Hell, she was getting tired of her shit.* Nobody uttered a syllable until they hit smooth highway. They started talking, avoiding the topic of ex-boyfriend's arrows. Strength shifted to fatigue as Kayn's brain recalled bringing Mel back to life. *She needed to close her eyes.*

Nudging her, Zach prompted, "Look at the message."

"So, I can see how ticked off he is? No thanks. I'll wait for the live show," Kayn said, yawning.

Zach instantly yawned. Yawning loudly, Killian scolded, "Stop that crap. I don't need to be yawning for hours."

He'd mentioned yawning. They all yawned again triggering each other in a ridiculous chain, except for Emery, which struck her as peculiar.

Snatching Kayn's phone, Mel read it, and gave it back, saying, "Yeah, he's pissed. At least he didn't seduce you into an elevator, tell you he loved you and get a Trinity to shoot an arrow into your heart when the door opened."

"Shit Mel, that's brutal, I'm sorry, hun," Zach consoled, caressing her shoulder.

"Why are you sorry? You didn't shoot an arrow into my heart?" Mel sparred, lightening the tension. Meeting Kayn's eyes, she assured, "It's not that bad. He just says you need to talk."

When though? How long would she have to wait? All Dragon excuses aside, if she wanted their relationship to last longer than five minutes, she had to start thinking about how her actions affected him. Ripping off the band-aid, Kayn texted Frost. *Full disclosure, Kevin has a thing for the Venom girl everyone wants. He must have had a vision. He asked me not to take her. You were asleep.* She gave it to Zach to read over. He looked at it and pressed send. "What in the hell, Zach? I just wanted you to read it."

He chuckled, "You'll thank me later. It would be silly for him to be ticked off after reading that. You didn't really do anything wrong, Brighton. You just omitted the truth so he wouldn't be ticked you were in bed with him, mind chatting with your ex."

Everyone else started laughing as Killian glanced back, asking, "Is Brighton American slang?"

"That's her mortal last name, Kayn's Canadian," Zach explained, grinning.

"I love that, Brighton," Killian stated. "Were you really in bed with Frost mind chatting with an ex? I'd be choked."

With her eyes on the snowy road ahead, as tires crunched on gravel-strewn icy highway, Emery shared, "If memory serves a night with Frost is many hours of cardio. I think it's badass that you bedded him and chatted with an ex. He's been a player for eight hundred years. He deserves that Karma."

Great, she wasn't going to be able to unhear that. Emery and Frost slept together.

Catching her reaction, Emery backtracked, "Sorry about just blurting that out, it was a long time ago. No big deal."

If you're going to get ticked off every time you bump into someone Frost slept with, you're going to be pissed off a lot," Killian chuckled, changing the music. Emery slapped his hand. Giggling, he playfully swatted back.

Mel changed the subject, "Where are we going?"

"We're driving east through northern B.C into Alberta to meet up with Markus' crew," Killian explained. "Who can drive? We should break this up into four-hour shifts."

Zach and Melody volunteered, Kayn admitted, "I drove once in a parking lot."

"I'll teach you how to drive," Emery laughed as the tail end of the truck swerved on black ice and recovered.

Unaffected by the drama, Killian suggested, "Pull over, I'm switching seats with Zach. Brighton stole my energy."

They stopped, leapt out into snow much deeper than it looked and comically switched up the seating arrangement. Kayn grinned as the mountainous Viking looking guy made himself comfortable, taking up a humorous amount of the backseat.

"Wake me up when it's my turn," Killian mumbled as he conked out.

She'd never seen anyone go to sleep like that. The musclebound Adonis had a breathy coo as a snore. *It was kind of adorable. Sleep was doable.* Closing her eyes, Kayn slipped into a dream, listening to Zach and Emery chatting like long lost friends.

WAKING UP, STIFF AND SORE, KAYN STRETCHED AS SHE SAT up. They were parked at a rest stop with a convenience store. *What time is it?* It smelled like greasy burgers. There was a gross amount of garbage in the back. *How long was she asleep?* She gathered up the trash into a bag. *They must have let her sleep. She couldn't go inside and leave the engine running.* Groggily, she searched for her cell. *There was another message from Frost.* Her growling tummy took precedence as she texted Zach. *I can't get out of the truck, please bring snacks and juice.* Her phone vibrated with Zach's response. *Already on it.* Grinning, she read Frost's message. *You can make it up to me today when you get here.* Joy flooded her senses. Forgetting her relationship paranoid boyfriend filter, she wrote, *love you.* She pressed send. *Oh, crap.* Mortified, Kayn stared at her phone. *Why did she do that?* Her cell vibrated. She read his response. *Ditto, Queen of mixed signals.* Giggling, she relaxed. *She hadn't wrecked it yet. She wasn't meaning to give him mixed signals. This wasn't how she imagined love would be. Loving him felt like she was always about to lose something. Things were much simpler when she was blissfully ignorant relationship-wise. The love she had for Kevin was pristine childlike certainty. Loving Frost felt like jumping out of a plane with a chute that may not open. What she felt for him terrified her. He must feel the same way. She'd been all over the place mentally since surviving the Testing, rarely in control of which ability surfaced. Only the Siren ability came easily.* She thought back to that night in Mexico when Frost tried explaining how hard it was going be with the complications of their abilities. *He'd vowed to keep trying, so had she, but hadn't understood what he meant. She did now. Trying, was all they could promise each other.* Her road trip buddies were on their way back to the truck with bags of snacks, chatting. Kayn silenced her inner dialogue as Emery fumbled with the keypad.

As everyone got in, Killian commented, "Sleeping Beauty has awakened and summoned the backseat cleaning elves. I'll run this to the garbage. Sorry, I knew it was gross back here. You've been out cold for a day and a half." He hopped out and sprinted to the trash can with the bag.

A day and a half? She wasn't a napper. That was strange.

Killian got back in and shut the door as Mel passed her a takeout bag. *Yes. She was starving.* Kayn peeked in. "You got me a burrito, you're amazing, thanks Mel." As they pulled away, she quietly observed Zach, riding up front flirting with Emery. Mel was pretending she wasn't devastated. Killian was trying to lift her spirits. *Being murdered by your ex dampens one's mood. She'd experienced that heartbreak. She barely knew Thorne, but the guy radiated goodness, what he'd done was hard to believe. It felt like there must be way more to the story. On the bright side, maybe Mel would finally be able to move on from the fantasy of what might have been.* A flicker of memory brought her back to Kevin slitting her throat in Immortal Testing, solidifying the truth of where they stood with him in Triad and her, in Ankh. *Yes, being murdered by someone you were devoted too made the situation crystal clear. She'd gone on an unhinged murder spree in the Testing. Melody wasn't like her though. Her friend was rational, calm, and innately good to her core. Naughty, on occasion, but those lines between right and wrong always seemed finite for her.* Unwrapping her burrito, Kayn dumped a disgusting amount of hot sauce on and devoured it.

Watching with morbid fascination, Killian commented, "You do the hot sauce thing like Lexy. Amar does that too you know. I've always been curious as to why?"

Shrugging, Kayn downed a jug of juice. *She was still hungry.* Ravenous, she dug through bags. *Nothing was appealing. Killian smelled good though. She'd brought Mel back from the dead, fed off his energy and he'd stayed on his feet. It was rather impressive. She didn't know him well enough to ask him for the kind of snack she suspected, she needed. Hi, nice to meet you. I'm Kayn, and I eat supernatural energy. Yours is rather addictive, I'd like more.* Her inner dialogue was getting crazy. Oh, fantastic. More immortal brain growing pains, when was this bullshit going to stop? Her stomach went off like a whale's mating call.

Eyes wide, Killian chuckled, "You alright, kid?"

Scowling, Kayn nodded, knowing it was a lie. The burly immortal carried on chatting with Mel about being Orin's daughter. Broiling, she wiped the perspiration off her brow. The crackling tires were echoing. *She should ask them to pull over, something was happening to her. She'd had this sense of ability related foreboding before, it rarely went well. Deep breath in. Deep breath out. Be calm.* Her peripheral vision flickered ominously. Her heart was thudding like she ran a marathon. *She'd been asleep for a day and a half. She needed to feed her ability but didn't want these new people to know she fed off immortal energy. It might make things awkward. Killian smelled amazing. He had sweet, tasty, potent pheromones. She needed to get out of here.* She wiped her brow. Her throat was so dry, she could barely swallow. *If she ate them all, they'd have a nice long nap. Usually, someone called her out on her feral inner commentary by now. Maybe they couldn't hear it? That was unfortunate, survival of the fittest wise. What was that? It felt like spiders were running around under her jacket. She didn't like it.* Imaginary arachnids scurried down her arms into her palms, making every hair stand on end. *Oh, no. There were dark veins on her hands. Something was bubbling up under her skin. If spiders exploded from the boils on her hands, she was going to lose her shit!* Struggling to remain calm, she cautioned, "Guys, I'm having an issue." Nervously, Kayn watched sparks glittering on her fingertips. *Shit. This was new.* She nervously warned, "Guys." Flames lit from the boils.

Nudging Mel, Killian declared, "Your friend is on fire."

Panicking, Mel barked, "Pull over! Quick!"

Looking back, her Handler cursed, "Shit! Calm down, Brighton. Breathe. Deep breaths."

Emery looked in the rear-view, the vehicle swerved to the side of the road. "I'm trying! Out! Get Away!" Kayn freaked, with her hands going off like sparklers on the Fourth of July. Everyone scrambled out, bailing into a snowbank as flames shot out her hands, igniting the interior. Power was coursing through her, it felt amazing. *This is so cool.* "Holy crap, I'm fireproof!" Kayn giggled as her flesh melted, laughing.

"Get out!" Zach shouted, running at her as everyone else frantically pitched snow at the fire.

Blistered, charred, engulfed in flames, Kayn hopped out. Zach leapt on her, smothering the blaze in a snowdrift. She giggled beneath her Handler. *Her back stung. Maybe she wasn't fireproof? That was stupid.*

Looking at her ash-covered face, Zach chuckled, "If you keep laughing like this, they'll think you're crazy."

Everyone was fighting to put out the fire. They should help.

Zach wiped her cheek, and beneath the layer of ash, her skin was pristine. Shaking his head as he got up, he reached out a hand and urged, "Come on, Brighton." With a peculiar grin, Zach enquired, "Feeling chilly?"

Not really. Kayn looked down at the dangling shards of burnt material. *Shit, her clothes were not fireproof.*

Emery shouted, "Run!"

Everyone sprang into action as fluorescent orange winter jackets and a nearly naked girl covered in ash sprinted away from the engulfed vehicle. They stopped to watch like it wasn't a big deal as it exploded.

Covering her with his jacket as they stood, watching it burn, Zach quietly teased, "Nobody can see anything, you're covered in ashes."

Her head was tingling. Kayn winced as she touched it and felt patches of stubble. *Crap. Seriously?* She sighed, "Am I bald?"

Grinning, her Handler confessed, "You're a little patchy. I wouldn't worry, it's visibly growing."

Launching a snowball, Killian announced, "Everyone left their phones in the truck, didn't they?"

"Mine was in my pocket," Kayn answered casually.

"A heads up on the pyrokinesis would have been nice," romance novel Viking looking Adonis, baited.

"Yeah, it sure would have. Am I still burned or is it the temperature on my ass?" Kayn saucily countered, winking at Killian. Almost cool for a split second, she tripped over her own feet. Zach caught her before she faceplanted.

"You're hilarious," Killian chuckled as they trudged away from the flame gutted truck through knee-high drifts, with nothing but snow-covered farmland for miles.

Everyone's auras were a trippy light show. *Nobody was too concerned. If their symbols went off so did the rest of their Clan's. They were coming.* She was toasty warm. So much heat was radiating from her, snow was conveniently melting, making her hike much easier but her head was crazy itchy. *Zach was trembling in his t-shirt.* She unzipped his jacket and suggested trading it for his shirt.

"I'm fine," Zach replied, shivering.

Feeling guilty, Kayn pressed, "My healing ability has me toasty warm. Take the jacket. I did this, not you."

Smiling, Zach said, "You only got to that point because I was so busy flirting, I didn't notice you were in trouble."

"She's hot, it's understandable," Kayn sparred, as they wandered down the deserted road. She took Zach's hand. *His fingers were so frozen.* She stopped, urging, "Trade me for the jacket, you are being ridiculous."

"Fine," Zach chuckled. "Now that I've felt how warm your hands are, I'll take it." The others stopped as Kayn and Zach swapped clothing.

They'd been trekking through the snow for a good hour when Kayn realised she'd drained her energy reserves. *If she fed on anyone, they'd go down.* Having faith, she could keep going until help arrived, she was a second from passing out when their ride showed up.

Markus rolled down the window and laughed as he saw Kayn staggering like she was drunk in a t-shirt with a melted trail of snow behind her. He commented, "Rough day?"

Oh, thank god. Kayn teetered over and was out cold before she landed in the snow.

Picking her up like she was as light as a feather, Killian placed Kayn in the back as exhausted Ankh squeezed in. Nobody spoke until Ankh's leader pointed out, "Wouldn't it have made more sense to walk in the melted snow behind her?"

"Behind the surprise Firestarter, you failed to mention?" Killian ribbed, laughing.

"Yes, the unconscious one," Markus replied with a grin.

"She's tuckered out," Mel decreed, lovingly stroking her hair. "Her Healing ability shorted out. She's been melting snow for hours."

Markus pressed, "I need the whole story, to figure out how to pre-empt this. What happened, Zach?"

"I was up front, I didn't notice she was in trouble," Zach admitted. "Mel started yelling for us to pull over. I tried to get her to breathe but she was already shooting flames from her hands. We all jumped out, except for Brighton, who thought she was fireproof."

"Our symbols went off, Zach started screaming at her to get out. He ran back, leapt on her, and smothered the flames in the snow. She was burnt to a crisp, but healed remarkably fast, and didn't seem to be feeling any pain," Mel disclosed, making sure their leader knew Zach acted heroically.

"Go back further, something happened after you three were left at the hotel," Markus prompted with his eyes on the road ahead. "Our symbols went off, one of you went down."

Mel confessed, "I thought I was playing Thorne, but

he was playing me. He convinced me to go to his room, and when the elevator opened, I took an arrow in the heart."

With soft eyes, Markus asked, "Are you alright?"

"Yeah, I'm okay," Mel replied, avoiding his gaze.

Markus quizzed, "Whose energy did Kayn use to heal?"

Raising his hand like a child in elementary school, Killian confessed, "I thought we were going to have to hide a body. When I looked down, Kayn was done healing Mel. I didn't even know she was a Healer. When I took her hand to help her up, she apologised and siphoned my energy. She only took a hair of what Amar's Healers usually take."

"So, she brought Melody back without an energy transfer and fed from Killian after. Where were you, Zach?" Markus questioned.

"I went with Emery to disable the security. I wasn't with her in the elevator," Zach admitted.

"Zach, her abilities are unstable. What happened to Mel could have hit too close to home and triggered the Dragon. Moving Killian's body would have been an ordeal. It's your job to keep her on an even keel," Markus reprimanded, scowling in the rear-view.

"I ordered him to go with Emery as backup," Killian explained.

Markus clarified, "We have no idea what she's capable of. You've heard about her Guardian paternity but she's also a Conduit. We haven't dealt with this ability before. She can siphon and replicate our powers. She's figured out how to summon Healing and Siren abilities but hasn't been taught how to shut them down. She must have fed off Grey to have pyrokinesis on the menu. Now, she may have your strength, Killian. It's my fault for not disclosing everything about the situation."

"How's Lexy doing with everything?" Emery enquired, looking out the window.

Watching the road as they hit the outskirts of the city, their leader answered, "Lexy rarely has deep chats with me about feelings. Normally, I'd tell you to ask Grey, but do us all a favour, don't open that can of worms." Noticing Zach's silence, Markus met his eyes in the rearview, reassuring, "Don't beat yourself up about it, kid. I get it, someone more experienced gave you orders, and you obeyed. I know you've had a lot on your plate. The Handler job is relatively new. Shit happens. I'm sure you've heard about Trinity sneaking in and stealing the girl we were after while we were fighting Triad. Thanks to you guys, we didn't lose our new Ankh. They're safe because you five distracted Trinity."

"Personal drama aside, Trinity was on the ball this week," Mel admitted, stroking Kayn's restored hair. She looked at Killian and questioned, "She brought me back and didn't go overboard feeding from you?"

"I was dizzy," Killian admitted, watching Mel playing with her hair. "She doesn't look dangerous now, she looks like a soot dusted angel. She's going to be freezing when she wakes up in nothing but that t-shirt. She's clearly chilly."

It took Mel a second to figure out, Killian was referring to her sleeping friend's headlights on high beam. She swatted him as he giggled.

4
ENLIGHTENING BRAIN GROWTH SPURTS

*G*roggily listening to crackling tires on gravel winterized road, Kayn questioned, "How long have I been asleep?"

"For future reference, you're not fireproof," Mel teased, with city traffic outside the window.

Confused by the tall buildings, Kayn sat up, wrapping her arms around her chest. *She was losing a concerning amount of time during these Enlightening brain growth spurts.* Zach took off his jacket and gave it to her, grinning as they pulled into the parking lot of a fancy hotel. *She wasn't dressed for this. She wasn't dressed at all. Awkward.*

Everyone got out. Markus looked back, asking, "Feeling better?"

It came back to her in an embarrassing whoosh of ability induced crazy behaviour. "I'm good," Kayn answered, doing up the jacket. *Her bottom half felt breezy. Oh, yes. She lit the truck on fire and burned her clothes off. She must have summoned up Grey's ability, Killian smelled like a snack. She should keep that to herself.*

"You can't eat anyone, Brighton. This is Lampir territory. We're here under the pretence of mending fences. After that unfortunate incident with part of Lucien's crew in Mexico, we've been sent to check the northern Hives for suspicious activity," Markus lectured as he got out into the snow.

Shit. She wasn't wearing boots.

Crouching, Killian offered, "Your chariot, my lady?"

"Thanks for not leaving me to run over there barefoot," Kayn giggled, climbing on his back, feeling like a kid as he jogged to catch up with the others.

Squatting in the covered area, Killian announced, "Front door service, my lady."

Knowing the jacket covered her, she didn't give her chilly toosh a second thought as they walked into the classy beige lobby, like worn-out tourists who'd been on the road for days. Handing out key cards, Markus directed, "Clean up, order room service and stay on your floor until morning."

Hearing Frost's laughter amidst humming voices, Kayn noticed the trendy bar and tried to look.

Picking her up to shift her position, Killian chuckled, "Nothing to see here, energy thief. You aren't going into a bar full of Lampir. We don't need an international incident."

She wasn't a moron. She knew what he did for the Clan. Hearing Frost's musical laughter again, she wanted to sneak a peek. Everyone was deliberately blocking her line of sight like kids. Kayn laughed, "Come on, I'm not going in there to attack whoever he's flirting with."

Staring into the bar, Zach cautioned, "Don't look."

Well, she had to now. Kayn giggled, "I just need to use the washroom." Manoeuvring past, she stopped cold as she saw what they were trying to prevent her from seeing. Frost was whispering in a scantily clad blonde's ear. He noticed her watching and didn't miss a beat pretending she wasn't there.

Putting his arm around her, Grey walked her out, saying, "He's trying to get information. Don't make a scene. Come on, let's go find you something to wear."

Crap. She forgot she was half-naked wearing a fluorescent orange parka. Squirming out of Grey's grasp, Kayn asserted, "I'm fine. I know what his job is, I'm not going to eat a bunch of Lampir." Embarrassed, she strutted adorably past the group, barelegged in a parka covered in soot, beckoning, "Zach! Come!" *She didn't even know what floor they were on.*

She was standing by the elevator stubbornly waiting as Zach wandered up, teasing, "What floor are we on?"

"I don't know," Kayn curtly replied in awkward silence. Trying to keep a straight face as it opened, she marched into the elevator.

As the door slid shut, he leaned against the mirrored wall, stating, "That was ridiculous."

"I know," she admitted, giggling.

"Let's go, half-naked weirdo," Zach chuckled as they wandered out of the elevator to a room conveniently across the hall. Opening the door, he stepped aside, grinning.

This week sucked. She was genuinely bad at her job. Going directly to the minibar to get herself a tiny bottle of vodka, Kayn tried opening it. *Oh, come on. She was a frigging superhero.* She passed it to Zach, he couldn't open it either. *That was strange.* "I give up, I'll go shower," she mumbled, shutting herself in the bathroom. Sighing, Kayn leaned against the door, reflecting on her behaviour. *It was silly to be upset. She'd used her mirrored ability many times for the sake of the Clan with no self-control at all. If she got pissy about this, he'd just come back at her with the half dozen times she'd done the same thing since coming out of the Testing. She was acting like a headcase.* She stuck her head back out, apologising, "I'm sorry, Zach."

With a smile, her Handler prompted, "I know, have your shower, so I can have mine."

Undoing the ugly parka, she grinned at her reflection in the mirror. *There were black veins on her chest. It looked like she needed an exorcism more than a snack. Before Immortal Testing, nobody thought she could hurt a fly, and now, everyone assumed she was an inconvenient emotion away from a murder spree. Looking at her Conduit anxiety response veiny situation, they may have a point. They were blocking her from seeing Frost because if she got pissed off, they were on the menu. It was hilarious. Her inner commentary was getting weird again. Be calm. Be Zen. Be chill.* She got into the shower, but there was no rushing the amount of soot she had to wash off. *Zach should have showered first. Shit, she didn't have clothes.* Wrapped in a towel, Kayn wandered out. *Her Handler wasn't there, just Arrianna.*

Lugging her backpack, Arrianna explained, "Markus told me what happened. Come on, let's go back in the washroom, I'm sure we can find you something of mine to wear."

How? She felt like a big oafish giant, who ate small children and lived at the top of a beanstalk next to her.

Shutting the door, the petite blonde made it clear she'd heard her inner commentary, taunting, "Shut that negative self-talk down before I chop down your beanstalk., you are beautiful." Inspecting her hungry Conduit ability situation, Arrianna explained, "Emotions are the trigger, that's why seeing Frost working wasn't a great idea when you were already having issues. Feed from me, Healers are the safest dish on the menu." Arrianna held out her hand.

She didn't know Arrianna well, but she seemed to know

what she was talking about. Taking her hand, the soothing warmth of her energy travelled up her arm into her chest. Fearing she'd take too much, Kayn quickly let go, saying, "Thank you." Metaphorical demons exorcized, she began sorting through options in the bag, opting for yoga pants and a t-shirt. *It was going to be a stretch.* Prying wideset hips into tiny pants giggling, she squeezed into an obscenely tight top next. Raking fingers through her curly damp mane, Kayn announced, "I can't believe I got into your pants." *Music was playing in the other room.* Arrianna laughed as they walked out. The party started while they were in the bathroom. There was a mountain of snacks from the vending machine on the counter. Zach was dancing with Mel, drinking from the minibar. Shimmying over, her Handler gave her a mini vodka. "You did it! You opened it!" Kayn praised, giggling.

Towing Arrianna to the fridge, Zach tempted, "Pick your poison."

Shaking her head, taking in the crammed minifridge and overflowing mountain of snacks on the counter, Arrianna toyed, "Which one of you stole liquor out of all of the fridges in the empty rooms and used telekinesis to steal everything from the vending machines?"

"They were all in there?" Zach fibbed, grinning. "Are you telling Daddy or joining us?"

Giggling, Arrianna swatted Zach, scolding, "You jerk that's going to be stuck in my head."

Rattling boxes of junior mints like maracas, Mel chanted, "Join us, join us."

Cracking a whisky, Arrianna drank it, strode over to the adjoining door, and loudly pounded on it, yelling, "Join us!"

Opening the door bare-chested with a shit-eating

grin and crinkled happy eyes, Grey flirted, "Hello trouble." Lured into their web of fun, he pissed himself laughing as he saw their mountain of stolen snacks. "This is a lecture waiting to happen."

"Look in the minifridge," Arrianna dared, grinning.

Following Grey into the room, Orin playfully shoved Arrianna, taunting, "I hope there's a Snickers in that pile. I recall Markus saying something about behaving ourselves."

Digging in the snacks, Grey pestered, "No, it was, stay upstairs and don't let Brighton eat anybody. I'll save him one just in case." Putting it in a drawer, he found another, wound up and called out, "Heads up, Brighton!"

Turning as the Snickers sailed at her, Kayn caught it, and declared, "I'm eating you first." Chasing her sister's Handler out of the suite, Grey raced down the hall, cackling. Ducking behind a housekeeping trolly, he rifled toilet paper rolls at her as Kayn superhero blocked each one with a wave of her arm. The elevator opened. They turned to see who it was.

Walking out, Killian saw the mess, warning, "Markus is going to lose his shit."

They chased Big Sexy rifling rolls as he ran for the room, laughing, "Stop! I surrender!"

Gathering armloads of toilet paper ammo, they busted into the room, pitched rolls at everyone and left the mess to do shots.

Looking out into the hall, Arrianna sighed, "Seriously?" She went to go pick them up.

Flinging her over his shoulder, Killian strode across the room and tossed her on the bed. As Arrianna bounced, Big Sexy pointed, comically reprimanding, "These assholes feed on our Siren. Nobody is cleaning up shit."

Now, she knew where Frost was. She didn't need that visual.

"Here," Zach said, passing her a whisky.

She drank it, shaking her head. *Three vodkas, a whisky, and a, your boyfriend is having sexy Lampir feeding time reveal. It must be Christmas.*

Putting an arm around her, Mel gave her a tiny bottle of tequila, whispering, "How are you doing?"

Downing it, Kayn teased, "Drinking vodka, whisky and tequila in the same night is the trifecta of stupidity, but I'm having fun." *Thorne shot an arrow through Mel's heart. She hadn't even given her a chance to vent.* Feeling horrible, she hugged Mel tightly, whispering, "Want me to kill Thorne?"

"Yes, make it hurt," Mel sniffled, giggling.

Swaying to the music embracing, Mel's chest shuddered. Kayn offered, "Let's order pizza and get you a Snickers."

Joining in their group hug dance, the trio swayed as Zach whispered, "I ordered pizza half an hour ago."

Giggling, Mel whispered back, "You're awesome, Zach."

"I have my moments," Zach chuckled, wildly rocking the trio back and forth as a fast song came on.

Tears ended, pizza came, and pointless talk of romantic entanglements ended as the endearing troop of joy junkies revelled in their unbreakable bond. When the rest of Ankh showed up, they were three sheets to the wind, leaping on the bed dancing and singing along to the music. The allure of mindless shenanigans was no match for the pull Kayn felt as Frost walked in. *He'd changed his clothes.* Far too tipsy to be coy, she ceased jumping. He grinned, sauntering over in a black fitted shirt and jeans. *Heaven help her.* The motion of everyone still leaping made her topple backwards. She fell between the bed and wall with a thud. Mortified, she decided to stay there.

Mischievously peering over the side of the bed, Grey baited, "Markus is shutting this down, if you stay there for a minute, we'll all be gone but I'd just own it."

Guru Grey was right. She got up and curtsied. The room of immortals cracked up.

Everyone's eyes turned to the door as Markus declared, "Who was the asshole that threw toilet paper everywhere?" They all raised their hands. Amused by their solidarity, he shut the party down, "My room is beneath this one, I need sleep."

Turning the tunes off, Zach pressed a finger against his lips, drunkenly motioning, "Shhh."

Giggles silenced as Emery rushed in, calling out, "Jenna!" Their eyes met in a movie worthy moment.

"Emery?" Jenna gasped, "How are you here?"

It always felt like a psychic shouldn't be able to be surprised.

Overcome by joy, they raced into each other's arms and seductively kissed. Everyone's jaws dropped. Fascinated as they left together, Orin just stood there.

With a supportive pat, Grey put his arm around Orin, saying, 'Digest it. Let's go, buddy. Time to move on."

Shrugging as they went into the adjoining room, Orin asked, "Where's Lexy?"

"Don't get him started," Markus scolded, pitching a toilet paper roll at him.

Sauntering over to Markus, Arrianna gave him a Snickers, toying, "Don't be grumpy."

Laughing, their leader hugged her, teasing, "It looks like you had fun."

"I did," Arrianna stated, strutting away, summoning him to follow with a finger.

As witnesses left, their eyes met. Placing a hand on the wall behind her, Frost whispered, "Hi."

"Hi," Kayn whispered as every hair prickled in response to his pheromones.

Pressing his body against hers, he whispered his breathy intentions, "I want to take you to bed and kiss every inch of you."

Caressing his dark hair, gazing into his seductive eyes, she leapt from a plane with no parachute, "Let's go."

They straight face walked past the Clan lingering in the hall. He swiped his card. As the light turned green, Kayn flashed back to a night in Vegas, when her attempt to sneak up to his room was foiled by their Clan's Oracle. He tugged her in and slammed the door as she laughed.

Flirtatiously walking her backwards to the bed, Frost chuckled, "I wanted you so bad when I saw you standing there in nothing but that parka. After I'm done making you scream, you'll have to tell me what happened." She lifted her arms over her head as he tugged her shirt off and tossed it with a cheeky grin.

Siren were similar creatures with volatile sensual energy hidden beneath the surface, ready to release incapacitating pheromones, able to change the rules of anyone's game. Neither was capable of G-rated behaviour, once their fuses were lit. The self-destructive Dragon in her yearned for the reckless way he made her feel like air to breathe. Pulling up his shirt, revealing inhumanly hot chiselled abs, she chucked it, biting her lip. Nuzzling her neck, feathering ticklish kisses on her throat, and chest, he shoved her onto the bed like a beast. Giggling, bouncing on the mattress as he crawled up after her until his lips were a breath away, Kayn whispered, "I'm not mad."

"I'm not either," he provoked, sliding his hand between her thighs, silencing her comeback with his lips.

She needed these leggings gone. It was torture, she wanted him. His lips left hers as she tried squirming out of her pants.

"Need help taking those off?" Frost laughed, seductively inching stretchy material over her rounded hips like he was unwrapping a present. Deviously peering up, feigning shock, he remarked, "No panties?"

Feeling his warm breath between her thighs, she arched her back, gasping. Chuckling, he continued struggling to tug her pants off. *It wasn't going to be sexy if they split and she burst out like Pillsbury dough.* The leggings were so snug, seductive removal was an impossible task. They were both laughing as he pitched the pants across the room. Kissing her ankles, he made his way up, nibbling on her calves, nipping sensitive flesh on her inner thighs. Kissing her abdomen, Frost peered up, enjoying her reaction as he tormented aching places with hot breath, pushing her to the edge of her sanity, playing his torturous games. Reaching for the button on his jeans, she demanded, "Quit messing around."

"Don't be bossy, Brighton," he reprimanded, naughtily caressing, toying with her until she shivered, releasing a gust of Siren pheromones. The game ended, as he lost control. Their lips merged with rapturous abandon as they were lost in savage intoxicating thrusts.

After an impressive number of blissful crescendos, with perspiration glistening on her skin, she lay spent in his arms. *All she wanted to do was tell him she loved him over and over until he believed it. Until she trusted it.* Toying with the mist of hair by his navel, she whispered, "I wish we could have more time alone like this."

"You just want to see if I can go for days," he taunted, sweetly kissing her hair.

Naughtily caressing him, Kayn harassed, "I'll cheer you on. You can do it! Get er done!" She doubled over cackling as he retaliated with tickles.

Ceasing the ticklish torture, Frost kissed her cheek and prompted, "Spill it, when did he start listening in again and, why were you naked under a jacket?"

He was referring to why they'd parted in the first place. Had it been two days or three? "Smooth transition," she commented.

"I've been overthinking this for days. Lily says, I need to remember what my ability was like before I had control. No judgement, no fear. I'm not mad, I just want you to clarify things," he disclosed, honestly.

Looking into his eyes, she confessed, "I don't know how to stop him from popping into my head. Honestly, after being kidnapped by demons wanting to be sent through the hall of souls, I'm not sure I should." *That was a bold confession, hope that wasn't too far.*

In awe, he teased, "You didn't think out that response a speck, did you?"

"Not a word," she admitted, shrugging.

Grinning, tenderly stroking her hair, Frost affirmed, "It's one of my favourite things about you."

He loved it when she spoke her mind. She met his eyes and felt it to her core. *He was doing his best, trying to understand her. She needed to know his favourite colour. It was silly, but it always felt like important knowledge to have, like someone's birthday.* "What's your favourite colour?" She asked with a smile.

"I've already told you," he ribbed, caressing her hip.

Her memory was like a black hole, information goes in there and vanishes forever. She remembered, "It's blue."

"Yours is yellow," he taunted, cuddling her.

With her head on his chest, she whispered, "Why did you change and shower?"

"I had blood on my shirt, you know why," he divulged, kissing her hair. "Lily was the only one who spent the night in the penthouse. Yes, I was turned on, it's impossible not to be. No, nothing else happened."

Grinning, she admitted, "I was afraid to ask."

"Back to you showing up at a bar naked under a jacket covered in soot," he prompted.

"Full disclosure, our symbols went off, we found Mel's body in the elevator with an arrow in her heart. I healed her without feeding first. Surprised I was conscious, I fed off Killian. His energy is like drinking a dozen Red Bull. I fell asleep and woke up a day later. I was only awake for a while when my skin began crawling, my hands started sparking and I lit myself on fire. I burned off my clothes and hair. I've been on fire multiple times this month; I hope it's not going to be a thing," she commented.

"Full disclosure, it's a thing. I hope feeding from Grey isn't going to be a thing. It's a sensitive scenario, just putting it out there," he responded, playing with her hair, snuggling her.

Gazing into his eyes, she nodded, saying, "Noted."

"I'm glad you didn't light me on fire this evening," Frost taunted with a grin.

"Everyone was watching," she sparred, feeling his chest jiggle with laughter.

"We should sleep, we have a Lampir supported demon infestation to find. I need my beauty rest, we can't have Ankh's sexy bait frazzled," Frost whispered, closing his eyes.

She'd referred to him in her inner dialogue as sexy bait on many occasions, that was funny. Snuggling against Frost, inhaling his intoxicating pheromones, Kayn sighed, "You are sexy bait."

"I meant you," he mumbled, closing his eyes.

Well, now she wasn't going to be able to sleep. She had to many questions. Were they splitting up again tomorrow? She didn't want to be the sexy bait; she didn't know how to control anything. She didn't want to lose what they had by doing something stupid. Someone had to teach her how to shut these powers down. Good lord he smelled amazing. His chest started jiggling again.

He chuckled, "That hamster wheel between your ears is kind of amazing. Listen, we're together for the next week. Lily and I are going to try to help you with control. As far as doing something stupid goes, I can't stay mad at you, it's impossible. Don't worry about wrecking this. I can control myself, you can't. I knew what I was getting into. Go to sleep sweetie, it's going to be a great week."

With worries put to rest, she didn't say another word and drifted off into a dream wrapped in his embrace.

She felt his hands between her thighs as she stirred and whispered, "I love waking up with you."

Toying with her and leaving her there, Frost chuckled, "Shower with me, I have to leave in a few hours." Leaning out of the bathroom beckoning her, he seduced, "Do you remember accidentally coming into my room in that demon-infested hotel? Want a redo where I finish the job?"

The shower started. *Good morning to me.* She sprinted after him, shifted the curtain aside and cautiously stepped in, knowing her accident-prone life status knew no bounds. With his eyes closed under the spray, she altered the scenario near missing everywhere he ached to be touched, soaping him up.

Gathering her in his arms, he slid his sudsy chest against hers. Massaging her rear, he naughtily whispered in her ear, "You're not trying to mess with me, are you, Brighton?"

Boldly caressing him, Kayn encouraged, "No more chit chat."

"I love it when you're bossy," Frost chuckled as their lips met in rapturous abandon.

She didn't want to play games, she wanted him. Like he'd read her mind, he groaned, sliding in and roughly took her against the wall until she was whimpering, so happy she might burst with confessions of love teetering on her tongue. Waves of carnal pleasure detonated Siren pheromones, inciting frantic urgency until they wildly cried out in unison.

As she adjusted her footing, he chuckled, "Don't move. Give me a second, we'll fall."

Grabbing a handful of his wet hair, she harassed, "Get it together, we're not done."

"Oh, now you're in trouble," Frost vowed, starting again until the inevitable happened, they slipped and fell out of the shower onto the bathroom tile. Without slowing the pace, wicked adventures carried on all over their suite in a lusty blur of climaxes. Through their euphoric haze, someone loudly knocked on the adjoining door. *Oh, crap. What time is it?*

Markus called out, "Thirty minutes!"

Awkward, everyone was hanging out in the room next door. They looked at each other giggling.

With an outstretched hand, he lured, "If we're not fast, we'll miss breakfast."

She was starving. Rushing to put clothes on, she scowled. *She didn't want to wear those leggings.* Squirming into boa death grip pants, Kayn caught her shirtless partner in debauchery watching, thoroughly entertained by her plight.

Looping arms around her waist, Frost tugged her to him, vowing, "We'll pick up where we left off later."

Moulding into each other, their lips met. Content, she pulled away meeting his vulnerable eyes. *Everything about her tested his boundaries. He should run away screaming.* Wishing they had more time before reality tested their patience, Kayn said, "We'll see."

Greeted by raucous hooting and applause as they walked into the adjoining room, her sense of humour rolled the dice. Bowing, Kayn commented, "This isn't awkward at all."

Frost kissed her cheek and explained, "I have to change into something more business, less frat boy."

He left her, post applause. *Fantastic.* Everyone involved in today's job was dressed underwhelming like it was casual Friday at the office but weren't allowed to wear anything risky. With her lustrous black mane, Lily flounced out of the washroom like a fairytale princess. *One of these days, forest creatures were going to come out of everywhere and climb all over her. She'd pay to see that.*

Grinning like she'd heard her thoughts, Lily passed a bag of toiletries, rushing, "Quickly, we're running out of time."

Damn it. Her inner commentary couldn't be left unsupervised. Her thoughts were a train wreck. She was a twisted, mangled, beautiful mess of a girl who was granted a reprieve from isolation. She gazed at her reflection. *With blushed cheeks and swollen lips, her extracurricular activities were obvious.* Putting the shower curtains in the tub, she reminisced. *They were going to have to pay for that.*

The door cracked, Frost asked, "I'm going to the buffet, cereal or bagel?"

"Surprise me," Kayn flirted. He gave her a peck on the lips and disappeared with his aftershave lingering like a place marker. Applying pink lipstick, she raked fingers through her curls and put her hair in a ponytail.

Lily stuck her head in and passed her jeans, assuring, "These will fit, they're mine. Take the day to relax, check out the mall." Smiling, Lily shut the door.

It was wrong to want bad things to happen, so she'd have an excuse to let the Dragon out to play. The euphoria in the aftermath of their love was always short-lived. If she just went to the mall and didn't kill anybody, maybe the content glow would stick around longer? Freeing herself from Arrianna's leggings, Kayn tugged on Lily's jeans and was able to breathe, until she squeezed into the t-shirt she was given. Her cleavage was out for the world to see, so was her midriff. *Arrianna was a tiny built girl, why didn't one of the guys just give her a t-shirt? Now, her chest was pried in like sausage contents.* She wandered out to find the door connecting the rooms propped open with everyone lounging having coffee. Frost was on their bed eating a random assortment from the buffet. He passed her the plate with a heaping pile of bacon. "Best boyfriend ever," Kayn praised, snatching some.

With his eyes on her navel piercing, Frost sighed, "You look hot in everything."

He was full of shit, but she'd take it.

Grinning, Markus commented, "Doesn't anyone have a baggy shirt?"

"Best we can do, it's laundry time," Lily stated, perched on the dresser by the door.

"What's this job?" Kayn enquired, peeling a banana.

"We've been invited to a gathering," Lily responded with a smile.

That banana hit the spot. Maybe she was low on potassium? Did that kind of stuff even matter anymore? She felt eyes on her and innocently peered up. *It felt like she was missing something.*

Zach walked up and offered, "Let me put that peel in the garbage for you."

She gave it to him and reached for another one. Markus cleared his throat. Kayn looked up. *What? She was listening.* Markus held out his hand. She looked at her Handler. Zach snatched her banana away and gave it to Markus who rifled it past Lily into the other room. *That was harsh. She was going to eat that.*

Zach nudged her and whispered, "I'll explain later."

Grinning, their leader said, "Ready to pay attention?"

She was paying attention.

"We have a cluster of mortals who went missing under suspicious circumstances. They returned home weeks later," Markus announced their next job.

Zach questioned, "Passivist Lampir hive?"

"That was my first thought too," their leader confessed. "Abducting mortals, grazing and wiping the hard drive, screams Lampir snatch and erase, but here's the plot twist, they don't speak or react to stimuli."

"Traumatised mortals?" Mel questioned, sipping coffee.

"Jenna suspects they're vacant shells, her abilities are being blocked. Lampir can't block Clan, it's in the treaty. We need to tread lightly. We don't want to offend anyone in their community, especially after that unfortunate incident with Lucien in Mexico."

That name made her nether regions tingle. Awkward. Recalling the job where she'd chased one of Lily's immortal boy toys in Dragon state, and granted him amnesty, based on a hunch. Only kill the ones with black auras. Those were her orders. The sexy mutual feeding session that nearly got out of hand wasn't.

"Melody, Kayn and Zach, you'll be observing the Siren's gathering intel," Markus explained.

Her eyes darted Frost's way. *He'd seen her reaction when Markus brought up Lucien. She had a confusing mixture of abilities making it impossible to be even close to normal for a breath. Lucien was delicious.* Her skin crawled. *Not now. Calm. Be mellow.* She inconspicuously glanced at her arm. *No veins. She might have to stab herself to take her libido down a notch. Bacon. She wanted bacon.* Kayn reached for the plate. *Whoops, she should pay attention.*

Patiently, Markus asked, "Do you have a question?"

"I was reaching for bacon," Kayn replied, manoeuvring past Frost, with cleavage in his face. He covered his mouth chuckling.

With laughter crinkled eyes, Markus chuckled, "The plan is for you to observe without distracting. Let's go with, make an honest effort and don't eat anyone."

Kayn nodded, munching on her crispy distraction. They carried on plotting and planning. *She didn't need to know details if they were just observing.* Everyone got up, preparing to leave.

Meeting her Handler's gaze, Markus directed, "I'll text our location later. You'll have hours to kill, use the Aries group card Jenna gave you to buy clothes and anything else you need. Do your best to fly under the radar. Mel, feed her before joining us. Eat up, Brighton. We're flying blind with our Oracle blocked. Pack up everything in the washroom, we have no idea where this night is going. Everyone else, follow me." They wandered away talking to Markus.

She didn't like shopping for clothes, nothing fit her properly. Sitting on the bed alone, she ate the rest of the bacon and wandered to collect their things, the door opened. *She thought he left with everyone else.* Kayn walked into Frost's arms. *She didn't want to screw this up.*

Nuzzling her neck, he sweetly kissed her cheek, pledging, "You can't."

She wanted to believe him.

Meeting her eyes, Frost tucked a curl that escaped from her ponytail behind her ear and divulged, "It's acting, I'll be playing Lampir for information, that's all."

"I know," she affirmed, tenderly kissing his lips.

Grinning, Frost confessed, "Admittedly, I don't do well with jealousy. I've stormed out a few times. If you can't reign in your reaction, they'll separate us. If we never spend time together, we'll end up booty calls."

She didn't like this conversation anymore. She was going to beat this to death in her mind.

From the hall, Markus hollered, "Come on, Frost! Let's go!"

He looked into her eyes, kissed her forehead, and rushed out. *What did he mean by they'd end up booty calls? She had no self-control, none. Truth be told, she wasn't sure she was capable of reigning in her reaction.* She sauntered over and flopped facedown on the bed. *He made her feel so many things but safe was never on the list. Before they started seeing each other the sight of him put her at ease, but now, thoughts of him brought a multitude of emotions to the surface.* She squirmed up the mattress and screamed into the pillow. *That helped.* She screamed until she felt the pressure of Zach on the bed.

Squeezing her leg, he probed, "Frustrated?"

That one word covered a lot of ground. Muffled by the pillow, she muttered, "I can't decipher half of the shit he says." She looked back at her grinning Handler. Curious as to why her dilemma was funny, she asked, "Why are you smiling?"

Crawling up onto the bed. Looking at her with his

head on the other pillow, Zach questioned, "What did he say?"

"Something about ending up booty calls if I can't reign in my reactions," she mumbled, watching his expression.

"You've misinterpreted something," he assured.

Kayn challenged, "It wasn't an ultimatum?"

"No way, he's into you, he's not going anywhere," Zach decreed, squeezing her arm. "We should get going, Markus wants you less distracting by this evening."

He seemed certain she was wrong. Maybe she was? "I'm going to need your help tonight," she confessed.

Looking into her eyes, he teased, "First things first, let's get you a baggy turtleneck, Mel's waiting downstairs, grab your jacket."

"I hate shopping," Kayn complained as they wandered into the hall.

With his arm draped around her, Zach chuckled, "No more than an hour and then, we'll find somewhere to have lunch."

Food, now he was speaking her language. A group was standing by the elevator surrounded by a black haze. Her stomach cramped. *Shit seriously?* Blood rushed through her. *She wasn't going to make it five minutes.*

Tugging her into the alcove by the emergency exit, Zach laughed, "You weren't paying attention to anything, Markus said, were you?"

Not a damn thing. As they stepped into the stairwell, the scent of bleach was overpowering. She picked up a hint of copper. *Covering up the scent of blood, didn't suggest good behaviour.*

As they jogged down the stairs, Zach gave her the short version, "Jenna's abilities are being blocked, so they're up to something. Lily, Frost and Emery are going to find out how and disable it."

Maybe Emery felt familiar because she was like her? Instinct prompted caution as they stepped out into a lobby with a sea of dark auras, "Zach," she gasped, her blood rushed as her Conduit ability took the reins.

Taking her hand, he met her eyes, calmly instructing, "I can't see it, but I can feel it. I'll get us out of here. Don't start siphoning until we've made it to Mel."

If she uncorked it, she wouldn't be able to control it. The urge to grab a Lampir and have a Conduit snack was so strong, she crushed her Handler's hand as he led her through the smoky vile haze, invisible to those who didn't have a healing ability. Physically ill as they stepped into the frigid air, they darted to the running vehicle.

When they got in, Zach yanked his hand away, cursing. Composing himself, he accused, "You broke my hand."

"The dark energy in that lobby was a little much for a Healer. It'll take the panic down a notch if you heal him," Mel suggested as they pulled away.

A wave of nausea washed over her. Wrenching as the tires bounced ill-timed potholes, Kayn groaned, "I'm going to barf, pull over."

Holding up his mangled purple fingers, Zach rebutted, "Heal first puke later, this hurts like hell."

Passing back an empty Tim Horton's cup, Mel suggested, "Puke it this."

Mid dry heave into a to-go cup, Kayn groaned, "Sorry, Zach." *She was going to blow this job. There was no way she wasn't eating someone tonight.*

Her Handler's eyes softened as he began massaging her back with his functional hand, soothing, "I understand, I feel brutal too and I didn't have a visual."

They turned into the mall parking lot and drove until they found a spot. Looking out of the window,

Kayn admitted, "I can't control this. We're going to be separated from the rest of the group again."

"We're going to stay with you all night," Mel assured. "If you need to leave, we'll go."

"I already need to go," Kayn mumbled into the empty cup, laughing. *She needed to reset herself, to stop jonesing for energy.*

"What do you need us to do?" Mel asked, from the front.

She looked at her Handler and directed, "Break my neck, I need to reset."

"I've killed you too many times this week, it messes with my head," Zach answered. "I can't do it, Brighton."

They looked delicious. They had to kill her.

Looking back, Mel volunteered, "You don't have to die. You need to be weakened. I can do it. Calm down, Kayn."

She didn't understand. "Don't touch me," Kayn cautioned, as her predatory Conduit ability broke free of its chains. The Dragon stirred.

"I can take care of myself, I'm just using your energy to heal Zach's hand," Melody explained, reaching for her.

She was too agitated. "Mel, no. Don't," Kayn advised. The instant their hands connected, Kayn's Conduit ability took over, siphoning her well-meaning friend's gift. Looking at her Handler, she panicked, "Zach, I can't stop."

Zach muttered, "Damn it, Brighton."

There was a sharp pain as the lights went out.

5
NEFARIOUS PLANS

Clutching a handful of sand, Kayn gasped, squinting in the sunshine. *Was that Killian?*

Holding out a hand, the blonde Adonis with flowing hair chuckled, "I guess you won't be coming to rescue me. How did they kill you at the mall?"

She was trying to remember what happened. It was coming back in fragments. Dark energy in the lobby made her sick. They drove to the mall. She was having issues, Mel touched her. Ohhh, Zach took her out. Opting for honesty, Kayn admitted, "The dark energy in the lobby triggered me. My Handler took me out." *He didn't need to know the rest.* "What happened, why are you here?"

Barefoot in the womblike warmth of velvety sand, Killian explained, "I was warming up the truck, someone knocked on the foggy window. I couldn't see who it was, so I rolled it down. That's all I remember."

"We'll find you," Kayn promised. Experiencing a tickle, she dissolved into dust and floated away.

. . .

STIRRING, IN THE LAND OF THE LIVING, SHE OPENED HER eyes to Zach's grin. *If he had pent up resentment about being bound to her forever as her Handler, he was getting the opportunity to work through it this week.*

Messing up her hair like a sibling, he teased, "Mel ran into the drugstore to grab a few things. Feeling better?"

Killian was with her. "Didn't your symbols go off?"

"For you, I texted Markus," Zach replied, as he got out. When she didn't move, he opened her door, urging, "Come on, what are you waiting for?"

Confused, Kayn asserted, "Killian was in the in-between. Didn't your symbols go off?"

"Ours only went off once," Zach stated, as Mel strolled over lugging bags.

Tossing one in the back, Mel said, "I bought you a baggy t-shirt to wear over the tight one so you can ditch that heavy jacket, it'll be way too hot."

Was it a hallucination? She'd promised to find him. She had to at least check. Slipping on the new t-shirt, Kayn instructed, "Ask Markus if he knows where Killian is."

Seconds later, Zach looked up, saying, "Killian's warming up the truck."

No, he wasn't. "He's dead, his story fits. Find out where they are and get in," Kayn urged.

Already texting the others, Mel announced the address. Zach punched it into the GPS, and they took off with the crunching of gravel-covered snow under their tires.

"What did Killian say?" Mel prompted, looking at their arrival time on the GPS.

"He was warming up the truck. Someone knocked on the window, it was fogged up, he rolled it down, and that's all he had time to say before I healed," Kayn explained. *They were thirty minutes away.*

Texting with one of the others, Mel relayed, "There's no response from Killian's cell. When we arrive, we're supposed to check for a black dodge. Someone might have his phone. They've messaged but there's no response."

Falling snow twirled past windows, nobody spoke. *There was something fishy going on, they knew it. No, stay away from this job. An hour later. Killian may be missing. Come check for a black dodge. They needed a tension breaker.* She looked at her Handler, saying, "I hope you don't get buried alive today, Zach."

Laughing, he fired back one of her traumatising events, "Hope you don't get chased and eaten by cannibalistic cave dwellers, disinfected by fire and bleached by scientists."

"That was brutal, well done." Kayn chuckled, "Hope you don't fall off a cliff." *They were all smiling, traumatic realism sure lightens up an atmosphere.*

"Touché," Zach sparred. "Hope you don't get skewered by a lizard demon." Mel giggled. Crushing on her as always, he added Mel to the game, "Hope you don't have to kill any of your old Trinity friends today."

Wincing, Kayn sighed, "That was pathetic. Shall we pull over so you can build Mel a snowman?"

Grinning, Zach needled, "Maybe if you throw a job for your ex, he'll make you a daisy crown?"

Bringing childhood into it, well done.

"Hope your ex doesn't slit your throat again," Mel one-upped, daring her to go there while innocently driving.

A direct hit to the chest. Taking slam fest for the win, Kayn went for it, "Hope yours doesn't seduce you into an elevator and shoot an arrow into your heart." When nobody reacted, she taunted, "Too soon?"

Shaking her head, Mel laughed, "You dick."

Stifling his reaction, Zach stated, "That just happened."

Come on, she used her ex killing her. His crush was getting old. Do it or don't. Stop dancing around it. This was a verbal jousting match, and she was the master. If she was going down, it would be in a blaze of glory. Looking at her Handler, Kayn provoked, "Hope I don't eat anyone at this party."

"Yeah, I hope she doesn't eat anyone at the party too," Mel ribbed, giggling as snow came at the windshield like they were travelling into another dimension.

They laughed, but her Handler didn't, not even a smirk. Zach glanced over, slamming, "Hope we don't catch your boyfriend with fifty Lampir in a sin cave."

Ouch. That might happen. The sin cave crack was rolling around in her mind like a wrecking ball, he won. Grinning, Kayn replied, "Well played."

The GPS announced their arrival as they detoured down a long driveway to a secluded brewery with a spa, tapas bar, and suites. *They should have been thinking up a plan.* As they pulled up a man waved them over. They braced themselves as Zach rolled down the window.

Smiling, the stranger over exuberantly greeted the group, "Welcome to Birchwood Estates, you can park over there. My name's Paul, I'll be giving you the tour."

A tour of a brewery? Telepathy was the only safe form of communication, knowing Lampir had a heightened sense of hearing. The trio got out to look around. *There were four black trucks parked out front. Footprints led to the entrance from all but one. Only one vehicle had return prints.*

As the man gave the trio a history lesson, Kayn tripped and faceplanted in the snow. *Son of a...* Kayn wiped her nose. *There was blood on her hand. Oh, shit. They were going to find out if the tour guide was Lampir in 3,*

2, 1. As Paul helped her up, she saw the predatory glint in his eye.

"You should be more careful, our patrons get squeamish around blood," Paul disclosed, with a wry smile.

Just like that, polite pretence was gone.

Watching Zach looking into one of the trucks, the tour guide stated, "The tour is over sir, your friend is bleeding, and I'm done pretending. I'm curious, what are you doing?"

Bending with the altered stakes like a pro, Zach sparred, "Looking for a big sexy Viking, have you seen him?"

Big sexy Viking. Go, Zach.

Sauntering over, Paul flirtatiously revealed, "I may have sampled sexy Viking today."

She'd been wrong about the truck.

Facing the smitten Lampir henchmen, Zach coyly lured, "Tell my friends where he is, we'll go somewhere private to discuss sexy Latino men."

"I have to babysit this tour group, Lampir loyalty and all." Their pretend tour guide toyed, "I can bring you inside, now that we understand each other."

Summoned by a flick of his wrist, they followed Lampir Paul inside.

It looked and sounded like a spa. Well, done. Relaxing music soothed her senses as they strolled by botanical gardens with a trickling fountain into an emerald green marble area where Ankh was enjoying cocktails having massages lounging on giant silky jewel-toned pillows. *It was remarkably like an Ankh tomb. Rough job.*

An eccentric woman with lush auburn hair zeroed in on her. Extending a delicate hand, she coyly enquired, "What might your name be?"

Kayn glanced at Markus. *Were they using fake names?*

She suspected she knew what Frost, Lily and Emery were doing but she didn't see Jenna either.

Giggling, their leader prompted, "Go ahead, be truthful with Georgia, tell her why you're here."

This felt like a trap. "Kayn," she responded, shaking the woman's icy hand. "I died earlier and had a visit with Killian who was here but seems to have vanished."

"Sexy Viking guy?" Georgia spun slowly, checking the room, commenting, "No, he doesn't appear to be here. If he let a new Lampir feed for recreational purposes, it may have gotten out of hand. We have similar restraint issues. Come, let's look, he can't be far. Do you mind if I steal your new Dragon, Markus?"

How much did she know? Wasn't this all supposed to be a secret? She'd never seen Markus this relaxed. Mel's face was scrunched like there was a nasty scent in the air. Yeah, she smelled bullshit too.

Raising his drink, Markus ribbed, "Not Dragon playtime, no killing anyone. Bring her Handler if you have nefarious plans."

Nefarious plans?

Looking directly at Zach, their host summoned, "Come Handler." She snapped her fingers and strutted away.

Confused, their eyes met as they left the group. *This place was many levels of unexpected weirdness.* A seductively attired girl passed by with a drink tray.

Their host stopped and enquired, "Fruity, sour or spicy?"

Sexy. There was the sexiest fragrance in the air. She couldn't think about drinks. Georgia was hot. Everybody was, what was this place? Her mouth was dry. Yes, she needed a drink.

Passing her a drink, her Handler whispered, "We have no idea what's going on, might as well."

It was long island iced tea. Smiling, she drank it as they strode past feverishly making out strangers. *Free-spirited group.* Her peripheral vision was silver and shiny like tin foil. *This can't be good.* Lusty wanton strangers were everywhere. Entangled limbs with vacant predatory eyes surrounded her, she slowly turned, losing sight of where she was going and why she was there. *The walls were a trippy, spinning ancient painting.* A door opened at the end of the hall. Siren pheromones wafted out, snuffing out inhibitions. Her heart thudded wildly as ration funnelled the drain faster than water in an unplugged tub. Vaguely aware as a girl in lingerie grabbed Zach's shirt and naughtily towed him away in slow motion, Kayn ventured into elegant Victorian décor with an out of place metal door by a painting of a robust gentleman with sunken eyes and a Basset Hound. *How did she get here? Where was she?* Beneath her bare feet was a sketchy painting on the floor. *She'd seen that symbol before. When did she take off her shoes? A fragrance drew her back to the here and now, she was missing time. Someone behind her was humming.*

Massaging her shoulders, a woman's voice cooed, "You smell delicious."

It felt nice. Nails tickled her scalp, Kayn shivered. Giggling as her ponytail was removed, hair escaped trickling down her shoulders like a wheat-hued waterfall. She recalled where she was. *Lampir spa job, she wasn't supposed to be participating. That ship had sailed. She liked it here. Where was Zach? She had magical fingers.* Every place the Lampir touched tingled and hummed. *It felt good.* Succumbing to hedonism inducing pheromones, Kayn's eyes raised to the woman's stroking her like a coveted pet. *She was still with the same person.*

Georgia confessed, "The opportunity to feed on Siren

is used to sweeten a deal when bargaining with Lampir. You were spoken of as a delicacy to be savoured. It was kind of Markus to lure you here as a gift."

The Dragon within stirred with the urge to storm back out there and throat stomp Markus. He knew she had no control. He didn't want to risk this job by having her there. It clicked, there must be something else at play. He knew she'd react if provoked.

"This is where we keep enticing creatures until deals have been solidified. You're far too tempting to be left out there with the riff-raff," the auburn-haired seductress cooed, with warm breath on her throat, raking nails along her flesh.

With the Lampir's breathing on her neck as sedating as a cat's purr, Kayn closed her eyes, as silky hands travelled her curves. *She'd known the pleasure of being fed on by Lampir. With her Siren ability at the helm, all she had to do was let go.*

Stroking her, the bewitching Lampir confessed, "I can be territorial if I covet someone. I was disappointed to learn of Frost's romantic entanglement. I was assured you have an understanding. Humour me while I test it."

She was about to see her boyfriend in a compromising position. Confidently striding into their exclusive club, it was a let-down. The hallway was a triggering hedonistic blur but this behind a metal door super-secret tavern wasn't. With an icy stroke of her spine, instinct cautioned her to see behind the veil of normalcy. Scanning the suspiciously aura free bar, she saw Frost in a secluded corner. *It served nothing to give herself a visual.* Siren curiosity kept Kayn's eyes locked on his erotic games as he toyed with a woman's necklace, gazing into her eyes. *Why was she watching this?* Looking past his mark, Frost's eyes met hers. *She'd needed to understand a Siren's role within the Clan. Seeing the situation clearly, she* deciphered what he'd been trying to say. *This was going to be brutal. They were destined to be messy, but she didn't need to care.* It only stung for a second before her heart sunk into deep nothing and she didn't.

Leaving his playmate at the table, Frost swaggered past, teasing, "Stings a little, doesn't it?"

Detached, she appreciated his rear as he walked away. *Nothing had to make sense anymore. She had a primal guidance system and he was the shiniest thing in the room. She was hungry and this was a Siren hunting ground. Anyone would go with her believing themselves more powerful. Carnivorous beings had no sense of self-preservation.* Ordering a drink, Kayn noticed an attractive man in a suit sitting there.

Grinning, he complimented, "Sexy hair."

She felt for her ponytail. *Oh, it was gone.* "Always," Kayn baited, raising her drink. Grinning, they clinked glasses like they weren't at a secret suspicious Lampir bar at a day spa.

"Do you have a name?" Her roguish admirer asked.

Toying with her straw, Kayn sparred, "Does it matter?"

Getting a kick out of her, the Lampir chuckled, "Not really."

Sipping her drink, she peered up, enquiring, "It's my first time, what's going to happen?"

"You can't be Georgia's, you're not dressed to allure," he teased, pointing to her baggy drugstore t-shirt with an easy button on it. "It's funny though."

She put it on without looking. Peering down at her chest, she giggled. *Mel got her a shirt with an easy button on it. She'd walked in here with this shirt on, that was hilarious.* Kayn boldly took it off, tossed it and ribbed, "How about now?"

Laughing, her Lampir flirting buddy, took in her

exposed abdomen and cleavage. With crystal clear dark intention, he warned, "Exposing that much skin is risky here."

Feeling Frost's eyes on her, Kayn smirked. *Stings, doesn't it?* Innocently looking his way. He shook his head grinning and stripped off his shirt, blatantly tossing it in her direction. His ravenous flock got all worked up, one licked his chest. Holding her gaze without even attempting to move, he was daring her to take it a step further.

Presumptuously tracing a pulsing artery on her neck with his finger, her ignored friend teased, "If I were him, I'd be too jealous to play striptease Russian Roulette in a room full of Lampir."

He knew way more about her than he was letting on. Curious, she asked, "Why can't I see your aura?"

"It's a diet thing," her Lampir said without noticing he'd given her information. "So, we're not doing introductions at all?"

"Why bother?" Kayn enticed, placing her drink on the counter.

"I like you, come with me," he requested, holding out a hand as an invitation to whatever came next.

Like taking candy from a baby. As he led her away, she asked, "Where are we going?"

The nameless man playfully backed up, towing her with him, flirting, "I promise you'll enjoy it."

She was a Trojan horse, just a girl on the outside, but inside, she was a Dragon with the power to leave any being ashes in her wake. In this state, she had no fear.

He towed her into a cubicle. Someone shut the door as he declared, "Time for the show."

The walls on either side slid into the floor. Through a see-through barrier between rooms, she saw Frost being fed on by a squirming mass of women and men, enjoying it. She relaxed against her nameless Lampir.

With hot breath on her throat, he whispered, "I'll stop when you say no."

His teeth sunk into her creating such sweet agony, Kayn shivered as euphoria-inducing venom coursed through her and wept as pheromones released luring more strangers in. Her Siren soaked in their pleasure like a sponge as everyone fed in a hedonistic blur.

HEARING STEADILY HUMMING TIRES WITH RISQUÉ SIREN snippets flickering through her mind, Kayn groggily opened her eyes, mumbling, "What happened?" *Nothing made sense. Zach and Mel were out cold.*

Driving, Frost asked, "Feeling alright, Hun?"

With a flash of crawling out from under a hoard, Kayn sighed, "I killed everyone, didn't I?"

"No worries, the job was a success," Lily assured, looking back. "They dosed us to test a cloaking vaccine. Survival of the fittest, no harm, no foul. We fed information to Jenna via psychic link. Markus and the others dealt with it."

Meeting Frost's gaze in the rearview, Kayn confessed, "After strip Russian Roullette, my memory is scrambled."

"Lampir toxin," Frost disclosed, winking in the mirror.

"No fair, I didn't get to play strip Russian Roulette," Mel complained, yawning and stretching.

"Anytime," Zach taunted. Mel swatted him as he sat up, giggling. Looking around, she questioned, "Where are we?"

"We're doing a solo job. They'll catch up with us when they're finished," Lily said, switching the subject.

If the steamy visuals didn't stop, she might blow up another vehicle. Watching Frost being fed on by a writhing hoard totally did it for her. Flashes of shiver worthy hedonistic pleasure made goosebumps prickle everywhere. Concerned abilities were unstable, Kayn reached for Frost's shoulder, directing, "Pull over, I need a minute." They stopped, she got out into the crisp air and stood by a snowy field, watching her breath pirouette into the sky. *Snow rarely stuck around growing up, they'd have a day or two of it, but winter on Vancouver Island was mostly overcast and raining. It felt good to stand in the sunshine. It was too cold for rain.* She heard a door close and footsteps crunching in the snow.

Zach whispered, "I promised I'd stay with you, I don't know what happened."

"Extenuating circumstances," Kayn teased as he put his arm around her, giving her a buddy squeeze.

"It's cold out, you're not planning on lighting yourself on fire and blowing up another truck are you?" Zach ribbed, goofily swaying her, trying to lighten her mood.

Smiling, looking up at a cloudless sky, Kayn admitted, "I rarely plan for anything."

"It's been a wild six months, hasn't it? How much of last night do you remember?" Zach asked, shivering.

An x-rated flash of Lily and Zach going at it flickered in her brain. Kayn confessed, "I'm not sure what's real."

"I'm having flashes of something that must be a dream, I get it. There's only half an hour left in our drive, we're almost there," Zach walked her back to the truck.

Messing his hair, she kissed his cheek, praising, "Thank's for being you." Their eyes met as he opened the door and got into the middle next to Mel, who was texting away with someone. Curious, he peeked. There was no name on the number. Rolling his eyes, Zach baited, "Grey?"

"Hell no," Mel laughed. "It's just Arrianna making sure everyone is okay."

Switching Zach's focus would be easy if he knew Lily might be into him. She couldn't say anything about it when they were together.

"In an hour we'll be having room service in robes," Frost announced as they sped away leaving sketchy memories in the past.

With titillating visual of Frost being fed on by a hoard, swimming in her brain, she wanted to get him into the shower because he was impressively dirty. She had a sneaky suspicion her freaky Siren also knew no bounds. She'd only slept with Frost, and that happened for the first time a few months ago. Kayn peered down. *Oh, good, she was still wearing Lily's jeans. This wasn't her jacket.* She unzipped it and snuck a peek. *Awkward, she had no top on and was wearing a bra that wasn't hers. That was concerning. She'd had a few layers on. She lost an easy shirt flirting with Frost. Only one thing was going to calm her hampster wheel spinning at warp speed. Was she wearing underwear?* Stealthily unbuttoning her jeans, Kayn peeked. *She wasn't wearing any. Oh, no.* Everyone howled laughing. *They'd heard that unfiltered inner commentary. Fantastic.*

Giggling, Mel disclosed, "I was in a room with everyone else, nobody touched us. They let us out saying Lily was the only one awake."

"I don't pass out, I haven't slept at all," Lily said, smiling while texting.

Unable to resist, Kayn prodded, "Where was Zach?" Mel grinned like she had a secret. *That sly fox, she knew.*

Following the exchange like a tennis match, Zach grilled, "Where was I?"

Sighing loudly, Lily looked back and revealed, "You were with me."

"Our Zach, I can't believe it," Frost razzed, shoving Lily.

"I may never shower again," Zach flirted, grinning.

"You're not sleeping in my room without showering, you get stinky," Mel slammed, looking at her phone.

"Right in the groin, Mel," Zach rebutted, embarrassed.

Leaning her head back, Lily stated, "Don't overthink this, Zach. Those two set off my ability, you were the only one in the room, it could have been anyone."

Cringing, Mel quipped, "Ouch, awkward."

Awe, Zach. It felt like Mel was being nasty. Jealous?

"I'm going to jump out of this truck," Zach threatened.

"Drama queen," Mel teased, pushing buttons.

Zach tried to open the door. "Child lock," Frost giggled. He looked back at Zach as he unlocked it.

Without hesitation, Zach leapt out and tumbled down the highway behind the truck. *Holy shit. He did it.*

Backing up, Frost glared at Lily, saying, "This isn't the first time you've made a man jump out of a moving vehicle."

Impressed, Lily decreed, "He's way hotter now."

"He is," Mel mumbled, "I'm an asshole, I'll heal him."

"I've got it," Kayn jumped out and jogged over, knowing those two were the last people Zach wanted to see while writhing in agony by the side of the road.

In excruciating pain, her Handler looked up, groaning, "That was so much cooler in my head."

It always is. Placing her hands on his chest, Kayn assured, "I love your crazy." As her palms heated, she sensed she'd summoned the wrong ability. *Shit, she was going to siphon not heal.* Visualizing what she had to do, sedating warmth filled her chest and shivered up her spine into her brain, tingling before heading back down her arms into Zach, healing him instantly. With not a speck of fatigue, she helped him up. *That was different. She'd never felt that spine to brain part before.*

Walking back with his arm around her, Zach kissed her cheek and whispered, "Thanks for being you."

This was going to be a thing.

Zack slid into the backseat, baiting, "Anything else?" Not a syllable was uttered as they drove away.

He'd done something crazy to get her attention. It was romantic. The timing was downright idiotic, but he'd been standing outside of Mel's window with a metaphorical ghettoblaster professing his undying devotion since they met. With Mel's fling with the leader of Trinity and booty calling Grey, it was obvious she wasn't ready for what he wanted. Outside, hauntingly serene prairie slopes were blanketed in snow for as far as the eye could see. *It was beautiful.* Her eyes were drawn to Mel silently letting the ache in her heart settle. *She'd been disillusioned like that before. Love was magical enough to survive anything until you found out first hand it was bullshit. She hadn't been able to let go of the fantasy of her first love either. Kevin slitting her throat in the Testing had drawn a line in the sand between their Clan's and kicked her over it. Thorne may have done the same thing. Solidifying a relationship's demise with an arrow to the heart oughta do it. That was going to sting for years.*

"Getting out of the truck, Hun?" Frost teased, holding the door open.

Everyone was gone, she must have gapped out. What wild shit did her Conduit ability soak up at the Lampir Hive? Getting out, Kayn stepped into Frost's arms. After a prolonged embrace, they sauntered towards rustic cabins lugging mystery bags.

Lily walked out with keys, announcing, "I'm giving Frost and Kayn the single cabin. Am I correct in assuming we're adults capable of sharing a room without jumping out of a window?"

Peering up from tying his shoes, Zach bantered, "Fair enough, I'll assume you'll stop drugging me for sex."

Impressed by his witty comeback, Lily knelt, gazed deep into his eyes, caressed Zach's cheek and enticed, "Like I'd need to drug you." Gracefully rising, she left him squatting in the snow.

Helping him up, Mel suggested, "Let's go check out this horror movie cabin."

Mesmerised by the sway of Lily's hips as the breathtaking seductress walked away, Zach commented, "It's like winning the lottery and losing my ticket." He left Mel's side to pursue the alluring Pied Piper.

With a grin, Mel sighed, "Guess I'm the third wheel for a few days." Irritated by their flirtation, she took off.

"Have fun!" Kayn called after her. Mel laughed. *She wasn't sure who'd she'd root for if he asked for her opinion. She didn't want to see her Handler hurt. Mel just hit a bump in her life path and Zach was nothing but smooth road. Her friend Mel usually chose the windy route, even in the in-between where everything can be as simple as you envision. Then, there was Lily, coasting through the afterlife like sexy royalty with shiny black tresses and come hither everything, lighting up a room each time she walked in. It didn't matter where they were, the world stopped for Lily. Her dormant fire played oneliner peekaboo and vanished, rarely leaving a room breathless. She'd left many rooms laughing. It was better than nothing.* Watching the trio unlocking the door to an eerie shack, grinning like a Cheshire Cat, Kayn whispered, "That combination has the ingredients for a shit show." *Saying they were cabins on the website was a stretch.*

With arms looped around her waist from behind, Frost friskily nuzzled her neck, walking her forward, urging, "Let's find our cabin so we can be alone." Intending to mess with him, she reached back, he dodged out of her way, cautioning, "I'll take you right here in the snow."

Even walking in slush with soaking wet, freezing feet, he made everything feel like a sexy adventure. Crunching their way down the trail, they came upon their shady hut cabin by a frozen lake. *Wow. At least someone already lit the fire.*

"This masterpiece of false advertising is ours for a few days," Frost announced. Wincing, in preparation, he shoved open the door and laughed, "It's so bad."

"How bad can it be?" Kayn questioned, shimmying past him. There were single bunks, a kitchenette, an old recliner with a TV, and a fire going.

"You were saying?" Frost teased, tossing his bag.

Dropping hers as he locked the door, her pulse raced. Knowing what to say to make him snap, Kayn unzipped her jacket with no shirt on, enticing, "You mentioned seeing me through that glass wall."

Cockily removing his coat, revealing his chiselled abs, he toyed, "You were watching me too."

With only a breath of standoff, they frantically tore each other's clothes off. Lips met, as seductive tongues incited frenzied abandon so intense, he savagely took her against the wall with rage like urgency until they were crying out in limb trembling rapture. Panting, he held her captive whispering his kinky plans. Floating on euphoria, she shared a fantasy in flickering firelight.

He nibbled her ear, vowing, "Anything you want, I'll do. I'm yours."

Crazy in love, Kayn whispered, "Ditto." They hit pause to look at the room. *She needed to use the washroom.*

Checking the mystery door, she was so happy there was a tub. As she went in, Kayn called out, "Our next job isn't to find a serial murder at a campground, is it?" *He didn't hear her. Wrapped toothbrushes, bubble bath, toothpaste. No shower. It smelled clean.* She turned on the water.

Naughtily observing her bent over the tub, Frost trifled, "I might be the luckiest guy alive."

She glanced back and got an eye full. *He was a machine. So was she though. Were they alive?*

He took it G-rated, announcing, "Good news, there's a stocked fridge, clothes that look like they'll fit, and phone chargers." He placed a makeup bag on the sink.

That was hers. That bag should be long gone. Kayn reached into the tub to adjust the plug.

Clutching her hips, he mischievously instructed, "I'll be back with a treat. I'm trying to be romantic. Stay here, get in the tub."

Born in different times, she was a fetus in comparison. Not even that, she was the urge to copulate. Did he just tell her she was going to get a treat if she stayed? Holy crap, he did. She was obligated to call him out as part of the female species. Music was playing as she slipped into the tub. Lounging, closing her eyes, she heard him come in. He turned off the lights. Smelling something, Kayn peeked as he lit a candle and passed her a bottle of wine. She shimmied up so he could get in behind her, relaxed against him and took a drink. *This was nice.* In his arms with the sedating warmth of the water, her body melted against his.

Lathering his hands, tenderly kissing her shoulder, Frost whispered, "I adore you, Brighton."

As skilled hands slid over her soapy curves, enraptured by caresses, Kayn sighed, "This may end up being one of my favourite places." With a song she loved playing in flickering candlelight, she faced him. Straddling his lap, she washed his chest with slippery sudsy fingers, taunting, "I can't believe you took off your shirt in the bar."

Grinning, Frost countered, "You walked in with a shirt that said easy and took it off."

"I had a shirt on underneath," Kayn sparred, soaping him up beneath the bubbles.

Playing her game, he caressed her, baiting, "The rules of strip Russian Roulette say it had to come off." Their lips met seductively. Testing with her sanity beneath bubbles, Frost confessed, "Watching you through that glass barrier will be in my dreams for decades."

Ration tapped out as she gasped, "Don't stop." Their lips met, muffling moans and they were lost in a soapy blur of erotic games until the water grew cold. They towel dried each other off and wandered out. *Mattresses and blankets were by the fire. Music was playing, there was another bottle of wine and no way, Twinkies. So many brownie points.* Pheromone love drunk, Kayn whispered, "It's perfect."

"You don't miss the expensive honeymoon suite?" Frost teased, running a damp tendril between his fingers with raw emotional eyes.

Gazing into his eyes, Kayn admitted, "I don't care where we are. If we're never simple or normal, it's okay with me, I'm in this." Tenderly kissing his lips, she left him standing there speechless to sprawl like a feline by the fire. Feeling his pressure as he joined her, she faced him. They lay looking at each other in flickering light and shadows.

Inching closer, Frost probed, "What happened last night occurs regularly, can you deal with it?"

"I may eat all your friends and kill you in your sleep, can you deal with it?" She harassed, nibbling his ear.

Rolling her on top of him, he chuckled, "See, I know it's wrong to find that crazy sexy, but I can't help it."

Tracing his abs with a finger, Kayn whispered, "Can I be honest?"

"Always," Frost said, watching her.

"I'm going to need a minute if you sleep with Lily," she admitted.

Suggestively gripping her hips, he explained, "We're in a magically reinforced friend zone, it's highly unlikely. I can't promise it's not going to be gong show of epic proportions if you continue having conversations with your ex about departments I'm lacking in."

Where did that come from? "Explain," Kayn prompted.

"Picture this, we show up to steal Triad's Venom, and Tiberius is on a hookup date. Lexy goes dark, Grey full-on loses his shit. Mortals are fleeing, chairs are flying. Triad and Ankh are in a deep south no holds barred, biting, scratching, broken beer bottle shanking brawl. Kevin goes off about me being an emotionally vacant sociopath as we're beating the snot out of each other, then starts spouting off about how cold our first time was. I chased him around the hotel while he tossed in intensely personal shit, telling me answers to every question I've ever had about you because he paid attention to your needs."

Holy crap. What in the hell, Kevin? Unwrapping a Twinkie, she took a bite, dipped her finger and licked off the cream. Meeting his eyes, Kayn disclosed, "Remember the job in Alaska where Mel snuck into a hospital to heal a Correction survivor, Astrid and Haley took off, and we distracted Triad. I may not have mentioned how choked Kevin was about being forced to watch me move on in visions. We talked, I stole his phone and left. If opting out of telling you every detail was the wrong decision, I'm sorry. During that fight, he was flinging shit at you to hurt me for not warning him."

"He's psychic, that sociopath crack is stuck in my head," Frost admitted. Confiscating her alluring snack, he took a bite.

With ringlets concealing her chest in firelight, she kissed his sweet lips, provoking, "If you're concerned you might be one, you're not. A sociopath wouldn't care."

Sliding a hand between her thighs, he whispered, "I'm yours for as long as you'll have me."

Their lips met in lusty seduction as they lost all need for anything but pleasure, christening every surface until the wee hours.

6
REEL HIM IN OR LET HIM GO

There wasn't a speck of drama left in Mel as she wandered into their cabin and saw bunk beds with a recliner. Normally, she would have shared a bunk with Zach, but he was angry with every right to be. She couldn't keep him dangling on a hook forever. She had to reel him in or let him go. Tossing her bag on the top bunk, Mel watched Zach joking with his forgotten fantasy consort, ignoring her presence. *Her friend won the guy lottery by hooking up with Lily. If she wanted to make up with him, she should go sleep in the truck.* After checking out their slasher film worthy accommodations, Mel decided to just do her best to stay out of their way. Claiming the top bunk by climbing up and lounging on top of the sheets, she dug out her phone to entertain herself. *Lily was in the kitchen, making something to eat. Zach was having a bath. She'd already made plenty of bad choices this week, why not make one more?* She texted Grey, *What's up?* When he didn't respond, she regretted it. She'd used Grey because she was bored and blown him off when she found out Lexy was hurt by it. She'd never wanted more from him than a pleasurable way to kill time. *She had time to kill now, Lexy was moving on, why not?* Her phone vibrated. Mel grinned as she read Grey's text. *Who dis?* Shaking her head, she flirtatiously messaged back. *You can have me if you can guess who it is.* Her cell buzzed. She read his response. *I'm intrigued by this nameless naughty offer. Give me a hint.*

This was stupid. What was she doing? Bored, Mel hinted. *Is my dad with you?*

Grey texted back. *Lily?*

Ouch. Enough of this game. Flopping on her back, staring at the ceiling, Mel grimaced. *The mattress was horrible. Going to sleep wasn't an option.* Leaving her phone, she climbed down.

Dancing and singing with her shimmering black hair like a scantily clad fairy tale princess, Lily turned, announcing, "I made you a sandwich and here's a glass of wine. I know you prefer white but red is all we have."

Why did she have to be this likeable? Smiling as Lily passed it, Mel said, "Thank you."

"I'm sensing tension," Lily whispered, so Zach wouldn't hear. "You know how out of control Siren get when you add Lampir venom to the mix. We were locked in a room. I hope you know, I'd never purposely do anything to hurt you."

She felt like a jerk. "Don't worry about it," Mel assured. "We're just friends. It was just the timing after what Thorne did. Zach's always had a crush on me. I know it's wrong to string him along. It feels good to know someone will always want you no matter what."

Sipping her wine, Lily admitted, "I have one of those."

"Grey?" Mel asked curiously.

Nodding, Lily said, "I try to stay away, but sometimes my libido snuffs out ration."

"I texted him a few minutes ago, I was bored. He thought it was you," Mel confessed, smiling.

"Really? See, that's what I mean," Lily whispered as Zach walked out, silencing their gossip.

"Should I just assume you were talking about me?" Zach teased with a towel wrapped around his waist. "I left my bag at the door. This is a tiny towel, look away if you don't want to see my ass."

Sipping wine, they kept watching as he walked to his bag. *Knowing he'd been with Lily made him so much hotter. What was wrong with her?*

Catching them staring, Zach flirted, "See anything you like?" Grinning, he strutted back to the washroom.

Curiosity, that's all this renewed interest was. As he shut the door, Mel whispered, "How was he?"

Lily challenged, "Find out for yourself."

"It'll wreck our friendship, he's all yours. Go for it," Mel dared, eating her sandwich as Lily got up to grab the bottle of wine. *Zach might have a shot with her. It blew her mind. She was equal parts proud and jealous. It was wrong to stand in the way when she didn't have a logical reason.*

Placing the bottle by her, Lily revealed, "I was irked when I found out you'd been sleeping with Grey."

"Not jealous, just irked," Mel teased, pouring another glass.

Smiling, Lily confessed, "Maybe a little. Don't tell him, I'll never admit it. I'm sure you remember how chilly it was between us for a year. In retrospect, I knew better. There's a drama toll to pay booty calling someone who has feelings for you." Watching the crackling fire, Lily disclosed, "I heard about what happened. An arrow in the heart was excessively harsh but maybe it needed to be. One of you was always going to have to take out the other. You'll feel better after you've had a chance to get even."

Maybe. Blinking away revealing tears, Mel kept her gaze on the soothing fire. Sucking back self-pity, she couldn't find the words to respond. *It felt like his arrow was still in her heart.*

Reaching for Mel's hand, Lily consoled, "Toss those rose coloured glasses, he arranged an arrow in your heart. I know it feels like the conclusion of each chapter is the end of the world, but it's only the beginning of a new one."

Something crashed in the bathroom. They raced in and found Zach writhing in agony, shrieking for Kayn clutching his head. By his side in a breath, Mel soothed, "I'm here. You can do this. I've got you."

"Enlightenings happen for the first couple of years after coming out of the Testing. There isn't much we can do, his brain's changing, new areas are lighting up. I'll get Kayn," Lily announced, taking off.

Her symbol heated beneath her glove. Mel yelled, "I hope that was you!"

Sticking her head in, Lily chuckled, "It was me! Just cut my hand to summon the honeymooners!"

7
SHIT WAS GOING DOWN

With her chest burning, Kayn opened her eyes, panicking as the brand of Ankh on her hand heated and flashed. *Shit was going down.* She scrambled up. Frost was dressed, tugging on boots. She whipped on clothes. He tossed her a knife, she caught it in midair. In a flash, they were sprinting for the other cabin through crunching snow in the dark, guided by instinct. As they grew closer, she heard Zach shrieking and her blood ran cold.

Standing in the doorway, Lily waved them in, explaining, "It's Zach's Enlightening. He's screaming for Kayn."

Panicked, Kayn rushed past her into the bathroom. Zach was naked flailing in Mel's arms. Looking up helplessly, Mel sighed, "It's hard to just sit here. I wanted to try healing him but intuition was screaming to let it run its course."

Switching places with Mel, Kayn consoled, "I'm here. I'm with you Zach, it's me." He went limp in her arms as their Handler Dragon bond worked its magic.

She stroked his hair as he trembled, slick with perspiration.

Frost stuck his head in and said, "Lily is making coffee, he could be like this all night. Do you need a pillow?"

Looking up, Kayn answered, "Coffee, when it's ready, would be fantastic." Smiling, Frost tossed Zach's towel and closed the door. She shimmied backwards until her back was against the wall, covered him up and stroked his hair. *She could have used that pillow.* Staring at the closed door, bored stiff, her mind travelled back to the one, Frost carved their initials on. *It felt like it was a long time ago, but it wasn't. Testing was less than six months ago. Maybe it was four? She wasn't sure. The concept of time was difficult to grasp now.*

Lily came in and passed her a coffee, asking, "How's he doing?"

"Feverish but less agitated," Kayn whispered.

"You'd better drink that coffee before he starts flailing," Lily suggested, quietly closing the door.

Kayn spent hours thinking up scenarios to keep herself occupied. *What if this wasn't Zach's Enlightening and he'd caught a supernatural std last night?* She smiled at her inner dialogue. *It was more likely she caught something.* X-rated steamy snippets flowed through her mind as she dozed off.

Kayn opened her eyes. *Shoot, she'd fallen asleep.* He was out cold on her lap. *He wasn't shaking anymore.* The door opened.

Peering in, Lily whispered, "How is he?"

"I think it's over, it looks like he's sleeping. What are you guys doing?" Kayn quietly replied, not wanting her to leave.

Catching the hint, Lily whispered, "It's morning, Frost is out cold in the easy chair, Mel fell asleep. I slept for an hour or two. We have a job, I let them rest. I bet you're sore from sitting on the floor all night?"

Dawn's first rays were streaming through the bathroom window with dust particles floating magically in light. *Was it really morning?* Kayn stroked her Handler's hair, Zach opened his eyes.

With a strange look, Zach whispered, "Is there a reason we're bonding on the bathroom floor?"

Smiling, caressing his hair, Kayn whispered back, "You had a rough night, brain growing pains."

"What are you talking about?" Zach asked, sitting up and stretching. "I was having a bath." Seeing the towel over his junk, he chuckled, "I bet this wasn't the night you pictured." Holding the towel over his situation, he got up and held out his hand to help her as Lily came back in.

Grinning, Kayn suggested, "Cover up."

He spun around and saw Lily standing there. "Whoops." Zach giggled, trying to wrap the towel around himself but it was too small. With his backside facing the tub, he clicked, "It's all coming back, I had a brutal headache." He looked at his hands, saying, "I don't feel different."

Funny, her badass superhero healing powers didn't cover sitting on a bathroom floor all night. Stretching, Kayn hinted, "I'm sure someone is dying to use the washroom." She reached for the doorknob.

"Hey," Zach called after her. She turned back. Smiling, he added, "Thank you."

"You've done it for me," Kayn answered, gently closing the door. Smelling bacon frying, she snuck across the room and leapt onto Frost's lap, kissing his neck.

Groggily grinning, he opened his eyes, saying,

"Morning beautiful." Hugging her, tickling her sides as she laughed.

Strolling over with a coffee in each hand, Lily teased, "You two are far too adorable. Breakfast will be ready in a few minutes. One of you needs to wake up, Mel. I've had to pee for hours."

From her bunk, Mel shouted, "I'm up. Carry on being cute."

They couldn't, they had coffee in their hands. Kayn whispered, "I'm sorry, our romantic night was cut short."

"We didn't come back here until after one-thirty, I have no complaints," Frost whispered, giving her a peck on the lips.

Wandering over with his coffee, Zach apologised, "Sorry I wrecked date night."

"How you feeling?" Frost asked, drinking his coffee.

"Refreshed, like I just had a full night of sleep," Zach admitted. "What's the job?"

"We'll talk over breakfast," Frost answered, playing with Kayn's hair.

Closing her eyes, tempted to have a nap in his arms, Kayn relaxed against him. *He always smelled incredible.*

Nuzzling her, Frost whispered, "No rest for the wicked. Who's watching the bacon?"

"It's on the counter, grab a plate," Lily prompted as they all went to the kitchen.

Sitting with plates on their laps in front of the fire, Frost filled everyone in, "Okay, we're doing a large Correction. We have a demon, pretending to be a prophet. He's gathered a following for the purpose of mass suicide as a sacrifice to bring back his girlfriend. Now, he can't just kill thirty people, they have to do it themselves. Everyone in his following must be marked by us and put down to prevent it. This demon he's trying to bring back is a pain in the ass, we've dealt with her before. Any questions?"

"Can't we just get rid of the demon?" Mel asked.

"These people have been infected with his ideology. The Oracle gives the orders, we obey. If there were a way around this, trust me, Jenna would have found it. I promise once you've spent five minutes with this flock of mortal assholes, you won't be feeling the need to save anyone. For those capable of operating without feelings, it'll be a walk in the park," Frost stated, winking at Kayn.

Intrigued, the Dragon stirred as Kayn enquired, "Where do I find these brainwashed zealots?"

"We," Zach corrected, irritated, glaring at her.

Rolling her eyes, Kayn sighed, "Where do we find these zealots?" *Lambs to the slaughter.*

"Not funny, Brighton," her Handler commented on her inner dialogue.

"I was a sacrifice yesterday," Kayn rebutted, with a wink. *In theory, so were you.*

Grinning at his girlfriend's eagerness to go on a murder spree, Frost teased, "Back up Jason Vorhees, there's a way it has to play out. Those with a shot at redemption need to be marked with our blood and sent back through the hall of souls. Dark auras go elsewhere. We have to subdue and sort these people. Lily will go through the wounded with me. Zach, can keep up with Kayn as she takes them down?"

"One demon and thirty mortals, I've got this, you guys clean up," Kayn replied, bringing her plate to the sink. *She'd heard all she needed to hear.*

Frost asserted, "Earth to Zach, are you confident you'll have control over the situation or is Kayn just going to go on a murder spree and blow the job?"

Watching Kayn rinsing off her dish, Zach sparred, "Are you confident she'll listen to you?"

Cackling, Lily choked on her last bite. Frost patted Lily's back, teasing, "Karma got your lungs?" Redirecting his witty banter, he clarified, "I'm not her Handler, Zach. Be straight with me. Do you have enough pull to give her direction?"

Answering for Zach, Mel reminded, "Kayn can see auras, she stopped herself from killing Lucien. If the orders are clear when she slips into the Dragon state, she'll play along."

"That was a Lampir Correction. These are mortals, we must designate their soul's destination. She can't kill anyone tonight. No mortals perish within the walls of that building until they've been marked to diffuse what he's done," Frost stressed. "We have information for ten people who need to meet with accidents before this evening. If they survive until tonight our odds change. The daytime portion of this job is brains before brawn."

Sauntering over, Kayn provoked, "No murder spree till this evening, got it."

Entertained by her selective hearing, Frost maintained, "No murder spree for you, honey."

She wanted to smack him. He had this polarizing effect on her. Meeting his entertained eyes, Kayn knew he'd caught her unfiltered inner dialogue.

With a hip check, Frost flirted, "Smack me later."

Or now. Kayn slapped his ass so hard it stung her hand. *Oh, pain totally did it for her.*

With mesmerizing eyes locked on hers, Frost cautioned, "Keep sticking kinky ideas in my head and I'll be the one that blows this job."

"As entertaining as this game of Siren chicken is, we have to kill ten people before midnight," Lily reminded, walking over.

Frost bargained, "Twenty minutes, I'll owe you one. PG promise."

Looking at the others, Lily rushed, "Shoes on, if they go back to that cabin for their bags, we'll lose hours."

Brushing her teeth, Kayn paused as Frost came in. With a foamy mouth, she mumbled, "Noob bubbis umba ba bink."

Grinning, he wrapped his arms around her waist, kissed her neck and whispered, "Noob bubbis?"

She spat out her toothpaste and repeated, "Toothbrushes under the sink."

With hands naughtily travelling her curves, he baited, "I promised I wouldn't do anything."

"I didn't," Kayn taunted. Grinning, she spun around and planted a minty kiss on his lips.

As they embraced, Frost whispered, "No killing anyone tonight, you'll get me in trouble."

Giggling as he nuzzled her neck, Kayn sighed, "You drive me insane in so many ways." As their lips met, hers parted, urging the G-rating up a notch. Darting her tongue against his, she boldly caressed him. Frost groaned, picked her up and put her on the counter. She wrapped her legs around his waist so he couldn't get away as their lusty game of chicken intensified, lines blurred as they fogged up the mirror, lost their shirts and were scrambling to get their pants off when they heard a noise in the other room. *Shit. No.*

The door slammed, Lily's voice announced, "You're not alone. We have your things, it's time to leave."

Frost called out, "Noob bubbis!"

Kayn shoved him as he giggled. Smiling, she tossed him an unopened toothbrush.

Jaw-dropping hot, with his chiselled chest and six-pack abs, he patted down her hair, tenderly kissed her and urged, "It's difficult to plot and execute ten accidents in one day. We should hurry."

As he brushed his teeth, she wiped off the steamy mirror and freshened up her makeup. *It felt like they were a married couple getting ready for their workday. Creatively murdering ten people wasn't a normal couple pastime, but for them, it was just another Wednesday.* Trying to put on eyeliner while watching him put on his shirt in the mirror, she poked herself in the eye. "Crap," Kayn cursed, blinking and tearing up.

"You okay?" He enquired, with a hand on the doorknob.

"All good, I'll be another minute," she answered, smiling at him in the mirror.

"Bring anything you want to keep, we don't know how this job will play out," he suggested, closing the door.

Everyone was in good spirits driving into town, singing along to music like they weren't on their way to murder ten people. *Serial murderers and demons were easy to execute, the innocent weren't. She'd never done a job like this.*

Turning down the music, Lily explained, "All we have is the address of our first accident, and the name, Martin."

They pulled up in front of a house with a swing set and miscellaneous toys scattered on the lawn. *At least one child lived here, she didn't want to think anymore.* Kayn slit her palm with a blade, the wound seeped and healed instantly. She went to pass Mel the knife.

"I'm good, mine never dulls, I always see auras," Mel answered.

"Mine dulls when I'm Siren," Kayn admitted as a child dashed out the door to the swingset."

Watching the child play, Lily remarked, "Siren's are built to overlook things."

The little girl leapt off the swing and raced towards older children walking a dog down the sidewalk. *She loved dogs, she hadn't had the opportunity to pet one in a long time.*

Nudging Mel, Zach questioned, "What's that goofy look for?"

"I miss being a kid," Mel confessed, glancing his way.

Zach taunted, "We're about to blow up this happy kid's life, I bet Martin's her dad."

"Thanks," Mel sparred, shooting him a dirty look.

"Wait here," Lily said as she got out and walked over to the child, "Hi honey, does anyone else live here?"

"Nope, just my Mom," she replied with an adorable grin. "Want to see what I got?"

Playing along, Lily humoured her, "Sure, what do you have?" She followed the child around the side of the house.

Nobody ever worries about beautiful female strangers.

Texting, Frost looked up and assured, "Jenna says this is the address. "Where did Lily go?"

"She went with the kid," Kayn commented. "Do we get to know why Martin needs to die?"

Meeting her gaze in the rearview, Frost disclosed, "These deaths set off a chain reaction of events, they're sacrificial lambs like us, that's all we need to know."

8
MARTIN MUST DIE

*I*n the backyard, the excited child showed off a bucket full of wood bugs. "Wow, did you collect these by yourself?" Lily praised, noticing bruises on the child's arms.

"I did," she happily preened, wiggling with excitement as five-year-old's often do.

Sensing her happiness was an act, Lily enquired, "What's your name?"

"Chelsea," the child announced with a toothless grin.

Smiling maternally, Lily stated, "That is the perfect name for you."

"It's stupid, I don't like it anymore," Chelsea declared as her smile vanished. She turned it back on, and changed the subject, "I have a hamster named Winston. Stay here, I'll get him."

Something was off. Instinct led her up weathered mint green steps into an open backdoor. Detecting a hint of copper, Lily peered around the corner. Blood spatter on linoleum led to an unconscious woman on the carpet in the living room with a pulse. The coffee table was covered in empties. There was a bloody belt on the floor. Disgusted by abuse, Lily solemnly walked back to the door.

The child came downstairs with a shoebox. Beaming with pride, she opened the box and showed her a dead hamster, whispering, "He's sleeping."

"Your Mom's hurt, I want to help," Lily whispered.

Frightened, the child whispered, "Don't take me away."

"I wouldn't do that but I have to leave to get help for your Mom," Lily urged, seeing pictures of a mother and her child in the hall.

With trembling lips and tear-filled eyes, the child stressed, "Promise you won't take me away?"

Lily knelt to meet the child at her level, whispering, "They won't have any reason to. I'll make sure he leaves and never comes back. Where is he?"

"In the shop," the child disclosed, pointing to a shed.

Smiling, Lily wiped away her tears and said, "This is very important, go to your room and hide in your closet until the police come. He'll never hurt you again, I promise." Lily held out her pinkie, pledging the most powerful of all childhood oaths, "Pinkie swear."

They shook pinkies and Chelsea ran upstairs. Enraged, Lily marched to the shed at the back of the property. He was using a drill. *This was going to be quick and painless for her.* She texted Frost. *Drive around the block. This will only take a minute.* Taking a breath, Lily composed herself. Feeling nothing but contempt, she knocked on the garage door.

A male voice hollered, "How many times do I need to tell you to stay the fuck inside, you dumb bitch!"

Footsteps stomped to the door, it swung open and stale beer wafted out. A man in his mid-twenties who might have been attractive if she didn't already know he was disgusting was standing there. Placing a hand on his chest, Lily walked him back into the shed, flirting, "Don't you remember me? You asked me to come see you."

Intrigued, Martin slurred, "Of course I remember you, baby."

As the door swung shut, Lily picked up a nail gun and innocently enquired, "What is this for?"

Snatching it from her, he laughed, "Someone as pretty as you, shouldn't play with nail guns."

Sensually caressing his stubbly jaw, gazing into his eyes, she seduced, "What do you want me to play with?" Under her spell, she ran her hand down his arm to the hand holding the nail gun and whispered in his ear, "I have a sexy idea. Point it at my head, I'll pretend it's a gun. That would turn me on." Holding it to her temple, evil glinted in his eyes as Lily suggested, "Or we can do this." She moved the hand with the gun to his head and squeezed it. He slumped to the floor, with wide eyes. Satisfied the world was better off, she walked out, vanished down the alley and called 911, "My neighbour was screaming. That abusive asshole must have come back. Her car is there, she has a little girl. Nobody is answering the door. Oh, God. I hope he didn't kill them, please hurry." She gave the address, hung up and texted Frost. *It's done. I took the alley, keep driving around the block you'll find me.*

9
FLYING BLIND

Frost's phone buzzed. Smiling while reading a message, he started the truck, explaining, "It's done. Time for hall of souls contestant number two."

"We're not going to be sitting in this car all day, are we?" Kayn commented as they spotted Lily and pulled over.

Looking into the backseat, Frost teased, "I thought you newbies were sensitive about this stuff."

"Ditch the newbie tag we survived Testing," Mel sparred, shaking her head.

Chuckling, Frost baited, "Alright, which of you new full Ankh immortals with no control over your abilities and less than six months experience wants to fly blind?"

Raising her hand, Kayn offered, "I'll do it."

Intrigued, Frost toyed, "All by yourself, no Handler?"

Meeting his eyes, Kayn shrugged and said, "Why not?"

Peering up, her Handler decreed, "You might set fire to a hair salon full of mortals?"

"Details, killing strangers is my thing," Kayn joked, just messing with Frost. *She didn't think anyone would be stupid enough to send her in alone with her track record.*

Giggling, Zach didn't bother looking up from his phone while commentating, "This is a horrible idea."

Mid text Mel peered up, saying, "You can't be serious? She just lit a truck on fire."

"Just one person, I can pace myself," Kayn responded. "If I'm having a moment, Zach will sense it. Better yet, I'll text just like Lily did if there's an issue."

Lily got in, oddly satisfied for someone who'd just killed an innocent.

Frost asked, "What was Martin like?"

"He was Mom's abusive boyfriend. I found her beaten to a pulp in the livingroom. The child had bruised wrists and a dead hamster in a box. Martin tripped and shot himself in the head with a nail gun in the shed," Lily revealed.

Feeling good about the next job, Kayn pressed. "What's the next guy's name?"

Snatching Frost's phone, Lily read the Oracle's message, "Jennifer works at Jiffy Cut. I'm guessing she's a hairdresser. Who is up to bat next?"

"Me," Kayn said, googling, toxic products to mix in a hair studio. *This was going to be fun.*

Elbowing Frost, Lily quietly reprimanded, "Really? Why are we risking this?"

Ouch. She didn't even try to hide her opinion by just thinking that slam.

"Why not? We're supposed to be helping with control. She's not turning her emotions off, she'll use ration when it counts. Right?" Frost asserted, staring into Kayn's eyes.

Shit. She took a joke so far it was real. Now, she had to own it.

Reading the article on Kayn's phone over her shoulder, Mel sighed, "She's looking up which toxic chemicals to mix to knock out people in a hair salon."

"That's a good idea," Lily praised, impressed.

"Right?" Kayn answered, sending her the article.

Mel stammered, "No, it's not. Are you guys insane?"

"Probably," Kayn replied, winking.

"It's a prerequisite for surviving Immortal Testing," Lily taunted, grinning. "It's quick in and out rules. Slow and easy doesn't win the race when there's a time crunch."

As they pulled up at the hair studio, Kayn held out her hand, saying, "I need an Aries Group card."

Digging it out of his wallet, Frost passed it to her, teasing, "I'm texting the address to the Aries Group. No witnesses. Fast in and out, text if there's an issue."

It was adorable. He believed in her. Semi confident, Kayn got out, loudly saying, "I've got this," walking away. Bells jingled as she walked into a full hair studio. *She didn't have this at all. This just became complicated. She'd planned on getting a haircut and mixing a few products before she left. Now, she had no idea what she was going to do.* Scanning for a camera, smiling warmly so it looked like she knew how to people. *Everything smelled fresh and lovely.* Perusing products on the shelves, she checked out service prices on a flyer at the desk. *Three stylists were working and they had name tags. Perfect.*

A girl with burgundy hair and a dull aura, approached, enquiring, "Can I help you?"

Smiling politely, Kayn asked, "Do you have anyone free to give me a quick trim and style?"

"I'm Jessica, I'm free. Feeling adventurous?" She sang as Kayn followed the girl to her station

She motioned to her set up. Kayn sat in the swivel chair, instructing, "Just split ends, I'm okay with my hair."

Playing with her curls, Jessica scrunched up her nose as she remarked, "I get it, you're earthy. It's greasy, can I wash it. I understand for people with busy lives and no romantic prospects showering isn't a priority. With hair like yours, you should try to wash it more than once in a week. I just want you to be the best you."

Earthy? She wasn't allowed to kill the heinous bitch. Looking in the mirror, Kayn sighed, "I guess."

Jessica massaged her scalp, droning on about products that would clear up her gross dandruff situation. Ignoring the jabs the stylist was making, Kayn closed her eyes. *She was going to prove she could ignore this dumbass.*

"I can fix this dull, lacklustre colour, amp it up a touch with a few streaks," Jessica suggested, rinsing her hair.

Gripping the armrest, Kayn kept her eyes closed. *This wasn't Jennifer. She wasn't allowed to kill Jessica.*

"I think Jennifer is free. Do you want her to fix your nails? When people have dirty nails, I'm concerned for their well being. All of your hygiene issues aside, we touch our faces thousands of times per day, you'll give yourself pink eye," Jessica lectured.

Holy shit. Holding back the intense need to slap her, Kayn met her eyes, agreeing, "Sure, Jennifer can do my nails."

"I'll get her," Jessica declared and left.

She texted Lily. *Are you sure I'm supposed to kill Jennifer? My hairstylist Jessica might be the antichrist. She insinuated I never bathe and might get pink eye from my nails.* A second later, her phone buzzed with Lily's response. *People like that will insult anyone. I'm coming in, let's see what she has to say about me.*

Grinning as the girl with a Jennifer name tag strode over and shook her hand, apologising, "Jessica is having a social media break. Her dad owns the salon, she does whatever she wants."

"Says whatever she wants," Kayn sighed, scrutinising her clean nails.

Looking at her nails, Jennifer whispered, "She told an elderly customer a rash looked like syphilis." Jennifer passed a basket of polish, urging, "Pick a colour. Once I've started, you'll be granted a reprieve for twenty minutes, loose hair sticks to wet nails."

The bell dinged. Lily strutted in like an Arabian princess. Jennifer rushed, "I'll get her to wash this girl's hair. Maybe, she'll switch customers with me?"

Jennifer was nice. Jessica was Satan, and she was intrigued. Would she try to pick apart perfection? Kayn picked a colour as Jennifer slipped into the backroom, returning with the horrid thing. She passed the nice girl the colour she'd chosen.

Sitting on a rolling stool next to her, shaking the polish, Jennifer whispered, "You're all mine."

"I'd like to see her pick that girl apart," Kayn whispered.

Leaning closer, Jennifer whispered, "She's going to try, watch."

Washing Lily's hair, Jessica tried her dandruff speel. Lily calmly retaliated, "I don't have dandruff, I've never even had a split end."

Sneering, Jessica probed, "Where did you migrate from?"

"Everywhere," Lily replied, crossing her toned legs like a dare.

Smirking, Jessica goaded, "I thought Indian women were docile?"

Smiling, Lily countered, "You were misinformed."

Focused on drying her hair, Jessica sighed, "I don't care."

"About getting tips, I can tell, " Lily stated, winking at Kayn.

The lady doing her nails, whispered, "If you know that girl, you might want to tell her she's playing mind games with a diagnosed psychopath."

Wild. "What's the difference between a psychopath and a sociopath?" Kayn asked, fascinated.

"One might kill you," Jennifer disclosed as she left to diffuse the situation.

Kayn texted Lily. *You are messing with a diagnosed psychopath.*

Touching Lily's shoulder while she was reading Kayn's message, Jennifer suggested, "Why don't we let Jessica take a break?"

"I don't think so tip vulture," Jessica bantered, shooing her away. "Flee pathetic loser, before I get you fired." She raised scissors.

Fleeing as most reasonable people would, Jennifer shook her head, sitting back down, whispering, "I feel obligated to warn people. Sorry about that."

"It's not your pile," Kayn responded, feeling shitty about the hand fate dealt the lady.

Filing her nails, Jennifer whispered, "Everyone working here should get danger pay."

Waving psycho Jessica away, Lily gagged, provoking, "Your breath smells like garlicy deli meat. Hope you don't have low carb diet-induced rage issues, you lost your tip ages ago. I've changed my mind, if your hair washing skills are this mediocre, you aren't touching my hair."

Lunging at Lily as she swivelled her chair, Jessica tripped and stabbed, Jennifer in the neck. Coldly watching as her blood spurted, she taunted, "Bye bitch."

Holy shit, Jessica.

The psychopath kept trying to stab Lily as she scooted around on the chair, giggling, "So scary. Stop, I'm going to pee."

Everyone gathered in a terrified cluster. Pretending to put pressure on the wound, Kayn called out, "Help! Call 911!" Looking into Jessica's eyes, she whispered, "I'm sorry this happened." Jennifer went limp in her arms and sailed away into her next life as a lone cop rushed through the door. *Wow, that was fast.*

"Jessica! Put the scissors down!" Raising his weapon, the officer, demanded, "Now!"

Everyone raced out in the chaos. They grabbed their jackets, slipped out, got into the truck and took off. Kayn's shirt was covered in blood, Lily was pissing herself laughing. Stripping off her shirt, Kayn asked Zach to grab her a new one from someone's bag.

Passing her a baggy shirt, Zach enquired, "Things get out of hand?"

"My hairdresser tripped and stabbed Jennifer in the neck. Where are we off to next?" Lily prompted, smiling at Kayn.

Glancing in the rearview, Frost tempted, "Want to go on a murder date, Brighton?"

Romantic. Peering up at Frost's reflection, Kayn baited, "Can you keep up?"

"Can I keep up?" Frost scoffed, with an amused smile. "Haven't we already determined, keeping up isn't an issue?"

"You try," Kayn sparred. The truck pulled over. *What in the hell was he doing?*

Frost got out. Opening her door, he leaned in, tempting, "Coming, Brighton?"

He wasn't going to leave her by the side of the road to make a point, was he? Playing along, she got out. They were at a rest area.

"Follow me," he instructed, leaving her standing there wondering what he had up his sleeve. She glanced back at the truck. Everyone was watching. She sauntered after him, saying, "Are you going to explain why we pulled over? Am I in trouble for being sassy? *In theory, he was her boss.* They walked around the building.

When they couldn't be seen by the others, Frost swooped her up in his arms, seducing, "After we're done this job, you're in so much trouble." Playfully kissing her neck, she giggled as he whispered, "I'd take you right here if I didn't know there were cameras. Look up, there's one by the door and another on the pole. The guy in the tiny tourist office over there needs to meet with an accident. Any ideas?"

"So many. Most involve shoving you into the bathroom and having my way with you," Kayn taunted in his ear.

Pulling away, Frost caressed her cheek, sweetly kissed her and provoked, "Can your one-track mind hold that thought until we murder this guy?"

She was so into him, it was crazy. "I'll try," Kayn replied, looking at the teeny office. "That has to be the most boring job in the world, we're doing this guy a favour."

His phone buzzed. Grinning as he looked at it, Frost suggested, "The peanut gallery votes for the tree behind his office."

She'd had a tree thrown at her before, by Lily. "If he's playing music, there's electricity. Loose wires? I'll go say hi and see what we have to work with," Kayn toyed, sauntering away with an exaggerated hip sway.

Glancing back, she saw Frost laughing. *She was never sure if he was laughing with her or at her.* A few drops of rain fell. She looked up at the dark clouds, as it started pouring. Thunder rumbled and lightning flashed as she jogged over to the frail man in the booth, saying, "This job has to suck?"

Smiling, he said, "It sucks way less when people don't remind me. Where are you newlyweds off to?"

About to correct him, she opted to just go with it, "We're headed back to B.C."

"You're in B.C," he chuckled, over the pattering of heavy rain on the roof.

"I was asleep for a few hours," Kayn laughed. "I feel like an idiot." *She didn't even know what province she was in. They were just in Edmonton? It didn't really matter. There was a coffee machine.* Resting her arms on the counter, she enquired, "Is the coffee fresh?"

Frost snuck up, kissed her cheek and flirted, "Hey baby."

"When was the wedding?" The man asked, passing her a coffee.

Expecting Frost to bolt back to the truck, she winked and glanced his way.

"Three and a half amazing months, he gushed, messing up her hair. "I guess she's a keeper."

He was a talented liar.

"I'll use the next rest stop, there's something gross in the men's washroom," Frost commented, towing her away.

"Thank you!" Kayn called out as they walked back to the truck.

When they were out of earshot, Frost tugged her into his arms in the pouring rain. They rocked back and forth, nearly dancing as he whispered, "See that power-line behind you?"

She did. She whispered, "I see it, why?"

"What you can't see from this vantage point is the line in the puddle, he'll step in when he goes to check the men's washroom. We need to stick around to make sure he doesn't avoid it. "Race you to the ladies washroom," Frost tempted, sprinting away.

Grinning, Kayn chased him. Drenched by the downpour, he grabbed her as she came around the corner. Their lips lustily fused as he tugged her into the washroom. The door swung shut. He backed her into a stall, undid the top button of her jeans and slid his hand in. She gasped as he kissed her neck, whispering suggestive things until she was moaning his name. Her back arched as euphoria rocked her so hard her knees buckled. He sat and undid his pants. Whipping a leg out of her jeans, she took what she wanted. He was clutching her hips groaning as the power flickered out.

Catching their breath, they began laughing. Playing with her silky curls, Frost whispered, "Is marriage something you wanted?"

"After graduating, university and a thousand other things I'll never do," she confessed in darkness.

Tenderly kissing her lips, Frost chuckled, "I gave you a bubblegum machine promise ring months ago."

"It was romantic, tossing a plastic ring at me when we hadn't kissed yet." Kayn countered as someone pounded on the door. *Oh, shit. That guy was still alive.* They scrambled into their clothes, giggling. Frost sheepishly opened the door. Their friends were standing there.

Unamused, Lily sighed, "This romance is cute but did you forget to do something, Frost?"

"Oh, shit. I'm sorry," Frost apologised, looking at Kayn.

It could be anything. The job, everyone else waiting in the truck. The time they had left to kill eight people.

Irritated, Mel answered her thoughts, "Seven, your guy's been dead for half an hour. Next time you lovebirds hookup, please make sure you're far away from us."

"Rose quartz to dull the pheromones would help," Lily suggested. "Come on, there are seven people left, it's past noon."

Giggling, they strolled back to the truck holding hands. As everyone else got in, they kissed. Frost whispered in her ear, "It was worth it."

With her heart glowing, she got into the back next to Mel. Curious, Kayn whispered, "What happened?"

"I left to make sure the job was finished. When I came back, the windows were so steamy I thought I'd just walked in on Jack and Rose from the Titanic," Mel replied, shoving Zach as they drove away.

Pressing his lips together to stop himself from smiling, her Handler said nothing as their eyes met. *She'd get it out of him later.*

Looking into the back, Lily praised, "Good idea, having him step in the puddle with a live wire."

"That was Frost," Kayn clarified, rubbing his shoulder as he smiled at her in the rearview. *She couldn't even think rationally when he was close by. All she wanted to do was have her way with him. Anywhere, everywhere, Always. The truck smelled amazing. Too good. Oh, no. Not again.* She unzipped her jacket, her chest was covered in veins. "Zach," she whispered.

"Pull over!" Zach asserted, reaching across Mel trying to touch her.

She swatted him away, the truck swerved to the shoulder, stopping. Scrambling out to get away from everyone, Kayn stood in the snow by the side of the road, with her breath rising into the air. *It felt like the afterlife couldn't grant her a moment of peace.* Taking deep breaths, she felt Zach's presence.

He passed her a knife, suggesting, "Cut yourself and heal, it might take it down a notch."

This was going to get old fast. She was a predatory species. Reality would destroy what he felt for her. It was only a matter of time. Kayn took the knife, whispering, "Is everyone watching?"

"They're just worried, you're overthinking it. Cut yourself and move on," her Handler urged.

She sliced her flesh, the blade didn't work. *What in the hell?* Kayn stabbed herself in the stomach, it didn't break the skin. Panicked, she turned to her Handler, stammering, "I can't stop it. Get away, go back to the truck."

Racing back to the others, Zach banged on the window, shouting, "She can't stab herself!"

Lily passed a knife and Frost got out. Marching over, he gave it to Zach, ordering, "Stab yourself."

"You, stab yourself," Zach bantered.

"Do it, it's harder to kill you," Frost rationalised.

Wincing, Zach sliced his palm, commenting, "There."

Dumbfounded, Frost scolded, "Go big or go home, kid. There's an Enlightening bomb about to detonate."

Blood was whooshing through her veins. Her palpitating heart grew louder and more volatile until it was deafening. Dropping to all fours in the slushy snow, Kayn shrieked as a pulse of energy blasted Frost and Zach through the air. The truck moved, screeching sideways onto the road. *She felt better.* She peeked up. Frost and Zach were frozen in time, twenty yards away, suspended in midair, posed like they were shielding themselves from the energy blast. There was no sound, nothing but the eerie echo of her heartbeat, it was like she hit pause. *This was crazy.* She looked up, a flock of geese were in a motionless perfect v above her. *What had she done?* Suddenly, life hit play. Her Handler and Frost dropped into thawing muck with a splat. The geese honked as they flew away.

Zach leapt up and sprinted to her side, "Are you alright?"

"I think so," Kayn mumbled in awe. Frost was sprawled in the mud howling laughing. "Glad you found that funny," Kayn taunted, walking over to help him up. *He was comically covered in mud. They all were.*

"We might not get through this list before time runs out if you keep blowing things up," Frost ribbed, with an arm around her as they strolled back to the truck, "Now, we need to change."

They didn't know what happened.

Lily got out, declaring, "I'm not sure what you did there, but we gapped for a second, and the vehicle was on the road. Mel's digging out clothes for you three, change outside."

It felt like she shouldn't say anything about this development. They changed by the side of the road like she hadn't frozen time. Feeling equal parts powerful and frightened, Kayn got into the back beside Mel.

"Are you alright?" Mel probed, sensing her distress.

Empaths were difficult to fool. Kayn gave her a touch of the truth, "I hope I can learn to control whatever that was."

"You will," Mel affirmed as they pulled away.

Eavesdropping on the hushed conversation, Kayn opted to say nothing. Lily was lecturing Frost, still pissed about her restroom rendevous induced makeout session with Zach. *It was an irresponsible stunt. They'd set off abilities without thinking. Her brain rarely functioned in*

Frost's presence. The instant their lips met the hedonistic pleasure-seeking pull of their powers nullified ration. She peered past Mel at Zach. As their eyes met, they started giggling.

Looking back, Lily remarked, "I'm getting Jenna to make you another bracelet. I can't be taking advantage of Zach every time we do a job together."

Grinning, Zach flirted, "So, we're clear, I'm fine with anything you need at any time." Their gaze held.

Shoving Zach, Mel accused, "Are you trying to piss me off?"

Where did that come from?

"It hasn't been a week since your elevator makeout with Thorne. Catch me up next time you decide to switch the players in your game," Zach countered, shutting her down.

"That wasn't what I meant," Mel said. "You aren't acting like yourself, there's a weird sexy vibe."

Turning to Lily, Frost teased, "You gave the kid a sexy vibe, whatever will he do with that?"

"Pheromones hang around, it's us," Kayn explained.

"I know what I'm feeling," Mel stressed, fuming.

Intrigued, Zach naughtily taunted, "Maybe, you're finally ready to admit you're into me?"

"Stop the truck!" Mel asserted, loudly.

Humouring her, Frost pulled over, and declared, "We're almost at the next job, we don't have time for relationship phobia issues, Mel."

Shoving Zach until he got out, Mel marched around the truck and ordered, "Move over, Brighton. I'm not sitting by him when he's like this."

Whatever floats your boat, Mel. Shrugging, Kayn shimmied into the middle.

Zach sarcastically cautioned, "Are you sure you

want to sit beside me? I'm too sexy, your boyfriend is right there, what if you can't control yourself?"

Kayn rolled her eyes. Laughter erupted from Frost as he pulled onto the road. Mel was livid, staring out the window. Touching her leg, Kayn assured, "It's just pheromones, it'll wear off."

"You four can kiss my ass," Mel bantered, angrily.

They pulled into a parking lot. The truck barely stopped when Mel got out and stormed off. Looking at Zach, Kayn grilled, "Did something happen between you two?"

"We kissed once, months ago. I've been waiting for her to decide she likes me back for years. I'm moving on," Zach answered, his eyes darting to Lily.

A door started dinging. Frost leaned in, saying, "I'll talk to her."

"I'm coming," Kayn replied, reaching to open the door.

"Stay here, you need a breather," Frost corrected, taking off after Mel.

There was a concerning amount of sexual tension, she should go. "Sorry, it's getting hot in here, I'm better off elsewhere," Kayn explained, fleeing the vibes.

Glancing back at Frost, Mel admitted, "Taking off was stupid, I know."

Walking with her, Frost interjected, "I get it, ration and jealousy rarely rear their heads at the same time."

Mel shook her head and denied, "I'm not jealous."

He chuckled, "So ration won then?"

"I'm an empath, I know what I'm feeling," Mel insisted.

Tilting his head, Frost probed, "Do you? You've had a rough week. My brother shooting you in the heart had to stomp on the fantasy. Hooking up at banquets happens but you were more than that, making it clear where his loyalties lie was the right thing to do. You're soul level adversaries. Thorne gave you the out you needed, take it in and move on."

Strolling through the plaza parking lot, Mel commented, "You put work into that speech."

"I did. I've been saving it," he disclosed, pointing to the pet store. Noticing Kayn, Frost sighed, "Not listening to me is going to be a thing, isn't it?"

"I love pet stores," Kayn toyed, giddy at the prospect of petting a kitten.

"Okay, his name is Mike, he works here. So you're not disappointed, I heard there aren't puppies or kittens in B.C pet stores," Frost replied, smiling.

"Party pooper," Mel muttered as they walked in to the ding dong of a bell.

The store was empty. Wandering by empty glass enclosures, Kayn pouted. *This sucked, there really weren't any kittens to pet.*

Touching the coffee sitting at the till, Frost said, "It's hot, Mike must be in a washroom. You have two minutes, go pet a hamster." He walked around, searching for cameras.

Mel took a fluffy hamster out. Frost locked eyes with Kayn, silently mouthing, "Move." Kayn yanked Mel out of the aisle as Frost shoved the shelves. They toppled with a domino effect, landing on the worker. He knelt by Mike, checked his pulse and confirmed, "It's done, let's go."

Putting the rodent in her pocket as they strolled out, Mel said, "I hope there weren't cameras, I have a hamster in my pocket."

"I sent in the IP address. The Aries group will erase the footage in the plaza," Frost chuckled, smiling. As they got in the car, he suggested, "I know where we can drop off that hamster in your pocket."

Smiling, Mel passed Lily a fuzzy rodent peace offering. "You finished that job in record time." Petting the hamster, Lily praised, "Aren't you adorable." She glanced back at Mel, asking, " Is it a he or a she?"

"I didn't have time to look," Mel replied, grinning.

Looking up from whoever he was texting, Zach noticed the rodent, pestering, "Who stole a Teddy Bear Hamster?"

"I knocked shelves over on a guy, we had to leave," Frost answered with smile crinkled eyes in the rearview.

Sheepishly, Mel extended her apology tour to include Zach, "I'm sorry, I'm having a bad week."

Reaching over Kayn, Zach touched Mel's leg, assuring, "We're all good."

They were driving back the way they came. Kayn smiled as her heart warmed. *They were bringing the teddy bear hamster to Chelsea, weren't they?* Familiar scenery blurred by her window as they passed the rest stop with police cars and yellow tape around the office. She asked, "Isn't returning to the scene of a crime frowned upon?"

"Our next accident is a few blocks from the kid's house," Lily revealed. Drop me off, I'll exchange her dead hamster for this live one. Jenna says the next job is Zach and Kayn's."

Watching Lily with the coveted hamster, Zach enquired, "Is it possible Jenna put the jobs in this order knowing we'd have a hamster to give the kid?"

"Oracles always have a reason. It would have made more sense to do this job right after the last. Sometimes, it's just a feeling. Ask next time we see her," Lily explained, caressing the furry rodent.

They pulled up at Chelsea's house, and nobody was there. Kayn said, "How is this not a crime scene?"

Meeting her eyes in the rearview, Frost answered, "They would have rushed Mom to the hospital." He glanced at Lily, saying, "We'll drop them off and come back." Lily got out and ran around the side of the house. Driving away, Frost gave them details, "Offing two dealers, shouldn't spin your moral compass." Parking by a sleazy apartment complex, he texted Zach the buzzer number, urging, "Take them out fast, we'll go get Lily."

They got out and watched Frost drive away. Walking to the panel at the entrance, her dormant conscience twitched. *Normally, they'd call a bunch of numbers to be let in.*

Shrugging, Zach punched in the number on his phone, chuckling, "This feels way too easy."

A female voice directed, "Come up."

Plot twist, she'd been expecting a male voice. As they climbed the staircase, Kayn admitted, "I was expecting a guy."

Shoving past her, Zach raced upstairs, teasing, "It's the age of equality, Brighton. Girls can be dealers too."

He thought he was funny. Slowly following, she laughed, "Do you have a plan?"

Stopping to wait for her, he confessed, "No."

"Are we pretending to buy drugs?" She probed, climbing up the musky staircase.

"Sounds good," Zach agreed, grinning as they reached the landing. Beaming, he provoked, "You have experience with balconies."

Funny. Kayn suggested, "Murder-suicide? I'll toss one off the balcony, while you write a life isn't worth living without you note for the other."

"Good enough," Zach replied, startling as the door at the top of the stairs opened.

An attractive girl with deep-set blue eyes leaned into the stairwell, questioning, "Have we partied together?"

The vibe the curvaceous girl with short jet black hair was throwing down, surprise lit up her Siren. Their eyes locked as Kayn seduced, "Last summer we snuck away together at a bonfire. I told you I'd visit the next time I was passing through town."

Lost in her magnetic pull, the mystified stranger took the bait coming closer. The door to the hall swung shut behind her. Caressing Kayn's arm, she played along, "It's all coming back to me now."

Swiftly snapping her neck, Kayn launched her over the railing. She plummeted down the stairwell, making a hollow thud on the landing. Looking at Zach, Kayn coldly decreed, "Next."

Concerned by her lack of emotion, Zach suggested, "I'll deal with the next one, why don't you go back to the car?"

The door opened. A guy with crazy hair stuck his head in, asking, "Where's Cheri?"

"She went downstairs to grab a new life, we're waiting for you," Kayn explained, truthfully.

Stoned, the scruffy guy, flirted, "What's your name?"

Summoning the stranger with a smile, the magnetic pull of her Siren disarming caution, Kayn toyed, "Karma."

"Cool name," he mumbled, mindlessly stepping into the privacy of the stairwell with b.o so pungent the Siren up for anything vanished in a poof of hell no.

"Karma's a bitch," Zach commented.

Snapping his neck, Kayn launched the next body into the stairwell. Hearing pitchy shrieking, they booked it into the hall. *Every time they did a job alone, shit went wrong. There had to be a fire escape.* Laughing, Zach pursued her down the hall. *Oh, shit. They didn't check for a camera. There was an elevator, no second staircase. Shit, that was the fire escape!* They raced from door to door, looking for an unlocked one. *Score!* They slipped into an apartment with an elderly woman in a chair knitting.

The elderly woman called out, "Is someone there?"

Tugging Zach into the galley kitchen, Kayn whispered, "We'll go out a window."

"We're on the sixth floor," he whispered.

They slipped into the bedroom, dashed to the window and tried opening it. *Holy shit, someone childproofed. Crap. Son of a bitch. Think, think, what were they going to do?* The hall creaked.

Panicking, Zach hissed, "Get in the closet, you maniac!"

They scrambled in as the door opened. Shaking, silently laughing. *You maniac? She was going to pee.*

Muzzling her with a hand, Zach cautioned telepathically, *'I will snap your neck right here in this closet if you move a muscle.'*

"I must be hearing things," the sweet old lady mumbled, hobbling away.

Her cell beeped. *Crap!* Zach swatted her, she scrambled to silence it. The woman paused, fiddled with her hearing aid and left. They exhaled. Kayn whispered, "You unlock the window, I'll see what they want." As he tiptoed away, she read Frost's text. *Having problems?* Zach looked back, shaking his head. She crept over to the window. *There were police cars and ambulances with a crowd gathering below. Crap. How did they get here this fast? She didn't want to admit defeat.*

He whispered, "We can't get out this way."

She texted Frost. *We're stuck on the sixth floor in an old lady's apartment.* Her cell vibrated. She read Frost's response. *You're immortal, figure it out.* Zach cursed under his breath. *They were being shoved down a hill with no training wheels.* Her cell flashed with another message from Frost. *I've called in your location. If we need to get creative with the cover-up, so be it. Hurry, we have five more people to take out. It's four pm. We're parked on the left side of the building. Get out of there.* She passed the cell to her sidekick.

After reading the messages, Zach stated, "We'll bust in a door on the other side of the hall and jump."

With a plan, they snuck out of the bedroom, tiptoed to the door and peeked out the peephole. *Zach's plan was out. Six officers were going door to door. Think, come on, think. Brains before brawn. Maybe they could go up and out?* Soundlessly opening the hall closet, Kayn peered up. *No attic there.* Summoning Zach to follow, she slipped back into the bedroom, whispering, "We can hide in the attic." She opened the closet. *There it was.* They scaled the shelves, shoved open the slab of wood, climbed into the confined crawlspace style attic and slid the wood back in place. Her mind darted to how creepy it was that they all attached. *You could get into any apartment this way.* They crawled left, manoeuvering missing plywood until they reached the end and sat. *Which apartment were they going to climb into? They were checking rooms.*

"We'll wait here until they've searched the apartments on this floor," Zach whispered, leaning against the wood.

Her skin was crawling. *Don't think about it. You are a badass immortal, spiders shouldn't freak you out anymore.* In the dark, she answered, "You read the message, we can't wait." Looking up, Kayn whispered, "Maybe there's a vent large enough to crawl out through onto the roof?" Light was filtering in. She crawled over, Zach followed. *They couldn't fit through there. If they busted out, it would make too much noise.*

Zach's phone buzzed, he quietly chuckled as he read the message and whispered, "You have a strange relationship."

Her Handler passed her his phone. She read Frost's text. *We had to move. Make-out with my girlfriend, pheromone bomb the place and walk out the backdoor. We have shit to do.* She passed the cell back. *She wasn't sure how to take this?* They sat in the dark. *Knowing they were training her to control her Siren ability didn't make it sting less.*

Her Handler confessed, "You smell fantastic, it'll go too far up here. I'll forget we're trying to escape. Think you can find your way back to that old lady's closet?"

She needed to see. Knowing it may not work, she felt for something to cut herself with, found an exposed nail and instructed, "You look, I'm putting a nail through my hand so we can see."

"I'll do it, you couldn't break your skin earlier," Zach offered.

Removing the fingerless glove, concealing her brand of Ankh, she drove the nail through her palm. It lit up, strobed once and healed. Smiling, she asked, "It worked, where are we going?"

"You're going to hate me, but I missed that. I was texting Frost, so they don't come running. You heal too fast, I'll do it, you look," Zach offered, crawling closer.

She sighed, "You'll make a mess you're a bleeder. I'll keep doing it, you look." She slowly sunk her hand down on the nail this time, giving him a few flashes of her symbol to adapt to the light, removing it at a snail's pace.

Prying the wood off, he whispered, "Once more while I look in the closet to see if it's the one."

It was so wrong that pain did something for her. Kayn slowly shoved her hand on the nail and light strobed in the attic, as a spider scurried over the nailed hand. *Oh, sweet lord. Her fear priorities were messed up.* She shivered, as it moved up her arm, squirming. *Spiders, spiders, no. Nope, she couldn't.* "Zach, spider, I can't. Smacking it off with a strobing hand.

Giggling, as he climbed down shelving, he urged, "Come on, superhero, this is it."

She scrambled down the shelves away from her phobia. Zach flicked on the light. Noticing a spider on her shirt, she removed it so fast Houdini would have begged for pointers. Squirming, shaking it off, Kayn asked, "Is there any in my hair?"

Smiling, Zach picked through her messy curls. Cupping her cheeks, he assured, "You're fine. There's nothing in your hair. Your cheeks are all rosy though."

"I'm sorry you keep getting dragged into Siren games," Kayn apologised, meeting his brown eyes.

Shrugging, he whispered, "Dealing with your issues is my job. I was going to suggest this, but your boyfriend is here, I didn't want to get my ass kicked. You pulled the Siren vibe up earlier, I saw that. What shut it down?"

Grinning, she quietly confessed, "It's a toss-up between the smelly dealer who looked like Shaggy from Scooby Doo and the screaming."

"He did look like Shaggy," Zach quietly chuckled. His eyes changed as he stroked her rosy cheek with his thumb, enquiring, "Pain turns you on, doesn't it?"

Instead of admitting it, she silenced her Handler with a kiss. Following her lead, Zach cupped her face, deepening the seduction with his tongue. Their bond altered perception as entangled souls meshed. Lost in their Handler Dragon connection, seven seconds in heaven went dark as the Siren ignited. A burst of morality blinding pheromones frenzied passion, squashing reason. No longer playing a game, void of ethics and consequences, they were tearing each other's clothes off when their phones started vibrating. Their lips abruptly parted. With their eyes locked, they knew they'd almost gone too far.

Buttoning his shirt, Zach raspily directed, "Respond to those texts before Frost panics."

With swollen lips and a pheromone frazzled mind, Kayn covered her chest. *Where did her bra go? What just happened?*

Embarrassed, Zach passed her bra, whispering, "Maybe, we shouldn't tell anyone I got this off?"

With every inch of her tingling, she put it on and picked up her shirt. The closet door opened. *Oh, no.*

Menacingly pointing a knitting needle at Zach, an irate elderly woman scolded, "Richard, you swarthy fornicator. How dare you come into my home and take advantage of my sweet Rebekka. Put your clothes on and get out of my closet, you heathens."

They didn't need to kill her, she was senile. They looked at each other, shrugged and followed her as she hobbled down the hall. Zach reached for the doorknob. The old lady smacked him with her knitting needle, "You may not touch anything else in my household, Richard." Someone knocked on the door. Swatting Zach again, she threatened, "Don't you move a muscle, dirty boy!"

The old woman swung open the door and spat, "What!"

It was an officer. Holy shit. The elderly lady shoved Zach out into the hall, reprimanding, "Go home closet fornicator, my granddaughter wants nothing to do with you!" Slamming the door on Zach and the officer. Swatting Kayn, she pointed to the bathroom and decreed, "Clean that filthy boy off."

"Okay," Kayn agreed, going to the washroom. *Hope Zach wasn't getting arrested.* She took the stick out. Thankful relatives hadn't gotten creative with the bathroom window security, she opened it, pulled herself up and peered out. *The crowd had dispersed. Nobody was out there. Her hips were going to be a tight fit. This might suck. It wasn't going to be a controlled fall.* She texted Frost. *Long story short, drive to the front, I'm breaking something for sure dropping out of this window.* She took the piece of wood out, tugged herself up, squirmed through the tiny opening and dropped. Hitting the grass with an excruciating thud, she lay gasping with the wind knocked out of her. *Shit, that hurt. She wasn't feeling optimistic about this job tonight.* Struggling to get up, she couldn't move, burning up as her healing ability repaired her injuries. She saw a shadow in glaring light above her and heard Frost's voice, "Bad day, sweetheart?"

The lights flickered and went out.

STIRRING, SHE TWITCHED HER FINGERS IN WARM SAND. *Crap, she died.* Rolling over, Kayn squinted in the sunshine, giggling. The endless splotchy blue sky brought her heart back to the first time she'd been granted access to this magical place as Ankh. *Her perception of everything had been altered on that journey. She was just a girl with an immortal destiny. It had only been a few years, but everything changed. The afterlife reconstructed her being and made her into something new. Whenever her mind slipped back to the beginning, it hit refresh on her browser reminding her of everyone she lost along the way. Her family, Kevin's family, Kevin. He was her enemy now. They'd evolved to survive in the darkness.* Sitting up, shaking off mortal memories. *There was no point in dwelling on things that didn't matter anymore.* Sensing, she wasn't alone, she saw a child playing in the sand. *This was new.* Wandering over, Kayn asked, "What are making?"

The toddler peered up, grinned and lisped, "I'm making a gawage."

Garage? Garbage? It didn't matter. Sitting in the sand

by the wispy blonde-haired child, she said, "That sounds fun. What should I make?"

"A gawage," the child repeated, creating his masterpiece.

Grinning, Kayn declared, "I'm going to make the same thing." They sat next to each other, peacefully moulding sand. Tingling, she explained, "I have to go. See you later." Smiling, Kayn magically disintegrated into floating sand and blew away on a breeze.

Spinning tires, they were on the road. With the magic of playing in sand with a toddler fresh in her heart, Kayn opened joyous eyes, smiling.

"I told you we couldn't survive that fall," Zach harassed.

She'd jumped out of the bathroom window. That was stupid. Kayn enquired, "What happened to you?"

"Sure you want to discuss it here?" Her Handler ribbed.

Meeting Frost's grin in the rearview, she disclosed, "You were Richard, I was her granddaughter Rebekka. We were caught in the closet. You were swatted with a knitting needle, called a swarthy fornicator and shoved out the door at a police officer." Everyone lost it. Peering up, Kayn saw Frost laughing, and the knot in her gut unwound.

"Swarthy fornicator," Mel provoked, shoving him.

"You've had a studly day, Zach," Frost aloofly remarked. "Want to do the next job with, Mel? She's the only girl in the car you've missed." His icy comment shut down the jokes. Meeting Kayn's gaze in the rearview, Frost questioned, "So you're saying the makeout session wasn't hot enough to set off adequate pheromones to chill out an old lady?"

She knew what he wanted her to say. Kayn incited, "Can I plead the fifth even though I'm Canadian?"

Titillated, Lily grilled, "What happened?"

Ignoring Frost's catty need to have his ego stroked, Kayn overshared the job recap like a pro, "I had a sexy moment with a hot dealer before snapping her neck and tossing her downstairs. The next guy I killed looked like Shaggy from Scooby Doo. A mortal started screaming, my Siren ability shut off, and we were forced to improvise. Officers were searching apartments, that's how we ended up in the attic." Aware of Frost's annoyance in the rearview, Kayn provoked, "My boyfriend told my Handler to set off my pheromones and get out, but a sneak attack from an old lady stopped it."

"That's everything?" Frost challenged, unsatisfied by her recollection."

What was he getting at? Filter off, Kayn carried on, "He got tossed out in the hall, I was sent to wash up because I was dirty. I texted you to pick up my body and dropped headfirst out a sixth storey bathroom window."

"When I bump into your ex, he'll enjoy feeding me the details you left out," Frost slammed, turning down a crunchy gravel road, toppling everyone over.

She wanted to strangle him. He hurt her first. They parked at an abandoned farmhouse. *He wouldn't even look at her now.*

"Come on, Mel," Frost instructed. "Lily, find Zach a shirt that isn't missing half its buttons."

That ignorant ass.

Staring at the ceiling, Zach commented, "There's a time and place for passive-aggressive Scorpio bullshit, this wasn't it. Next time just tell your boyfriend I do nothing for you."

She was hurt. "He told me to be honest," Kayn responded, with shit disturbing eyes.

Looking back, Lily explained, "He's aware he told you to do it. He wants you to embrace the part of you that's like him so you'll understand Siren related hurdles. That's why you're doing these jobs with us. Give him a minute, he'll come back and apologise." Lily got out to search for a less antagonising shirt as they sat in tense silence.

Zach got out. Lily winced, he said, "What?" She pointed at his fly. He did it up and swore, "It didn't go that far."

"I believe you, you're a good guy. Anyone would jump at the chance to be with you. Don't take what he says seriously. He's in love her, it's a tricky situation," Lily answered.

Curious, Zach asked, "What about you?"

"What about me?" Lily sparred, doing up the buttons on his new shirt.

"Would you jump at the chance?" Zach flirted, grinning.

Smiling, Lily admitted, "Maybe."

"Really?" he probed, undoing the button choking him.

Laughing, Lily prompted, "Get in the truck, Zach. Next time, check your fly."

Zach got in, saying, "I know why he freaked out."

"I heard everything, Romeo," Kayn teased, messing his hair. *Frost and Mel were already coming back. That was fast. It didn't look like anyone lived here.* She questioned, "What was the job?"

"Hunting accident, we had the location. They must have found him right away," Lily explained.

Kayn got out so Mel could sit in the middle. Frost gently grabbed her arm. She turned to him.

Closing the door for privacy, Frost apologised, "I'm a hypocrite and an idiot, I'm sorry. I told you not to overreact, and when the tables were turned, I lost it."

Folding like a cheap deck of cards, Kayn caressed his face and quietly replied, "You have to stop changing the rules. It hurts when you play games and walk away like that."

"I sucked back his missing buttons and your shirt being on inside out, but when I noticed his fly down, I got jealous and panicked, I couldn't reign it in," he admitted.

"It stung when you suggested that escape plan. There was a spider on me, I took off my own shirt. My pants stayed on. His fly being down was a random act of fate," Kayn taunted.

Embracing her, Frost whispered, "I love you, I'm sorry."

"I'm sorry you love me too," she giggled. *He said the words.*

Kissing her, he laughed, "Get in." Kayn scooted into the back. Frost leaned in, looked at Zach and said, "Can we just agree I'm an idiot and move on?"

"No problem," her Handler replied, trying not to grin.

A few more mortals met a creative demise. With the first part of their mission accomplished, they opted to eat at an eighties roadside diner with jukeboxes at every booth. The server came for her order, Kayn replied, "Surprise me." *She didn't even have the brainpower to read a menu. She was exhausted. If she closed her eyes, she'd fall asleep, right here at the table.* Zach selected tunes on the jukebox. The same song played four times before a giant burger appeared in front of her.

Their server declared, "Best burger in B.C."

Kayn looked at Frost and started laughing. *He'd*

ordered a steak sandwich after searching for decades for the best burger. Now, she had to eat it. She cut it in half, picked it up and took a giant bite. *It was delicious.* Wanting to devour it, she shoved her plate to Frost, offering, "Try this one."

Grabbing half, his eyes widened as he ate it. He gave her a ketchup kiss on her cheek. Laughing, wiping it off with his napkin, Frost teased, "Showing up at a demon fight with ketchup on your face might tank your Dragon street cred."

"I'm not sure I can go full Dragon and follow rules like, just maim thirty people," Kayn provoked, taking another chomp of the tasty burger.

Holding a chicken strip, Lily clarified, "If taking out ten people works, disciples won't show up and it'll wreck the sacrifice. We'll turn you loose on a demon, vanquish him and call it a night."

Frost cut his steak in half, putting some on her plate. He leaned closer, whispering, "There's a burger at a roadside diner in Arizona that tops it. I'll take you there next time we're passing through."

The waiter appeared with a tray of beer and placed one in front of each of them. Raising her beer, Mel saluted, "I'm thankful most of the people we killed today were assholes."

"I'll second that," Lily cheered as they all clinked bottles.

She was going to need a bunch of these to wake her up. Kayn chugged her entire beer, watching Zach continuing to select the song. Wincing, Kayn toyed, "Grey would be so proud."

Nudging her, Frost asked, "Want another?"

"I should have coffee, I can barely keep my eyes open," Kayn admitted as the room wavered.

"You died earlier, the Conduit hasn't eaten. Pass me

the keys to the truck, I'll feed her," her Handler suggested.

Shoving keys across the table, Frost baited, "Just feed the Conduit, I've got the Siren covered, Swarthy Fornicator."

"That's going to stick, isn't it," Zach chuckled, as they walked out to the truck together.

Poking him, Kayn ribbed, "It's better than Froggy."

He unlocked the truck. As they got in, Zach pointed out, "Only Frost called you Froggy. We all used your mortal last name, Brighton."

She called him Smith and Kevin called her Brighton. She blinked away the mortal memory.

Holding out his hands, her Handler pointed out, "We can downplay it all we want, but if nobody was there to stop us."

"You've been spelt to forget," Kayn affirmed, taking his hands. "I'll deal with it when it does." When she was lost in the emotionless void her Dragon self created to survive the violent purgatory of Immortal Testing, the light within her Handler led her home. Zach was her anchor to Ankh. Their souls were bound after the Testing. Reeling her in whenever she slipped into the Dragon state was his duty.

"Ready whenever you are." Zach chuckled. "Feel free to kill me, I'll have a Pina Colada in the in-between while you crazy kids fight demons and zealot mortals."

Squeezing his hands, she reprimanded, "I'm exhausted, don't make me laugh." Kayn willed her Conduit ability to siphon energy, nothing happened. Focusing, she tried again. *Nothing.* "I might be too tired," she whispered. *Her eyelids were heavy. Wait. Were they drugged?* She squeezed Zach's arms. He went limp and slumped in the seat. *He was out cold. Shit.* She felt for her phone and texted Frost. *We've been drugged.* There was no response. She messaged a listed number. *Drugged. Post St Diner B.C.* She slapped her face. *She wasn't going to make it back into the restaurant.* Her phone buzzed. Kayn read the message. *Hide.* She got out, her legs couldn't hold her weight. She flopped in the snow. Fighting to remain conscious, she clawed her way under the truck and passed out.

Shivering, Kayn heard a ding, ding, ding, tried to get up and smoked her head. *Shit. She was still under the truck.* She squirmed out and scrambled up. *The door was open. Zach was gone.* With the truck dinging, she stormed to the closed diner. *What time was it?* She squinted through the window at the clock on the wall. *She couldn't focus. Her phone.* She felt her pocket. Her phone was soaked. *Please work. Please work.* It lit up. *The battery was almost dead.* It powered off as she tried to text. *Damn it.* She tore off her bracelet, willing Kevin to hear her plea, "I know you're mad, but if you can hear me, I need help. We were all drugged. I hid, everyone's gone. I'm at the Post Diner in B.C. standing in a parking lot soaking wet. I'm supposed to fight a demon tonight. My phone's dead." *That was ridiculous. He was somewhere thinking, suck it up princess, you blocked me with a bracelet. That was the equivalent of unfriending someone on Facebook, immortal style. She was an adult. She could figure this out. Brains before brawn.* She searched the truck for Zach's cell. *Nobody is stupid enough to kidnap someone and take along a trackable cell. They'd ditch the phones. Maybe one was dropped in the diner?* She turned her phone on, it powered up. *One shot at this, Brighton.* She called Frost's number, listening. *Nothing. Guess this was happening.* Backing up, Kayn ran at the picture window shielding her face as she crashed through, and rolled on linoleum with the security system whooping. She raced for their table. *No phones.* She ran into the kitchen, tore the alarm off the wall and ripped the cords out. *Silence.* Snatching someone's plugged in cell, she leapt through the window and ran back to the vehicle. *She had to get out of here.* She got into the truck. *Please let keys be in here.* There was one behind the visor. Turning the key in the ignition, wishing she knew how to drive, she put it in drive and stomped on the gas. It jolted forward and took off way to fast. She lightened the weight on the gas, coasting out of the lot. *She needed to pull over and think.* Parking down the road, she took the battery out of one phone and put in the other. It juiced up. *All she had was her phone. She didn't have Markus' number. Calling Frost again wouldn't make sense.* She picked a number on the call list.

Grey answered, "What's up?"

Oh, thank god. "I need, Markus. They drugged us. I woke up under a truck in the parking lot. Everyone's gone, I'm supposed to be fighting a demon."

Laughing, Grey soothed, "Calm down Brighton, they're immortal. I don't have Markus' number. I'll talk you through it. Do you have a name for this demon you're fighting?"

"They told me. I can't remember. He's trying to get thirty mortal zealots to sacrifice themselves so he can bring back his girlfriend. We killed ten mortals today to wreck his mass suicide plot," she disclosed, struggling to remain calm.

"This sounds familiar," Grey replied. "Listen, you don't need the address. When they start torturing Ankh, instinct will lead you there. Calm down, who do they have?"

"Frost, Zach, Mel, and Lily," she replied.

"Chill out, relax, have a chat with me, you'll find

everyone no problem. How's Mel doing? I heard Thorne shot her in the heart with an arrow. That had to suck," Grey gossiped.

"I'm not feeling chatty, Grey," Kayn stated.

He chuckled, "Listen, Lily never gets tortured. Mel is a Healer, Frost is a badass, and your Handler Zach is screwed, but he'll be fine. How did they drug you? The Aries Group couldn't take you down a few weeks ago with large animal traquillizers?"

He was trying to distract her. "They must have something new. Is Lexy there?" Kayn tried, hoping for Dragon advice.

Grey answered, "Lexy just got back from wherever she was with Amar's crew but isn't speaking to me. I'm watching the newbies play Scrabble."

He was stalling, doing his best to Guru Grey her out of her panic attack. "How's Emma?" Kayn asked, playing along.

"Still pregnant so we haven't taken the newbies to the in-between much to train, but as soon as this baby is cooked, we're good to go," Grey answered. "Speak of the devil."

Lexy just walked in. He was a glutton for punishment.

Grey gave Lexy a quick rundown, "Kayn woke up under a truck. Everyone's gone, and she's supposed to kill a demon who is trying to get thirty people to sacrifice themselves to resurrect his girlfriend. Here's your sister."

Taking the phone, Lexy questioned, "How in the hell were you drugged?"

"No idea," Kayn answered. "I didn't even know it was happening until it was too late."

"This demon isn't the sharpest tool in the shed, call their phones and ask where they are," her sister suggested.

"They'd really be stupid enough to keep their phones?" Kayn commented.

"The window for opening demonic portals during a lunar event starts at eight pm and closes at two seventeen am. He'll kill time torturing Ankh. It's eight pm here, but we could be in a different timezone. What time did you pass out?"

"I have no idea," Kayn disclosed, feeling her hand warm under her glove.

"We felt it too, Dragon up. Let us know how it works out," Lexy directed, hanging up.

Snow delicately fell as her breath pirouetted into the sky. Her heart thudded like a tribal war drum. Adrenaline pulsed through her as predatory senses sprang to life, and emotions sunk into Dragon induced oblivion. Fury broiled beneath her flesh as her Handler's agony lit up her primal guidance system. Kayn bolted through bushes into desolate winter wild, leaving mortality an afterthought as branches whipped, slicing limbs, and sloshing feet rapidly propelled her towards unknown danger.

10
PRETTY BIRDS

Meanwhile, the rest of Ankh was waking up in a precarious position.

Voices were chanting, Jezebeth. Upright, with his arms bound, Frost opened his eyes, gave his restraints a tug and grinned. *Angel chains. Assholes.* They were in a hall of hateful mortals chanting, Jezebeth. *Lily was strung up next to him, untouched. Mel was a Healer, she was fine. Zach, not so much. Kayn wasn't here.* He started laughing.

An ignoramous with a protruding stomach strutted past with arms raised, dramatically announcing, "The hieratic has risen! Leonard, master of dark magic and sorcery, will expel those who defile this sanctuary. I bring forth Jezebeth to free you from mortal form and welcome you to the next realm." Riling up, his lynch mob of chanting townies, the irritating robust man decreed, "You stand accused of tainting sacred land. Do you have final words before we expel this vessel?"

He meant, Zach. Kayn was going to tear this guy a new asshole. Frost loudly declared, "I do!"

"Tell us, don't be shy!" Portly Leonard bellowed,

facing the chanting, brainwashed mortals. He turned, met Frost's eyes and provoked, "Speak."

Smirking, Frost declared, "My girlfriend is going to kick your ass." Zach was bound to a marble ceremonial altar, semi-conscious with hunks of missing flesh. *He'd taken the brunt of the torture, that was unfortunate.* "She gets pissy when anyone messes with her Handler. I'd stop torturing that guy if I were you."

"Only this one?" Leonard questioned. Motioning to Lily and Mel, he prompted, "No concern for the pretty birds?"

Confidently, Frost said, "They can hold their own. We're Ankh, you've violated a treaty. This will end badly for you."

The flamboyant demon in mortal flesh, provoked, "Will it? You've tried and failed to stop the rising of Jezebeth." Maintaining eye contact with Frost, Leonard sunk his blade into Zach's abdomen.

Sputtering up blood, braving the torture, Zach gave the demon in a skin coat no satisfaction.

Squirming on her post, Mel fought to switch his focus, yelling, "Come at me, you piece of shit!"

Amused by her silence, Leonard placed the knife against Lily's throat, coaxing, "Who shall I kill first, pretty bird?"

With Siren on standby, Lily met the depravities eyes, and naughtily seduced, "Take me somewhere private, I'll make you forget everyone else."

Intrigued by Lily's proposition, their captor caressed her jaw, huskily taunting, "Are you trying to seduce me, pretty bird?"

"Uncuff me, I'll show you," the Siren lured with flushed cheeks, luscious cherry lips and gossamer locks cascading like an onyx waterfall.

Grinning, Leonard confessed, "Tempting, I may take

you up on that offer after Jezebeth has risen, and I have enough free time to outwit a praying mantis." Trailing a blade along Lily's elegant olive neck, he licked the blood, savouring her essence. Shivering, he praised, "Delicious." He tore her shirt off, exposing her to the room, taunting, "Pretty bird's taste heavenly."

Knowing the show was for his benefit, Frost spoke to Lily telepathically, *"Kayn should be here soon."*

'I've got this,' Lily's voice answered, playing into his game, acting like she enjoyed it.

The creepy being, huskily whispered in Lily's ear, "Tasty, tasty, pretty bird." He sliced her bra strap and cut into her breast. A burgundy ripple ran into her cleavage. Lapping it up eagerly as calf suckling at a teet, the demon pulled away, fawning, "Tasty, pretty bird, I shall keep you as my pet." He sliced so deep, a fountain of sweet life nectar gushed out. Delighted, Leonard massaged her chest, licked his palms, painted his face with blood and went back to slurping from the wound.

This demon was impressively unhinged. Their Oracle's reading of events had been off but so were their internal warning systems. They should have been queasy long before they were drugged. Twice in a row, their danger detecting ability hadn't alerted them to air on the side of caution. Where was, Brighton?

Gleefully skipping, swaying arms, Leonard sang, "Pretty bird is bleeding, bleeding, bleeding, bleeding, and all mine." Playing with Lily's silky midnight tresses, he proclaimed, I shall keep you in a cage, and have my way with you every day, lovely dove."

Wincing, Lily thought, *'So gross.'* Frost pressed his lips together to stop himself from laughing.

Catching their reaction, Leonard looked directly at Lily and accused, "That was rude. I'll teach you to behave, pretty bird." Cackling, he sashayed over to

Zach, sunk his blade into their friend's stomach and gutted him like a fish.

As a pool of blood expanded beneath Zach, hot strobes beneath Frost's glove, let him know he was gone. *Have a Pina Colada on a sandy beach in the in-between for me kid.*

On his way back for Lily, Mel laughed. Leonard hissed, "Do you want me to gut you next?"

"Why not? I'll chill with Zach in the in-between and skip the bloodbath. When the Dragon shows up, everyone in this room dies. You just killed the only one capable of stopping her." Looking into his eyes, Mel dared, "Do it. Cut me, I'll heal."

Pressing the blade to her throat, Leonard grilled, "Where is this Dragon?"

With unwavering faith, Mel vowed, "She's coming."

Frost spoke to her in his mind, *that's enough, Mel. Kayn may kill everyone and leave us Angel Chained to poles.* There was a commotion outside. *He felt her, she was here.*

INSTRUCTING NEW TRIAD IN THE white sand desert of the in-between, Kevin and Stephanie were in a no holds barred battle match with their Clan raucously cheering. Kevin heard Kayn's plea for help. As the original choice for her Handler, their connection was strong, but he was pissed. They'd lost the girl he had a thing for to Trinity. He'd asked Kayn for help and she not only ignored him but magically blocked him from contacting her. Pretending he didn't hear, took his mind off the match for a split second. Swiping his feet from beneath him, Stephanie pinned him to the sand beneath her.

Undeniably hot with endless wit, Stephanie jumped up and tugged him to his feet, taunting, "That was sad Kev."

Brushing the sand off, Kevin confessed, "Vision issues." Addressing newbie Triad, he instructed, "Carry on fighting amongst yourselves, Stephanie's in charge." He abruptly left, needing space.

Pursuing Kevin, Patrick laughed, "Slow your roll, talk to me. What's going on?"

"She thinks I'm going to drop everything to help her." Livid, Kevin stopped and mimicked, "I'm wet and alone, everyone's gone, help me, Kevin."

Patrick giggled, "Think about what you said."

Grinning, Kevin clarified, "Ankh was drugged. She woke up alone in a parking lot, soaking wet."

"Maybe she needs to know you're out there somewhere, rooting for her?" Patrick answered as they strolled through the desert with warm, silken sand underfoot.

Noticing fluffy white clouds in the splotchy cerulean sky, his heart fought the urge to guess what each one resembled. Shaking his head, Kevin rationalised, "She ignored me and blocked me from contacting her."

"You're in different Clans, it's not that simple. You asked her to blow a job for you. She'd be in trouble with Ankh for entertaining the idea," Patrick replied.

He was right. Kevin admitted, "It's not healthy for me to be involved in her life. As much as I despise the thought of her being with someone else, he makes her happy."

"She reached out," Patrick pressed.

They squinted in white light. *What in the hell?*

Materialising facedown in the sand, his fingers twitched, Zach groaned, "That sucked."

Triad wasn't supposed to be able to run into Ankh. *Maybe his ability to find Kayn extended to her Handler?* "Hard night?" Kevin baited, helping Zach up.

Realising where he was, Zach whispered, "This can't be good." In a whoosh of torment, the Ankh recalled his death. Rattled, Zach panicked, "Kayn wasn't with us. When she shows up full Dragon, I won't be there to bring her out of it." His eyes lingered on Patrick as he addressed the pair, "How did you find me?"

Feeling the tug in his soul, as back up Dragon whisperer, Kevin sighed, "I can't promise she'll listen, but I'll try."

11
IN THE DRAGON STATE

In the Dragon state, decisions were made by an internal guidance system. Ration left the cerebellum, and in its place was predatory certainty. Avoiding roots and debris, skillfully as a cougar tracking prey through wilderness, wrath inducing spurts of extended heat informed her of an Ankh's demise. Free of trivial thought, she burst from the wooded area into a demonic mist, meant to subdue. It would have taken down any immortal, but Kayn was a rare breed. With her Conduit ability, she absorbed the fog through her pores. Gloriously euphoric, she cocked her head at the dark-eyed Abaddon guarding the door. *They feared her, they should.* They rushed at her with blades. Weaponless, Kayn dodged swings like they weren't trying, stole a knife like child's play and launched a hollow-eyed stranger through the air over the treeline with superhero strength. *That was new.* Without the blade used to purge demons from mortal shells, it was like trying to squash cockroaches beneath a shoe, the need for chaos was being quenched, but she wasn't getting anywhere. She commenced slashing throats as Abaddon sprinted at her from either side of the building. Baptised by arterial spray, she vanquished all who came for her. Drenched in blood, rolling on demonic vapour, the Dragon booted the door and strode into the rundown hall with only a hint of yellow in a sea of damned souls.

A voice spoke in her mind, *'Your Clan is restrained, snap the Angel Chains. Wake your Handler.'* On emotionless autopilot, she swatted mortal assailant's like bothersome flies, breaking arms grasping for her until she reached her Clan. She broke their restraints, rolled the dead one and snapped its chains. Placing hands on its stomach, she pulsed a burst of energy into it, tickling her spine. Confused, she touched her neck. Resurrected, Zach gasped as his eyes opened. She turned to the room of riled up chanting mortals fighting shiny things. A voice in her head instructed, *'Listen to your Handler.'* She stomped on something grabbing for her ankle. *Someone was behind her.* She spun, prepared to snap a neck.

A magical aura with a soothing voice instructed, "Don't kill any mortals, just wound them so they can't get away."

It felt like she should listen.

A shiny thing yelled, "Demon! Fire escape, Brighton!"

A trail of jet black smoke marked the exit. *She could eat that one.* She chased it outside, a sinister haze separated her from her snack.

"They didn't do you justice. You are magnificent," a dark entity encased in mortal flesh taunted, assuming it was safe behind the veil of demonic fog.

A voice reprimanded, "Don't do it, Brighton. That's too much dark energy."

She was hungry.

It grabbed her arm, asserting, "Honey, it's a bad idea."

Honey? She looked at where it touched her, felt a flicker of warmth, panicked and backed into incapacitating smoke. As it drained her lifeforce, Kayn turned the tables, inhaling demonic vapour through her flesh. *There was too much. Her head hurt. She had to get rid of it.* Her right hand pulsed. Curious, she looked at it. Energy was flickering like lightning between her fingertips. Her other hand pulsated, it was the same. *This felt good.* She placed her hands together, as they parted, there was a yellow orb. With unfortunate timing, mortals gathered, obscuring her view of her foe, chanting, "Jezebeth."

A sparkly thing, ran by, yelling, "Don't do it, Kayn! You'll get us in trouble, we've got this!"

She needed to throw it.

A soothing voice rationed, "It's Zach, please don't throw that. You're not allowed to use it. You'll send these people through the hall of souls. They need to be sorted by aura first or we'll be separated from everyone else."

With mortals in awe, Kayn clapped, the heavenly sphere vanished. *They all had to die now.*

"Thank you for reigning it in," shimmering Zach praised, cautiously inching closer. "Stand still, I need to help you."

Glowing things sprinted into the woods after fleeing mortals, vanishing into darkness. *She wanted to go but her feet wouldn't budge.*

Hypnotising aura, extended a hand, soothing, "Relax, I'm your Handler."

As he touched her sedating warmth filled her being. Reality came into focus. Looking at her blood-stained hands, snippets of what she'd been up to, sorted into chronological order in her brain. She looked up and said, "You died."

"I did. Nice to have you back. You're going to have so many issues, you ingested a crazy amount of dark energy," Zach commented, concerned. "What took you so long?"

She should tell him. Showing him would be easier. "Come with me," Kayn instructed as they strolled around the side of the building. *Frost was coming. He was going to bust her before she had a chance to confess.*

"Impressive body count love," Frost praised, grinning as he joined their stroll to her demon massacre. "Abaddon had this place locked down with shells guarding the doors. This job went so far off script. We don't have blades to disperse demons. I showed up as your stack of bodies healed and put them down. We'll have to continue inconveniencing them until Ankh shows up."

Taking in the macabre pile of corpses, Zach disclosed, "We would have been chained to poles for days if I hadn't materialised in front of Kevin in the in-between." Nudging Kayn, Zach probed, "Do you remember hearing his voice?"

"Someone told me to unchain my Clan and revive my Handler," Kayn stated, with no need to pacify anyone's ego.

Noticing her bare wrist, Frost commented, "Did you lose your bracelet or take it off?"

"I woke up alone in the parking lot under a truck with a dinging door and no juice in my phone. I didn't think he was going to help me, after cutting him off but I gave it a shot," she curtly responded.

Grinning, Frost confessed, "I deserved every slam Kevin landed. Now, I just want to thank him for having your back."

The pile of bodies moved. That was fast. Slitting risen demon's throats, Kayn peered up, enquiring, "Should I dismember these?"

Observing his girlfriend's unfiltered Dragon logic with admiration, Frost instructed, "Go wild. Don't let them heal. We have to figure this out." Looking at Zach, he suggested, "We should see if they need help."

Leaving Kayn creatively inconveniencing door guarding demons, they went back inside. Zach said, "She'll appreciate your confession when she cares."

Smirking, Frost harassed, "I wasn't sure we'd be able to be friends. We still aren't."

Following, Zach taunted, "You liar. You like me, I can tell."

Holding his thumb and forefinger a smidge apart, Frost winked. Looking at Lily, he asked, "Anyone worthy of the hall of souls?"

Perched on a wooden counter, Lily announced, "We've sent three people through based on their aura. We haven't had to do much, they've been poisoned. We woke up a few to ask what they'd taken but they're in a trance. I straight up told a guy, all he had to do was ask to be forgiven and we'd send him through the hall of souls, even though he took part in our torture. All he had to say was praise, Jezebeth."

"She's not even stretching the truth, watch this," Melody urged, as she laid her hands on a woman's chest.

Her eyes flickered open. Clutching her pearls, the mortal gasped, "Is it over?"

Mel innocently enquired, "Is what over?"

"Ridding our world of filth for Jezebeth," she hissed with hateful eyes.

"Right, it's almost over," Mel sighed. "Explain why you get to decide who is worthy of anything?"

"Devout need not share air with scourges of humanity," she scoffed, trying to sit up.

"Agreed. Define humanity," Mel prompted, with a hand on her chest to keep her in place.

The mortal hissed, "We are humane. Drifters, whores and non-believers of Jezebeth shall burn in the bowels of hell. We shall not feel safe with vermin in our midst."

"Humanity and humane aren't interchangeable words," Mel corrected, squinting.

Kneeling, Lily revealed, "It's true, immortals tend to be a tad promiscuous, but we can go to the in-between whenever we want. Your prophet was a demon and those pearls are fake."

Writhing on the carpet, the woman began shrieking like she was possessed, "Liars and whores! Whores!"

Zach snickered. Pointing his way, Lily cautioned, "I'll kick your ass."

Sucking back a touch of her energy, Jezebeth's sacrifice passed out. Mel muttered, "This drama-filled day of selective idiot population control was a waste of our time."

Marking her forehead with immortal blood, Lily spoke the words, solidifying the mortal's destination. Looking up, she asserted, "Find our phones. Ankh has to bring weapons. We can't leave demons roaming free. We have to hunt this asshole down before he collects enough morons to make a new cult."

"I'll take over," Frost offered.

Mel dusted off her pants, saying, "Go for it, they all drank Jezebeth's Koolaid."

Waving, Frost hollered, "Zach, we need bags of salt to contain the demons until Ankh shows up the with weapons to finish it. Clean Kayn up, and ask her where the truck is."

"No problem," Zach mumbled. "I'm sure the Dragon I left outside dismembering demons will stop no problem so I can clean her up and ask where the truck is."

Chuckling, Frost carried on marking disciples of Jezebeth as Zach walked away.

IN THE LIGHT FROM THE DOOR, the pile of corpses moved. *What was she supposed to do? They weren't staying dead long enough to waste time hacking off limbs. Why did she bother piling them up? Now, she had to dig through bodies.*

"Do you remember where the truck is?" Zach enquired as he approached.

Vaguely. Kayn answered, "I don't know how to drive, I ran through the woods in the dark and came out over there by that stump."

"I hope you remember how to get back. We should clean you up," Zach suggested, holding out his hand.

Looking back, Kayn asserted, "We can't leave, they won't stay down. I've been slashing throats since you went inside." The pile moved. An arm reached out. Kayn met the demon's vacant eyes, shook her head and stabbed it in the brain.

One grabbed his ankle. Shaking it off, Zach said, "I'll find someone to take over so we can run to the truck."

With a blade clutched in each hand, she slit throats until each demon housed in mortal flesh was momentarily down for the count. Everyone emerged from the building. Kayn looked up, commenting, "They won't stay dead."

Volunteering by reaching to pick up a blade in the snow, Mel asked, "Has anyone checked for salt in the hall?"

Passing Kayn a shirt, Lily teased, "Most demon's opt-out of salting their walkways but I'll look."

This was a soiled garment torn off a militant dead townie. Kayn took a sniff. *It smelled clean. She'd pretend it was.*

Lily instructed, "Get this wet in the snow and clean your face. If you go jogging in the woods like that you'll scare the crap out of hikers."

"Anyone out for a three am hike in the woods is looking for trouble," Frost stated. Wandering over, he offered, "I'll do it, Brighton. You don't have a mirror."

His hand grazed hers as she passed the cloth, making her pulse race. *Siren up to bat.*

Washing her face, Frost vowed, "First rest stop we find."

She wanted to do so many naughty things right now. Hypnotised by his eyes, Kayn switched topics, "Why are they healing so fast?"

"Demon's in mortal shells reanimate zombie movie fast, it's kind of cool," he explained, smiling.

"I love zombie movies," she blurted. *That was impressively nerdy verbal diarrhea.*

Continuing to clean her up, Frost said, "I know, I pay attention. I'm not always the idiot I was today." Taking an elastic band off his wrist, he announced, "I stole something off a dead body for you."

In the dark, Zach sighed, "He's a keeper. So romantic."

She'd forgotten Zach was there. He wasn't as shiny now. She didn't need Dragon eyes to see his soul anymore.

Putting her hair in a ponytail, Frost kissed the tip of her nose and decreed, "There, now you don't look like you've been running from a murderer in the woods."

"Dude?" Zach scolded, "Do not poke the Dragon."

That felt like it was a million years ago. Peeling her gaze from the pull of Frost's sultry eyes. *She had to burn off the tension, they were hours from the end of this job.* Stretching like it was the start of a race, Kayn looked at Zach, saying, "Can you keep up?"

Zach chuckled, "Try me." Kayn took off into the woods. "Brighton!" He shouted, chasing her.

The rustling of nocturnal creatures and mistimed hooting of an owl gave her a sense of normalcy. In the wee hours of a morning after foiling a resurrection, mortal expectations ceased to exist. Sprinting through trails into the midnight wild with the slushy swooshes of Zach's footsteps in pursuit, a foul stench revived predatory awareness. *Something wasn't right.* In remnants of snow, footprints marked the main trail. As they reached a fork in the route, instinct urged her to take the wrong path. *It smelled like someone farted.* Kayn stopped cold. *Unprompted, her heart sunk in preparation. The Dragon was a heartbeat from taking the reigns when her Handler caught up and touched her.*

Curious, Zach enquired, "Problem?"

Instinct to protect her Handler interrupted the Dragon's takeover. Abaddon's incapacitating smoke was only ever there to subdue you for a larger demon. "Do you smell that too?" Kayn asked, meeting his eyes.

Groaning, Zach sighed, "I was hoping it was just me."

A primal hum was advising her to take the other route, but she didn't know where that trail went. Her queasy demon warning system wasn't working, but the Conduit's instinct knew when there was dark energy close by. Kayn whispered, "This path isn't safe. We have no choice, they need the truck." *She had to get him out of these trails.* "Don't lag behind me," she cautioned, taking off down the trail with prints manoeuvered roots and leapt over a creek without slowing their pace until they saw the truck. About to step out of the woods, she tugged him back as a vehicle passed. Leaves rustled, the hair on the back of her neck prickled as droplets of water landed on her. *It was in the trees above her, she had to take him out of the equation. Only one of them had to make it back. She was so excited.* Reaching into her pocket, Kayn passed Zach the keys, speaking in her mind, *Do you trust me?*

'Sometimes,' he answered in his.

Looking into his eyes, Kayn thought, *There's a phone in the truck. The last number I called was Grey. It's one of us or both. Bring the truck back, I'll lead whatever this is away. You should go.* Out loud, Kayn announced, "I could use fresh air, I'll run back and meet you there."

'I can't leave you, Brighton,' Zach asserted, in his mind.

You won't. You'll find me. I love trail running. With a not so innocent smile, she declared, "I just need to stretch my legs before the drive."

Choked she was forcing his hand, her Handler clutched the keys, thinking, *'I don't like this. You've ingested too much dark energy.'* Zach answered aloud, "Twenty minutes," dashing to the truck.

As he drove away, she felt another drip and heard rustling branches. *Dragon time.* Chuckling, Kayn booked it into the trails. Hearing a thud behind her, she knew what it was. *The black fog accompanied a monstrosity, she didn't need the visual. The last time she fought one of these, she'd been skewered like a shishkabob. Usually, they were slow, but this one was speedy, and it smelled like Satan's asshole.* Reaching the fork in the trail, she chose the route away from the hall. *She couldn't bring it back to the others. She had to kill it or outrun it.* Sprinting through the forest avoiding roots, Kayn leapt over puddles and darted between trees, skidding to a stop to check out her odds. Many yellow glowing orblike eyes lit up the darkness like perfectly spaced hovering fireflies. *She needed to see everything.* Her eyes adjusted to night vision. In the moonlight, black scaly monster's were slithering along sparse branches, leaping from tree to tree. *She was about to be eaten by a hoard of young tar lizard demons. This wasn't her week. If she gave the last speck of control to the Dragon, odds would mean nothing, but she had to lead them further away first.* They closed in on her, pitchy wailing. Pressing her palms together, she parted them, willing the ability to surface. *No orb.* She pointed. *Come on fire. Nothing. Well, shit. This was going to suck.* Grabbing a stick, Kayn provoked, "Come on, let's do this." One leapt at her. Swinging a stick like a baseball bat, she hit a home run as it soared into darkness. Dodging trees, she sprinted away like she was trying to win a five hundred metre and leapt twenty feet over a stream like a superhero. Running so fast branches were whipping behind her, she miscalculated a step and tumbled down a ravine, smoking every rock, root, and tree on the way like she was in a pinball machine. With the wind knocked out of her, she laid at the bottom, cackling. Hearing pitchy wails, she tried to escape by scrambling under a log but was stopped by her butt. *Oh, the irony.* Tugged out by her legs, she clawed her nails into the dirt to slow demon snacktime. They yanked her free, she tried crawling away. They flipped her over. On her back exposed, glowing eyes encircled her. *Sacrificial lamb time. This was going to suck.* A mind-numbing blur of teeth versus limb tug of war commenced. *The agony was monotonous. Why wasn't she passing out? Oh, come on!* Her body was flung into bushes. *This was bullshit. Why wasn't she dead? If she was missing limbs, it was better to not have a visual.*

A voice in her head, scolded, 'Dragons don't give up. Dragons never give up.'

She wanted to though. She was exhausted.

Someone laughed, 'You're fine. Stand up and fight.'

There was no way she was in one piece. Humouring the voice, Kayn looked at her arms. *They were attached, that was good.* She felt her legs. *Wild, she was okay. Her skin wasn't even broken. She was strong and indestructible. She'd summoned up a new ability.* Her inner badass returned as a tar lizard's nose poked through the shrubbery. She slapped it. It wailed as she got up, cracked her neck, brushed off damp leaves and took off, continuing their savage game of tag.

12
HANDLER ISSUES

Driving down the road, Zach pulled into an empty grocery store parking lot. He picked up Kayn's phone with eight missed calls and pressed the number.

Orin's voice answered, "It's about time, we're almost at the diner."

"I'm down the road in front of a grocery store. We need salt," Zach responded.

"Name of the grocery store handy? You don't need salt, we're here," Orin chuckled.

Relieved, Zach checked the sign and said, "Super Save Market."

In the background, Jenna's voice announced, "Sit tight, Zach. We're two minutes away."

Closing his eyes, Zach took a beat. Hearing an idling engine and a door ding, he opened his eyes.

Getting in the passenger side, Jenna apologised, "Sorry, about the gong show, I only had pieces of this puzzle to work with. So, they drugged everyone, left

Kayn behind, and she called Grey. You were tortured and killed."

"That sounds accurate," Zach answered. "I woke up in the in-between by Kevin. That's the only reason we're not still angel chained to posts." He looked past her and waved at Markus and Orin in the lighted interior. Markus tapped his watch.

"A vision filled in the blanks, we knew you guys were in over your heads," Jenna disclosed. "I know how to get there, let's go."

As they drove, Jenna fired off questions, "You took out the ten people, but there was a full hall of sacrifices. Were you able to mark and send them off?"

"We were," Zach replied, impressed they were discussing murder like double-checking a grocery list.

Jenna asserted, "Turn right."

As they travelled the gravel road, Zach explained, "We didn't have blades to finish the job. We were sent to get salt to confine the demons and ran into trouble. Kayn's dealing with it."

Giggling, Jenna teased, "Why Zachariah, that's a nice way of saying, Kayn's gone Dragon feral in the woods."

"That goes without saying," Zach sparred, as they pulled up and got out.

Running over to the truck, Frost declared, "Tell me you have the blades, we're tired of killing these things." When everyone got out of the vehicles, he sighed, "Where's my girlfriend, Zach?"

"She didn't give me a choice. My symbol hasn't gone off, she must be outrunning it, leading it away," Zach explained.

"Did you see what it was?" Frost probed as they walked over to their friends, tending to a pile of reanimating bodies.

"It was too dark, I think it was one of those monsters that follow Abaddon's smoke," Zach replied.

Carrying a bag of salt over to Mel, Orin awkwardly said, "Hi kid."

Peering up at the immortal sire she barely knew, Mel disputed, "Kid? I'm far from a child."

Putting the bag down, Orin tried again, "Hi, Melody."

"Better," Mel laughed as Markus handed her a demon blade.

A flash of headlights through the trees signalled someone else's arrival. Jenna instructed, "Make it quick, we're about to have company."

In a fog, malevolent entities were vanquished back into eternal darkness as approaching tires crunched on the gravel.

"Look natural," Markus instructed.

Giggling, Zach baited, "Nothing to see here. Just hanging out by a pile of corpses."

As the car pulled over, they all squinted in the glare of headlights. When the door opened, the interior light turned on. Zach recognised the passengers. Thorne got out with his crew. *Holy shit.*

Looking up, Mel whispered, "Why me?"

Trinity wandered over with bows. Thorne questioned, "Do we need to lock down more than twenty miles?"

"That should be good," Frost declared.

Dropping the contraption, confining spiritual energy to a twenty-mile radius, Thorne explained, "We've been sent to help clean up. He glanced at Frost, provoking, "Job got away from you?"

Frost coldly slammed, "I'm surprised you didn't hide in the bushes and shoot us in the heart or do you just reserve that treatment for girls you claim to love?"

Thorne commented, "Touche."

Nudging Zach, Orin whispered, "Explain."

Zach filled him in, "Less than a week ago, Thorne lured Mel into a trap, we found her with an arrow in her heart."

Sheepishly coming over to Mel, Thorne implored, "Can we talk?"

"Don't bother," Mel curtly replied, walking away.

Thorne went after her, explaining, "I'm sorry it went down like that, I didn't intend to..."

"No. Making out with me and shooting an arrow into my heart made your intentions crystal clear," Mel insisted. "I'll get over it."

Out of nowhere, Orin hauled off and decked Thorne. Trinity raised their bows. Ankh gripped their blades.

Rubbing his jaw, Thorne stated, "Stand down, I deserved that."

Looking at Orin, Thorne apologised, "Falling for your daughter was wrong. I had to draw a line, I couldn't cross."

"Come get me when you figure out what we're doing," Mel commented, going into the building.

Wishing he'd punched Thorne, Zach followed her inside, wandered over and sat by her. He whispered, "I'm sorry I haven't been there for you."

Smiling, Mel admitted, "I know you're in love with me. I must seem like the most selfish person in the world, blowing you off every time you hit on me, then panicking when you move on. Listen, Lily is sweet and gorgeous, if you have a shot, you'd be crazy not to go for it." Holding out a curled pinky, Mel pledged, "Friends."

"Friends," Zach repeated, shaking pinkies. He took off his glove. Tracing the Ankh symbol, he noted, "Our symbols haven't gone off. It must be one of those super slow lizard demons that follow Abaddon's smoke. Let's go find her and reel her back in," he declared. Getting up, Zach held out his hand and prompted, "Come on, friend."

Accepting his gesture, Mel commented, "Those demons rely on the sedating fog, she ate. I bet she's walking away."

Grinning, Zach chuckled, "She'll be bored stiff." He let go of her hand as they wandered out to find only Ankh. He looked at Jenna, asking, "Where's Trinity?"

Their Oracle tossed each a demon blade, responding, "I had a vision of Kayn being chased by fifty fast, agile young Tar Lizard Demons. I know, she's not dead. Trinity has gone demon hunting. We can't call the Aries Group in to clean this up until the spirit world portion of the job is complete. We'll wait with the hall of corpses. Mel and Zach, go with Frost. If Trinity gets to her first, they'll have to give Kayn a Dragon time out."

Entering the woods, Frost directed, "We're following you, Zach. Activate those Handler powers, we need to tame a Dragon." Screams echoed, they sprinted into darkness.

13
BRING ME THE DRAGON

Tussling with the snaggle-toothed depravities, Kayn heard a whoosh. The monster trying to chow down on her innards went limp. Unharmed, she plucked an arrow from its scaly head and used it to impale the next one as another wrapped its spiked tail around her legs and whapped her with a spalt in the slush. Winded, but unscathed, she lay there giggling as one towed her away by her leg. A swoosh took out her ankle muncher, distracting her. Razer sharp teeth clamped on her face. Unable to puncture her throat, it thwapped her against a tree. Broiling hot, she shivered and pulsed, its jaw went slack. Unharmed, Kayn leapt up. Her fanged assailant was vibrating and shrieking. Pitchy wailing it exploded, shards of demon meat everywhere. Covered in moist gunk, she wiped it from her eyes. Noticing a faint glow in the trees, she turned and cocked her head as a portly man began a slow clap.

A voice declared, "Come to me, Dragon."
Who was this asshole?

"You chased me away before I finished my ritual. Now, I must wait for a portal," he reprimanded.

The remaining beasts were motionless. Trees shifted and the biggest Tar Lizard Demon she'd ever seen, nuzzled him.

Stroking its scaly face, he introduced his monster, "Magi is going to ingest you, trapping you in the bowels of hell for all time."

Kayn noticed her missing shoe.

The robust man, bellowed, "We are All-Powerful Beings! Bow in our presence vermin or be devoured!"

Vermin? With no filter, Kayn said, "No."

"Savage her!" The irritatingly insolent man commanded.

Kayn didn't move a muscle as the gigantic Magi lumbered over, hammered her with its spiked tail and sent her soaring through the air pissing herself laughing. Landing with a thud, she popped out of the foliage unharmed, brushed herself off and sauntered back, taunting, "Magi's babies hit harder."

"Nobody mocks Leonard the magical maker of mayhem and destroyer of souls!" The robust balding man decreed, wiggling his fingers like he was casting a spell.

"Who?" Kayn enquired, unconcerned.

The portly demon in a human skin suit, swayed his arms ominously, pranced and sang, "Broiling blood and mind, darkness cometh once per nigh." Pointing at her swaying his arms. Frustrated when nothing happened, Leonard shrieked, "What are you?"

"Bored," Kayn sighed, walking away. Sensing something, she stepped aside as an arrow missed her by a hair.

Leonard commanded, "Bring me the Dragon!"

Launching monsters into the air, avoiding arrows,

Kayn's stomach growled. *She was hungry.* Shuffling the food chain, her eyes locked with a beast's as she became the predatory species. It ran screaming. Pursuing it through the woods, she leapt on its back, soaking up its essence as it wriggled. *She wanted more.* Shrinking into the shrubbery to avoid detection, crawling soundlessly as a jungle cat, she happened upon a pack stalking shiny things. Waiting until they passed, she pounced on a straggler, drained its lifeforce and vanished into the woods without shuffling a branch. Glowing objects darted through the forest pursued by black scaly monsters, voices were yelling orders as arrows soared through the air. She climbed a tree and perched to observe the battle. From this vantage point, she had a visual of dark beings creeping in bushes and leaping from branches of one tree to the next. Radiant archers and beings on foot were in an epic battle. One soared at her from a nearby tree, she waved it away. It fell from the sky, tackling a shiny thing. *Whoops.* The gigantic depravity was moving through bushes, horror movie killer casual towards the battle as a hoard of demons leapt through trees, rapidly closing in on the group.

A voice yelled, "Brighton! Get your ass down here!"

Distracted, Kayn was knocked her off her branch. She felt a burst of energy. Everything paused, including her, mid descent. Hovering ten feet in the air like an astronaut in zero gravity, she tried to move and did a summersault. Unable to breathe, thrashing sent her into a stomach-churning spin. Dizzy, she thudded to the ground, and fighting commenced like she'd pressed play. Struggling to regain her bearings, a hoard of beasts came at her. Luminous beings encircled her, shooting arrows, swinging blades and screaming orders. The enormous Magi emerged, wailing like someone stole the last sales shoes. In a blur of whirling arrows, her fingers sparked. Grinning, Kayn placed her palms together and parted them. Mesmerized by the swirling luminescent green orb she'd created, time stood still.

A voice yelled, "Finish it, Kayn!"

She looked up. *Magi was covered in arrows.* Kayn pitched the swirling teal orb at the monstrosity, as it opened its mouth to wail.

Someone screamed, "Get down!"

Everyone dove away as Magi exploded, shards of meat and demon slime covered everyone. All of the baby lizard demons disintegrated in a black cloud. Drained of energy, Kayn's vision flickered, and the light went out.

14
IT'S A HARD KNOCK AFTERLIFE

After a choir of celebratory hoots, two wounded Clans of Immortals hobbled back covered in slimy hunks of Magi. At the start of this new day, Ankh and Trinity were good against evil, simplifying their differences. Frost was cradling Kayn in his arms, walking with Orin.

Lagging behind the pack, Thorne whispered, "Being this close to her is killing me."

"It's a hard knock afterlife," Glory whispered.

"Cute," Thorne said, watching Melody from afar.

Glory whispered, "In five minutes we'll be enemies again, stay strong."

"Maybe it won't always be like this?" Thorne whispered as they emerged from the bushes by the vehicles. Grinning, he picked up the device, closed it and rounded up the troops.

Smiling, Glory praised, "It looks good on you."

"You mean the slime?" Frost teased, carrying Kayn.

Laughing, Glory answered, "Feelings." She passed

Orin a box of garbage bags and instructed, "For the seats of your vehicle."

Orin went to work covering seats as Thorne strolled up, disclosing, "The Aries Group disposal team is outside of the thirty-mile marker, waiting for our go-ahead. We should take off before they show up."

Hugging Kayn as she stirred, Frost replied, "Thanks."

About to leave, Thorne added, "Tell Orin... Never-mind, it doesn't matter anymore." He walked away.

Placing Kayn on the backseat, Frost caressed her slimy hair, smiling.

"She's a crazy trainwreck of powers," Orin whispered.

Grinning, Frost said, "We're going to be the biggest gong show this Clan has ever seen."

Closing the door, Orin decreed, "Dethroning me will be difficult."

"Impregnating Jenna's mortal look-alike was next level breakup revenge," Frost chuckled as they walked into the hall of corpses and found everyone staring at the ceiling.

Looking up at symbols in blood, Orin stated, "Demons do creepy shit."

Waving everyone over, Frost urged, "Come on, let's call in the Aries Group and get out of here."

Hesitating, at the altar of immortal blood, Jenna insisted, "We can't leave mortals here by themselves. I'm certain this area hasn't been cleared. This is the beginning of something, not the end."

"Trinity left," Orin explained, stepping over bodies. "The Aries Group is waiting. Are you sure it's not just Oracle guilt speaking?"

"I'm not sure, that's the issue," Jenna mumbled, staring at the altar. "I need to talk to Markus."

Scanning the room, Frost said, "He isn't in here."

"He went with you guys," Jenna replied, looking around.

Panicking, Frost darted outside. He raced back in, saying, "I'm sure he wasn't with us."

An excruciating noise marking a four-minute warning dropped Ankh to the floor, clutching their heads, screaming. They scrambled up and sprinted for the vehicles.

Their wounded leader, limped out of the bushes, waving his arms, yelling, "Sorry, that was me. I found this checking out the perimeter."

Taking the Aries Group's immortal warning contraption from Markus, Frost questioned, "Where was this?"

"At the backdoor," Markus replied, wandering to their vehicles. "Trinity had a spiritual blockade, maybe it's theirs?" Preparing to leave, their leader asked, "Does everyone have phones and cards?"

"We found them a few phones, they have an Aries Group card and whatever is in those bags in their truck," Jenna answered, looking back at the hall. Grabbing Markus' arm, she cautioned, "This job doesn't feel done."

Smiling while texting away with the Aries Group, Markus teased, "Your premonitions have been off the mark lately, are you sure?"

Exhaling, looking at the building, Jenna admitted, "I'm not sure."

Their leader revealed, "We have a job in Vegas in two days. It's a long drive. We're way behind schedule, you need to be certain."

Jenna prompted. "Let's go."

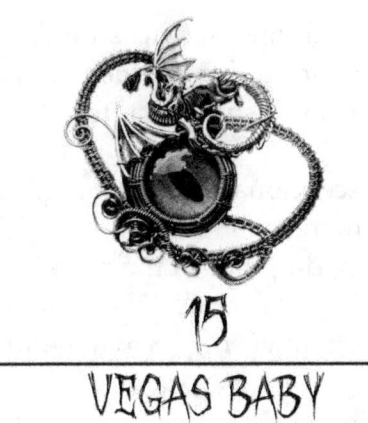

15
VEGAS BABY

Waking to the humming vibration of tires, Kayn opened her eyes. *She felt gross.*

"Welcome back," her Handler announced, stroking her demon innard stiff hair.

Focused on Zach's face, Kayn said, "You look like hell."

The truck cracked up. Her Handler chuckled, "You were sleeping on my lap. I didn't get to clean up like they did."

Frost was in the front passenger seat. Their eyes met, he grinned. *What kind of embarrassing shit had she done this time?*

"I missed you at the last three rest stops," Frost teased, tossing her a bag of salt and vinegar chips. Orin was messing with the stations. *Zach was the only one in the back with her. Mel and Lily must have gone with Markus and Jenna.*

Seat dancing, Zach sang, "We're going to Vegas baby."

Visions of naughty Vegas games swamped her mind,

she cracked her neck and sat up straight. Kayn caught sight of her reflection in the rearview. *Holy hell. She was hideous.* Afraid to ask, she went for it, "What is this green gunk?"

"Gross, it's exceptionally disgusting," Zach taunted as a song came on, they all knew.

Orin was serenading her in the rearview. *He a likeable guy. She rarely had jobs with Mel's surprise dad.* With shit disturbing Dragon lingering, Kayn enquired, "How's Lexy?"

Casually, Orin replied, "Amar was summoned by Third-Tier, Lexy went as backup. Afterwards, she was dropped off with our other group and the newbie Ankh."

Fiddling with Orin's playlist, Frost probed, "Did Jenna's fling stay? That was a surprise."

Orin sighed, "Yes, it was. Emery is still with us." Meeting Kayn's gaze in the rearview, he suggested, "Clean up, there are wet wipes in the console, we're stopping for lunch soon."

Now, he seemed fatherly. They made each other presentable while Frost and Orin chatted about Vegas. Kayn said, "Can I make a personal request?"

Undressing her with his eyes, Frost seduced, "Anything."

Slowly unzipping her coat without breaking eye contact, Kayn decreed, "I never want to wear an orange jacket again."

"Anything else you don't want to wear?" Frost naughtily baited, licking his bottom lip.

Provocatively shimmying stiff jeans over her hips, Kayn toyed, "These have to go." He caught his breath, seeing lacy black panties. She bit her lip, mischievously confessing, "I may need help getting these off."

The truck swerved. Frost wacked Orin, scolding, "What in the hell, Orin. Don't look."

"Don't play naughty Siren games, I'm driving. If we get in an accident, I have to explain why," Orin chuckled.

Smiling, Kayn said, "I seriously can't get these jeans off."

"Pull over, Orin. I'll help her," Frost naughtily suggested.

"Not a chance in hell, I'm starving," Orin laughed.

Reaching for a mystery bag, Zach searched through it and handed her a shirt, cautioning, "Put this on over that one. If you take your top off, Orin will crash the truck." Helping with her jeans, he pointed out, "You're missing a shoe."

She looked down. *She was missing a shoe.* As she peered up, her eyes locked with Frosts. *If he kept licking his bottom lip like that, she was going to tug him into the backseat.*

Frost silently mouthed, "Do it."

I will. She warned telepathically, biting her lip.

'You won't walk right for weeks,' he vowed, in his mind.

Cranking tunes, Orin shouted, "Cut that Siren shit out!" With Zach howling, Orin swerved into a restaurant parking lot, cautioning, "If you two get arrested for public indecency, I'm not bailing you out." He left them in the truck. Zach got out and took off.

Frost climbed into the back, laughing, "We're parked ten feet from the restaurant, we shouldn't."

"We'll wait," Kayn kissed his lips, wickedly caressed his junk, she got out.

Leaping out, he chased her to the restaurant, catching her before she reached the door. Provocatively making out with her, he backed her against the building. She was humming with desire as their lips parted. Frost whispered, "Game on," leaving her standing there, breathless.

Barely able to stand, she covered her swollen lips, exhaled and regained her poker face. *She was hardcore competitive; he had no idea what he was dealing with. Game on.* She composed herself and went in.

A waitress with a full drink tray, laughed as Kayn walked in, saying, "You must have been involved in the green slime prank. Follow me, I'm on my way to their table."

They'd come up with a backstory.

Leading her over, their server announced, "She looks like she belongs with you."

Kayn slid into the booth next to Zach. Frost was hiding behind his menu, laughing. *He was too chicken to sit beside her.*

Placing drinks on the table, their server looked at Kayn, asking, "Do you want a beer like these three?"

Someone was drinking a decadent shake at another table, Kayn replied, "I'd love one of those."

"Whipped cream and a cherry?" Their waitress enquired.

Meeting Frost's gaze, Kayn answered, "Definitely."

Picking up his beer, Orin shook his head and chuckled, "You're driving, Frost."

Searching the menu, Kayn peered over it as their server placed a giant milkshake on the table. *Oh, he had no idea what he'd uncorked.* She locked eyes with Frost, dipped her finger into the whipped cream, drizzled with chocolate sauce and licked it off. The waitress came back to take their orders.

Zach went first, "I'll have one of those milkshakes with a number seven."

She was planning on ordering whatever sounded

best but they all ordered by number. Kayn looked at the server and asked, "What's your favourite thing to order?"

"Chicken fingers with zucchini sticks and sweet potato fries," she admitted with a smile.

"I'll try that," Kayn declared.

Orin looked up from his phone and announced, "We're about to have company. They caught up with us. Can we switch to a bigger table?"

"Sure, no problem," the hostess said. "I'll put your orders in with the rest."

They carried their drinks over, she scooted into the back by Frost. He caressed her thigh. Kayn looked his way.

Kissing her, Frost licked his lips, teasing, "I might have to order one of those."

Pushing it over, Kayn whispered, "I'll share." Their Clan came in and sat down, chatting about Vegas, joking around. Resting her head on his shoulder, smiling, she baited, "You can have my cherry."

"Again?" Frost chuckled, kissing her hair. He snatched it out of the whipping cream and bit it off the stem.

He had cream on the corner of his mouth. She wiped it off with her finger. Snatching her hand, Frost massaged her palm, as he naughtily licked off her finger, gazing into her eyes. *Oh, she was going to tear his clothes off right here.* Not willing to let him win, she slid her hand further up his thigh under the table. The buzzing of conversation was white noise. *It was like they were the only two people in the world. She wanted him so badly it was crazy. Every nerve ending was humming with the urge to be reckless.*

Taking a tied cherry stem out of his mouth, Frost

placed it on his napkin and whispered, "Meet me in the bathroom."

Seeing what he'd done with his tongue, she crossed her legs. He excused himself and walked away. *Everyone else seemed preoccupied. Their orders were already in.* Squirming in her seat, her eyes darted around the table. *Maybe she could sneak away?* The excitement of the dare took precedence over ration as she slipped away and walked down the hall.

He tugged her in, locked the door and whispered, "If I set off your pheromones, we'll have someone knocking on this door. He undid her jeans, roughly tugging them down to her calves as she watched in disbelief. *He was really going to do this.* He buried his face between her legs. Clutching his hair, trembling, she gasped his name. *He was the naughtiest guy on the planet. She was going to lose it if he took off her panties.* Someone aggressively knocked on the door. *No.*

"Time out, lunch is waiting," Jenna laughed.

Kayn covered her mouth. *This was so embarrassing.*

"Kissing my girlfriend, be right out," Frost told the truth, deviously peering up at her.

He kissed her lacy panties again. Biting her lip as her toes curled, she arched her back. *This was so wrong.*

"Kiss her later," Jenna laughed as she walked away.

Looking up, he wickedly provoked, "Do you want me to keep going?"

So badly. Tingling, she gasped, "Don't stop."

He got up, whispered in her ear, "I win," and took off.

Oh, she was going to kill him. Looking at her reflection, her cheeks were rosy. *Well played.* Strolling down the hall, Kayn shimmied into her seat. She picked at fries, still tingly from his naughty games.

Nudging her, Frost urged, "Try this burger." She

took the biggest bite ever. Holding half a burger, he commented, "Hilarious."

Covering her mouth, chewing before she could respond, she mumbled, "I didn't think it out." Snatching a chicken strip off her plate, Frost ate it as everyone chatted about the Vegas job. He stealthily slid his hand up her thigh. *Everyone was watching, she couldn't react.*

"How are you feeling?" Markus asked.

Whoops, he was talking to her. Smacking Frost's hand, Kayn replied, "Alright."

Their leader probed, "What's in everyone's hair?"

"Demon slime," Kayn responded, eating a zucchini strip like they were discussing the weather. *Wait a minute, he was there.* She ribbed, "It's all over you too."

Checking out his dried crusty green slimy pants, Markus looked around the table, saying, "If I don't sleep, I'll be no help to anyone. We're driving straight through to Vegas. Is everyone good with the vehicles they're in?"

Winking at Frost, Orin teased, "If the Sirens reign it in."

Without looking at anyone in particular, Markus scolded, "Sirens behave!" He got up and declared, "I need to use the lavatory." He looked at Zach and instructed, "Pay."

Frost passed him a card. Shrugging, Zach got up to pay. *Markus was grumpy. Who says Lavatory?* Kayn got up, finishing the milkshake as quickly as she could. *Ahhh, brain freeze.* She rubbed her tongue on the roof of her mouth.

Entertained, by every weird thing she did, Frost hugged her to his side, chuckling, "Are you going to survive?"

"I'll do my best," Kayn sparred, strolling out to the truck.

Getting into the driver's seat of the other vehicle, Jenna shouted, "Behave for Orin!"

"I'll try," Frost replied as he opened the door.

With her arms around his neck, Kayn whispered, "How many hours until we're alone again?"

Tenderly kissing her lips, Frost whispered, "If you keep distracting me with lacy panties, we'll never get there."

"Kiss me and I'll behave," Kayn tempted. His lips inched towards hers.

Taking the lid off his ice water, Markus marched over and threatened, "Get in the truck Frost, I'll do it."

Everyone pissed themselves laughing as Kayn got in the back. Orin was texting with someone. She asked, "How are the new Ankh doing?"

"Lexy says, Molly is obsessed with me," Orin chuckled, grinning at a text.

"I like her," Kayn decreed. *She'd branded Molly, Ankh.*

Texting Lexy back, Orin said, "I'm not going there." He glanced at Kayn, adding, "Your sister says, hi."

"Hi back," Kayn laughed. *They'd had fun on their Handler Dragon road trip until Lexy and Grey started fighting.* She closed her eyes for what felt like minutes and woke up to everyone belting out a goofy pitchy rendition of Bohemian Rhapsody. Stretching, she joined in without missing a beat. A full day and night of karaoke roulette to the back noise of spinning tires kept the merry band of inappropriate lambs entertained as they switched drivers, only stopping for snacks. Sneaking intimate moments with Frost became their road trip game.

They stopped to stretch their legs on the outskirts of the city just in time to watch a vibrant Vegas sunset. They were grubby with crusty goo in their hair, but nothing mattered as Frost came up behind her and wrapped his arms around her waist, snuggling her. *She was happy. She loved him so much it ached. Even thinking those words terrified her.* Turning to face him, the stunning crimson backdrop was no competition for the allure of his magnetic eyes.

Caressing her face, Frost pledged, "I'm all in. All you have to do is believe it."

Her breath caught as he kissed her and everything melted away but desire. As their lips parted, she felt it in the core of her being. The tug of their souls drew their lips together, and they were lost under the Nevada sky.

"You guys are beautiful, get in the truck," Orin declared as he got in. "Everyone else is already at the hotel."

Kissing her once more at the door, Frost said, "We'll be in our room in less than an hour."

Anticipating their evening, they climbed into the truck as the sun vanished and the Vegas sky lit up like magic.

"It's nice to see you this happy," Zach whispered.

Squeezing her Handler's hand, she challenged, "Go tear up Vegas like the badass you deserve to be."

Driving by exciting scenery, Zach admitted, "I plan to."

Glancing into the rearview, Orin prompted, "Check my phone, it's buzzing. I left it back there on the seat."

Reading messages, Zach explained, "They're restocking our clothes, toiletries, buying dresses and renting tuxes for a benefit tomorrow. Did Lily's jeans fit properly or did you need more hip room?"

Grinning, Orin piped in, "Size thirteen heels, I'd prefer something in red."

"Ha, ha," Zach chuckled, texting his response. Laughing, looked at Orin, teasing, "You know she's buying you a dress now, right?" Grinning, Orin went back to driving.

"Lily's pants fit," Kayn answered, viewing the impressive display of lights. *They spent most of their time off the beaten path, staying in campgrounds, she felt like a fish out of water in the city. Everything about Vegas was exciting.*

They pulled up in front of the hotel, got out and grabbed their bags. Frost tossed the valet their keys.

A pretty brunette laughed, "You definitely belong to that bachelor party. Your friends are checked in."

Frost wittily responded, "You mean your patrons don't usually show up covered in green goo?"

Walking around to the driver's seat, shaking her head, she said, "You're the first. See Micheal at the desk for your room cards. There's a fancy benefit tomorrow evening, I heard you were all going. I can't wait to see everyone dressed up."

Wandering over, Zach flirted, "Will you be there?"

Smiling, she teased, "Regular people rarely go to balls."

"Can I see you later?" Zach boldly enquired.

Smiling, she replied, "I'll be out here until four am."

Holding out a hand, he introduced himself, "Zach."

Shaking it, she responded, "Emily."

"See you later, Emily!" Zach called out.

They were waiting at the door. With his arm around her, Frost sighed, "Our boy is becoming a man."

Zach strutted by. Orin chuckled, "I found a wingman." He took off after him.

As they wandered in, Jenna was by the desk, chatting with Orin. She summoned them over, gave Kayn a keycard and apologised, "Sorry, Brighton. We have something to discuss. Everything you need is in your room. Have a shower, he'll only be ten, maybe twenty minutes."

"This better be important," Frost groaned.

Waving as she walked away, Kayn checked out the card with their room number. *They might have a view.* She stepped into the elevator, rode it to the tenth floor and walked out. Everything was rich jewel tones as she wandered down the hall until she found their room. As she walked in, there was a king-sized bed and a large sunken tub. Checking out the bathroom, she gazed at her reflection. She'd washed her face and brushed her teeth on the road, but her hair had been in a messy ponytail for days. Stripping, she turned on the water and got into a luxurious shower. She'd washed, conditioned, and rinsed her hair before hearing him come in.

Getting in behind her, Frost kissed the nape of her neck, teasing, "At least one of us is clean."

Knowing he had demon slime and days of travel to wash off, she passed soap. Watching Frost lather up, she enquired, "What was that about?" *He was ridiculously hot.*

Rinsing his hair, he disclosed, "Relationship drama that's not ours."

Pressing her body against his, Kayn naughtily suggested, "Take me right here."

"Here?" Frost toyed, sliding his hand between her thighs.

She gasped as he caressed until she was shivering, got on his knees and made her's buckle with his treacherous tongue. Clutching the curtains, whimpering as he got up and groaned as he entered her. Whispered wicked sentiments, he roughly gave it to her against the wall until her toes curled.

"I want a chance to make love before this night goes full Siren," he seduced. Picking her up with her legs around his waist, Frost carried her to bed and placed her on silky sheets. Kissing the sensitive hollow of her ankle, his lips inched up her calves as she willed him to keep going. Teeth nipped her tender inner thighs. He feathered sensual kisses, as she pled, pleasuring her where it ached until she was squirming. With devious eyes, he paused as waves of euphoria swelled.

"You're horrible," she moaned, aching for release.

He chuckled, "Trust me." Hovering his hand, giving her magical shivers of pleasure without touching her, he kept her teetering on the edge, pausing once more.

Clutching his hair, she reprimanded, "I swear, if you do that again, I'll lose it." *He was making her crazy.*

"Do what?" Frost provoked, deviously locking eyes with her, finishing his carnal task.

"Frost," Kayn gasped, as he gave her a savage toe-curling, limb trembling climax. He leapt up to muffle her cries.

Removing his hand from her mouth, he taunted, "I know what I'm doing." Playing Siren feeding games, hovering his hand, heating her flesh, she reached for him. Mouths met in breathless abandon, and with soaring hearts, they merged as her lusty cardio god dynamically drove her to unimaginable heights of euphoria until she was clutching sheets, sobbing.

Rolling off, sprawling beside her, Frost gasped, "I'm so turned on, it's taking everything I have to slow down."

She didn't want him to. Yearning for the thrilling release of ration, she seized control, provoking, "Why?" Gyrating away his romantic intentions by indulging carnal wishes, enticing abandon with each perfectly timed grinding sway of her hips, ceasing all fantasies of regulating their combustible situation, she rode him to the edge of restraint. Clutching her hips, he cursed, groaning her name as a wave of euphoria shivered through her and simultaneous reality blinding explosions of pheromones detonated mirrored abilities. Hours were lost in a frenzied hedonistic haze of pleasure-seeking supernatural Siren bliss before they came up for air.

Caressing her hip, Frost whispered, "I wish we could stay in bed like this for weeks."

"Months," she sighed, sprawling like a feline in sunshine.

Smiling, he chuckled, "I'm starving."

Rolling onto her stomach, she said, "I could eat."

They ordered room service and wandered plush carpet out onto their balcony in complimentary robes to check out the view of Vegas. The city was alive with flashing lights and sounds, accentuating thousands of twinkling stars in a clear Nevada sky. Swept away, slow dancing with her head on his shoulder, she never wanted it to end, but their food arrived. They shared appetizers at a table on the deck. *It almost felt like a date.* Enjoying each others company, they filled the jacuzzi, sat at opposite ends, told stories and drank champagne.

"I almost forgot," he said, getting out and drying off.

Watching his magnificent rear walking away, she grabbed a towel and got out.

Placing a tray of chocolate-dipped strawberries on the nightstand, he didn't notice her there. He lured, "Come back to bed." She shoved him, he landed on his back, laughing.

Snatching one, she got in bed. Hovering a milk chocolate strawberry with white chocolate drizzle by his lips, Kayn seduced, "You first." Obeying by taking a bite, smiling. She straddled him, licking melted chocolate off her fingers and offered him another taste, admitting, "The strawberries are a nice touch."

Clutching her hips, Frost toyed, "I say we aim for

more chocolate strawberries in fancy rooms, less murder cabins in the woods."

"I'm in," she stated with a chocolate kiss. They made love again and she drifted off to sleep in his arms.

Waking with sunlight creeping up the sheets, Kayn saw a light flashing and reached for her phone. It was Zach venting about everyone. She giggled.

Frost snuggled her, groggily whispering, "What's making you giggle?"

"Zach's night wasn't as amazing as ours," she disclosed, rolling to face him.

Kissing her lips, he naughtily tempted, "We should make sure nobody has a better morning."

"Definitely," she affirmed, reaching for him as someone pounded on the door. "No, no," Kayn giggled.

He got up with his magnificent bare ass, covered himself with a towel and peeked through the peephole. Frost sighed, "It kills me to say this but get dressed Brighton." Cracking open the door, he asked, "Problem?"

"Cover up!" Jenna announced. "We have a time-sensitive Ankh issue, I'm coming in."

Of course there was. Kayn tugged up the sheets as Frost stepped aside, smiling.

Marching in, their Oracle declared, "Ambassadors from every community are here for a meet and greet that starts in less than two hours. Our fearless leader was breakup wasted last night. Markus is ghosting Arrianna. Only Zach is back at the hotel. Nobody has tried on their gowns."

"I've got this," Frost answered. "I'll shower and get ready to go in his place. Why don't you two order breakfast and try on clothes?"

Wincing, Jenna apologised, "I barged in, wrecking your morning, I'm sorry."

Reaching for the menu, smiling, Kayn assured, "It's fine, fate always interrupts us. It's a thing."

"Have you seen the dress we picked for you? It's ivory, lace and silk with chiffon. It's gorgeous," Jenna explained as they looked at the menu.

Frost stuck his head out, asking, "Can you pass me that bag in the closet, Babe?"

Tugging the sheet off the bed with her, Kayn wandered over, grabbed it off the hanger and passed it in.

He whispered, "Come in for a second."

She slipped into the washroom. Frost captured her in his arms, kissed her, and whispered, "Lily and I will be gathering information this evening. If you overhear anything sketchy come to me. The Clan's have ambassadors there, keeping an eye on things at the fundraiser. Afterwards, when a hundred drunk beings do Vegas, the Aries Group will be monitoring social media. We purposely do events in Vegas. People are used to the unusual. If anything happens, they'll assume it's a publicity stunt for one of the Casinos. Drunk witnesses have no clout. Stay with your Handler and don't eat anyone until after the banquet."

"Yes, boss," Kayn teased, wrapping her arms around his neck. Her sheet dropped on the floor.

With a pained expression, he taunted, "You are way too tempting, you should cover up and go."

Wrapping the sheet around herself, she provoked, "If I must." Kayn wandered to the closet to peek at her gown. Touching silky material, she said, "It's beautiful." *Yesterday, she was covered in demon slime, and today, she was going to a ball.*

"I hope it fits. Everyone will be wearing masks, dresses and suits from their favourite era. The point of this evening is to erase lines between us," Jenna revealed. "Did you figure out what you want?"

What she wanted was in the washroom. Knowing she meant for breakfast, Kayn replied, "I didn't get a good look at the menu. What are you having?" Frost walked out, insanely hot in a tux. She whispered, "Wow."

He sweetly kissed her, saying, "See you tonight."

She'd never envisioned their dynamics as a relationship scenario. Who would? Smiling as Frost left, Kayn announced, "I'll go shower quickly. Order me anything, I'm famished."

After brunch, Kayn was doing her makeup. Orin strolled in like a blonde groom on the top of a wedding cake, teasing, "Is nobody else ready but me?" Looking, he asked, "Where's Frost?"

"Covering for Markus," Jenna replied as her ex stretched out on the bed beside her. "Get up, you'll wrinkle your suit," she scolded, not so playfully shoving him.

Orin didn't move a muscle, provoking, "It's a good thing I'm not your responsibility anymore."

Getting up, Jenna left Orin making a point to no one, singing, "Fill your boots, fool with a wrinkled suit. I'm going to get ready. Go hunt down Markus."

Watching TV, Orin chuckled, "You're not my boss."

It was nice to see reality, behind the veil of perfection. For a good year, they seemed close to perfect. They did their jobs like badasses. Brains before brawn was the Clan's mantra. Apparently, nobody used that part of their anatomy when it came to hooking up. There was impressive behind the scenes drama. Fighting to keep a straight face applying eyeliner, Kayn fumbled and dropped it.

Raising her glass of champagne, Jenna disputed, "I may not be your boss, but I do pick your jobs. You might want to think about playing nice."

Leaning against the doorframe watching her strip, Orin muttered, "I spent all night reigning in drunk Markus, I don't want to be in charge of him tonight."

"Neither do I," Jenna stated, in underwear, pinning up lush chestnut curls.

Grinning, Orin flirtatiously offered, "I'll massage your back for two hours if you do it."

"What part of hard no, confuses you?" Jenna slammed, flouncing past with a seductive sway.

Jenna was drunk. This was entertaining.

Following her into the other room, Orin sparred, "Guess we're still stripping in front of each other. Good to know."

Stepping into her teal green gown, Jenna tugged it up and turned her back to Orin. On longterm relationship autopilot, he zipped up and buttoned her dress. Jenna compromised, "We'll watch him together."

"Agreed," Orin conceded. They high fived. He offered, "I'll go find the others."

Grinning, Kayn chuckled, "I wonder if he knows he's doing what you wanted him to do?"

"He'll be back when he figures it out. I'll do your hair," their Oracle offered, pouring another glass of champagne.

Entrusting her hair to an already drunk person felt like a bad idea but who was she trying to impress?

Pinning Kayn's curls up reminiscent of her first banquet before immortal Testing, Jenna explained, "Only Lily and Frost are working. Siren are a coveted food source. We use nights like this to foster alliances."

Code for, you won't be seeing your boyfriend after the banquet. "Why aren't you using me? You did a few days ago." Kayn probed as Jenna wandered out.

Jenna's voice teased, "I wonder?"

"It didn't go that bad, did it?" Kayn called out, messing with their Oracle.

"We've already fulfilled our Clan's shit show quota for the year," Jenna shouted from the other room.

Funny. Also, true. Barely recognising her reflection, Kayn stood in awe. *Was she sexier? There was something on the mirror.* As she moved, to rub it off, she realised it was teal flecks in her eyes. *This was new, she'd never noticed this before.* Her pulse raced. Her spine tingled. With the heebie geebies, she looked back. *No, she didn't have time for ability roulette crap.* She grabbed the hot iron, letting her fingers sizzle before yanking her hand away. *Healing might take her Conduit urges down a notch.*

Jenna walked in. "Feeling alright?" She enquired, twisting lipsticks and checking colours on her wrist.

That was dumb, they all knew what burnt flesh smelled like. A wave of nausea washed over her. Kayn covered her mouth. *Oh, no. Crap. This wasn't going to happen all night, was it?* As her stomach cramped, she said, "It's creepy when you do that."

Applying lipstick, Jenna revealed, "Abaddon just arrived, a spiritual blocker will be in place shortly."

Where was Zach? He should be here.

Playing with her curly updo creation, Jenna asked, "Have you had Enlightening brain growth issues since lighting the truck on fire?"

Her mind drew a blank. "Zach had a situation at the cabin. I wonder what he's going to be able to do?" Kayn hinted.

Finishing her final touches, Jenna sprayed her hair, slyly commenting, "I wonder?"

Kayn laughed. "Come on, spill."

"An Oracle has to have a few secrets," Jenna whispered. Changing the subject, she cautioned, "You'll be vulnerable after the banquet, stay with your Handler."

"Of course," Kayn answered, posing in the mirror in her skivvies.

Removing her dress from a hanger, Jenna urged, "Let's put your dress on."

Kayn stepped into it. Jenna zipped her up and she went back into the bathroom to look. Beaming at her reflection, she shook her head, laughing.

"What's so funny?" Jenna toyed, from the doorway.

Grinning, Kayn sighed, "This looks like a wedding gown. I hope Frost doesn't bolt out of the ball like Manderella."

Giggling, Jenna sparred, "I wouldn't get down on one knee and hand him any boxes unless you feel like chasing him around Vegas."

Now, she wanted an empty box to mess with him. She felt Zach.

There was a knock on the door. Jenna answered it and announced, "Everyone is ready. Orin, you shouldn't have."

"I didn't," Orin stated, walking in. He looked at Kayn and declared, "You assholes."

"It'll be entertaining," Jenna justified, winking.

The plot thickens, they'd dressed her this way on purpose.

Smiling, Mel revealed, "We've been dressed for hours."

Zach looked handsome in his suit, Mel was in a slinky black cocktail dress. It looked like they were going to prom. Jenna took Zach aside as they toasted to the night ahead with glasses of champagne. Curious, Kayn questioned, "Who is representing the other Clans?"

Smiling, Orin replied, "Thorne and Tiberius were arguing in the lobby at three am. I haven't seen anyone else."

"Fantastic," Mel sighed, downing her entire glass.

"Everyone will be wearing masks, if you don't look for him, you won't see him," Orin assured, meeting eyes with his offspring.

She'd know it was Kevin in a mask. She owed him an apology. It would be better for her relationship if he wasn't here. This dress was going to freak Frost out.

Orin razzed, "I hope you found Kayn a veil to go with that dress. Why half-ass a prank this epic?"

Whatever. She was going to own this wedding dress. This may be her only opportunity to wear one. Raising her champagne flute, Kayn announced, "Get me a ring box, I'll take this prank all the way." Looking at her feet, she said, "Do I have shoes?"

Jenna presented her with a shoebox. Kayn peered inside. *Glass slippers. Those assholes.* "These look uncomfortable," she complained.

Peeking into the box, Zach toppled over on the bed, laughing. Shaking her head, Mel decreed, "Let's pretend this is your wedding. We'll dance all night and give embarrassing toasts, it'll be fun."

Frost was going to have a jammer. Raising her glass, Kayn toasted, "It's on."

A few hours and far too many drinks later, Ankh strutted down the hall like a masked Vegas bridal entourage. As they approached, the elevator opened and they rode down to the lobby, grinning.

A couple got out, saying, "Congratulations."

Without missing a beat, Kayn grabbed her Handler's arm, gushing, "Thank you, he's so wonderful." As the elevator slid shut, everyone lost it. Silenced, as the door opened to the lobby so they'd appear united and powerful. *It was freeing to hide her face, but half masks were mediocre disguises.* She couldn't decide if it was creepy or cool as Ankh strolled into the ballroom of highly inebriated beings in masks. *She'd burned her hand but couldn't see anyone's aura.*

Jenna answered her thoughts, "This aura and cramp-free night comes to you, courtesy of the Aries Group."

Wandering under a delicate archway of sterling roses, Kayn took in the breathtaking display of twinkling mauve lights with fancy crystal chandeliers and music. Scanning the dance floor and seating area, there was lavender in vases at the tables. *Funny.*

Taking her hand, Zach whispered, "This looks like fun. If we overhear anything sketchy, we report it, but the night is ours. Feel like eating anyone yet?"

"So far so good," Kayn whispered, scanning the tables for Frost. *She could eat everyone in this room but didn't want to…yet.*

Kissing her hand, Zach pestered, "No eating guests until after midnight."

Jenna passed her a drink, suggesting, "Let's go find our table. We can have appetizers and try to figure out where everyone is."

Taking their seats, Ankh commenced people watching. Orin pointed and declared, "There's Glory."

Looking into her drink, Mel mumbled, "I plan to go out of my way to avoid Thorne."

The spiritual blocker didn't circumvent connections. Kayn's eyes were drawn to the dance floor. *Part of her mortal life was out there dancing.* Her eyes darted to Zach. *Her Handler understood.*

"Are we avoiding your ex this evening?" Zach enquired, seeing Triad dancing.

She should.

"To friends," Zach toasted, lightening the mood.

They clinked glasses. Kayn's broke slicing her hand. *Oh, no.* The scent of blood turned every head at the ball. *Of course, that impermeable flesh power wasn't permanent. She had to get rid of it. Cloth napkins. Damn it.* She licked her hand. *Apparently, being inconspicuous wasn't her thing anymore.*

Snatching the jagged glass away, Jenna reprimanded, "I'm impressed, you're bleeding and we've only been here for five minutes. Let's get rid of your bloody broken flute before a Lampir tackles you." All eyes followed their Clan's Oracle as she walked away with the broken glass.

The lights dimmed. Squeezing her hand, Zach assured, "Accidents happen."

Smiling at her Handler, she saw Jenna talking to Lucien. *Awkward. She tried to eat him.* The head of the Lampir caught her staring and grinned. Without uttering a syllable, Orin slid a flute of champagne across the table to her with his mind. *It probably wouldn't take her long to break this one either. Where was Frost?* Sipping champagne, she scanned the room. There was a flock hanging off a man in a black mask's every word. *There her boyfriend was.* With a hand on the small of a women's satin back, Frost whispered in her ear. *It's nothing, it's not real.* Her eyes darted to the dance floor. Needing a distraction, Kayn nudged her partner in crime and urged, "Let's dance."

Zach leapt up, held out his hand and announced, "Your wish is my command." Rallying Ankh troops, her Handler prompted, "Orin grab Mel, let's have fun!" Tugging her up, Kayn laughed as Zach danced her into the crowd of masked beings as eighties music played. Breaking tension with goofy antics, They mowed the lawn, washed windows and did the sprinkler. Laughing, others joined in until the song changed to a slow one. Her Handler took her in his arms. Swaying, Zach whispered in her ear, "If you start jonesing for energy, let me know. Mel and Orin will discreetly feed you."

"I'm fine, Zach," Kayn assured, finding it a tad peculiar. *Maybe she was alright because she hadn't left her Handler's side?*

Zach said, "Your fidelity challenged boyfriend is staring."

Peering over his shoulder, she saw Frost, watching. He raised his glass, saluting admirers. Siren worshipping smiles glowed in white light. Rhythmically moving, with her chin resting on Zach's shoulder. *She felt peaceful in his arms. It was his job as her Handler to make her feel this way. It was nice. She loved this song.* The music changed to a nineties tune they'd belted out on many road trips. Ankh mic free karaoke owned it.

Zach kissed her cheek and whispered, "I need to use the washroom. Maybe you should come?"

"I'm all good," she affirmed as mauve lights flashed orbs on dancers. *It was rather magical in here.*

Cupping her face in his palms, Zach cautioned, "If I feel hesitant to leave you, there's always a reason."

Having a conversation on the dance floor was making her uncomfortable. "Go," she laughed. Holding out a curved pinkie, Kayn vowed, "I pinkie promise I won't eat anyone." Someone shoved her. *Except that guy. She might eat him.*

Laughing, Orin grabbed Kayn's shoulders, saying, "Go! Get out of here, Zach. We've got her." He shimmied her to their group of Ankh.

She forgot about everything but having a good time with her friends dancing and drinking until she nearly went down. *Whoops.*

Orin caught her, laughing, "No passing out until four am, Ankh Vegas throwdown rules."

She was wasted, they all were. The dance floor was lit.

White Wedding by Billy Idol riled everyone up. The D.J shouted out, "This one goes out to the bride!"

A spotlight was on her. *Those assholes.* Orin, Jenna and Mel doubled over, howling.

Beaming, Zach danced over, daring, "You said, you were going to own this dress, Brighton. Bring it!"

Whatever. Tossing glass slippers like a drunken princess, Kayn twirled barefoot dancing in a circle of hooting masked strangers. Taking turns dorkily dancing their asses off, the lines between immortal species blurred as laughter lifted the room. The merriment carried on in a mauve haze of goofy comradery, evading those who may stir up the water in her snowglobe of happiness. *She was thirsty.* Manoeuvring past cavorting masked partiers barefoot, Kayn perched on a stool at the bar in her fancy gown. *She didn't give a shit now. She could care less what anyone thought.* The bartender passed her a glass of clear fluid. She smelled it. *It was water.* The music slowed. Kayn swayed to the song on her stool. *Couples were making out.* Tempted to look for Frost, she spun her stool, overshot it, and someone stopped her. A masked stranger placed her glass slippers on the bar in front of her. *Whoops, she'd left those on the dance floor.* Smiling politely, Kayn said, "Thank you."

The masked stranger asked, "You didn't really marry him, did you?"

Kevin's voice fractured her carefree demeanour. Shaking her head, she admitted, "It was a joke."

"I should go before Frost starts boiling rabbits," Kevin chuckled, inching his hand closer.

Grinning, Kayn sparred, "I'm sure Frost ran away when that song started, you're safe." Drawn to connect with him, she shifted her hand. A hair before they touched, she paused, saying, "I know you didn't have to help me."

"I was hurt. When Zach materialised in the in-between, I caved," Kevin confessed.

She knew Kevin was smiling but didn't sneak a peek. She couldn't even allow her heart to picture it. He reminded her of everything she needed to forget. Without glancing over, Kayn explained, "Lexy snapped my neck."

Kevin chuckled, "Seems legit."

"It caused drama," Kayn giggled, meeting Kevin's eyes. Feeling a hand on her shoulder, she winced. *Shit.*

Frost teased, "I imaginary marry you and the first chance you get you're chatting up your ex." He turned and said, "Hi Kevin."

Staring straight ahead, Kevin laughed, "Hi Frost."

"You were entertaining your harum, I didn't think you'd miss me," Kayn provoked, saucily looking back.

Leaning in, Frost whispered in her ear, "It's my job."

"Nice chat, I'll leave you two fake honeymooners alone," Kevin declared, getting up.

Blocking Kevin's escape, Frost admitted, "I owe you an apology. You were right, I'll try harder. Can you do me one favour?"

"What's that," Kevin asked, with a glowing smile.

Holding a hand out like a peace offering, Frost requested, "Avoid chatting when we're in bed together."

"For the record, seeing you two in bed is like having teeth pulled. Unless it's an emergency, I won't do it again," Kevin assured, shaking his hand.

Holy shit, they shook hands. This must be an alternate dimension.

Massaging her shoulders, Frost confessed, "I'd rather be dancing with my pretend bride but we have a job."

Enjoying his magical hands, Kayn sparred, "Of course we do." *He smelled amazing.*

Caressing wispy tendrils on the nape of her neck, he said, "The creepy guy who killed Zach is in Vegas. Hungry?"

"Now, I am. Are you suggesting murder date night?" She teased, giggling as he nuzzled and nipped her neck.

Sitting next to her, Frost took her hand, provoking, "We have Lampir backup, but there are lots of snacks here."

Zach was going to be choked if she wrecked his night by feeding and went off the rails. "I promised I wouldn't," Kayn countered.

Frost tempted, "No harm in showing these fools your place in the immortal food chain."

No harm. Right. Kayn sighed, "Spit it out, Siren boy. What crazy sacrificial lamb shit do you need me to do, and why?"

Caressing her palm, Frost replied, "New orders. Markus wants you to use whatever surfaces and move through the crowd siphoning energy, the Aries Group needs a reason to enforce early closure."

Whatever surfaces. She may light this place on fire. "How could siphoning a dance floor of immortals with a random mix of abilities backfire?" Kayn harassed, smiling.

Holding her hand, Frost whispered, "We can't question orders. I'll do anything you want if you pull this off."

Engaging in eye contact chicken with his ocular weapons of seduction, she toyed, "Anything?" *This was going to go badly. She was way too drunk. She might eat everyone at this banquet. If she sent a bunch of creatures through the hall of souls, Azariah was going to be pissed.* "I have no control," Kayn warned.

Massaging her palms, Frost vowed, "I'll make sure Orin is ready to take you out."

Only he could make plotting her own assassination sexy. Patting his hair to check for horns, Kayn sighed, "Alright."

Leaning in, Frost whispered, "Let your freak flag fly." He passionately kissed her, deepening allure with sensual darts of his tongue.

With the Siren ability idling as their lips parted, she stated, "Well played instigator, I see what you did there."

Running a hand down her arm, Frost disclosed, "Lucien knows we can't promise you'll do anything after uncorking your Conduit ability. His men are feeding on us after the job. I won't be back tonight."

"I know Siren blood is our currency, I'll do it if I'm not feral," Kayn agreed. "It just feels like there are so many ways this night could go wrong."

"Zach will pull you out before it gets out of hand," Frost assured, running a loose ringlet between his fingertips.

He couldn't promise that.

Gazing into her eyes like they were the only people in the hall, Frost whispered, "Do whatever you need to do. No judgement. No fear. We'll talk about it tomorrow."

That wasn't going to be a fun conversation. There was apprehension in his eyes. He wasn't okay with what he was asking her to do, that's all she needed to know. "Okay," Kayn accepted her mission like she had a choice.

"They're waiting for me outside. I need to trigger you and runaway," Frost whispered with his hand on her shoulder. It heated, making her pulse race.

With her heart thudding wildly, Frost vanished into the writhing crowd like a naughty hallucination. Thin threading restraint, she saw Lucien coming with a shot in each hand. *Shit, no way. Zach, if you can hear me, I'm about to go hardcore feral.*

Stealing Frost's seat, Lucien placed a shot in front of her, saying, "This situation requires a stiff drink."

Summoning the bartender, he raised a shot, instructing, "Eight of these."

Laughing, Kayn picked up the shot, toasting, "You have no idea what you're uncorking."

Lucien teased, "I have an idea." His eyes locked with hers as he touched her face feeding her carnal visuals.

She was full Dragon, killing every Lampir with dark auras. His wasn't like the others, she'd granted him a reprieve. Feeding on his energy triggered her Siren ability, their mutual feeding session got out of hand. Her Handler jumped in to stop it and was caught in her web. Damn it, Zach. I'm sorry. Concerned, Kayn stated, "I need to find my Handler."

With a dimpled grin, Lucien enticed, "He'll find you once people start dropping on the dance floor. I'll come by your room later."

Smiling, shaking her head as her stomach twisted into a knot, Kayn cautioned, "I may eat you."

"I have faith in our Siren Lampir chemistry," he taunted, squeezing her hand, revving her engine.

She wasn't only Siren. Blushing, she couldn't resist pointing out her place at the top of the immortal food chain, by taking a taste. Tilting her head, Kayn stroked his throat and smirked as her hand heated on his skin.

Leaning closer, he tempted, "Do it."

Unable to resist, Kayn closed her eyes as warm euphoria-inducing Lampir essence travelled up her arm into her chest. *Oh, this night was about to get out of hand. She had no control over her toe-curling reaction.* With goosebumps of pleasure on every speck of exposed flesh, she gasped, tightening her crossed legs, struggling to regain composure.

Beaming, he revealed, "Siren and Lampir, it's a Ying and Yang thing. Every magical species has a weakness."

Instinctual autopilot snuffed out concerns of

emotional recourse, Kayn cocked her head, revealing, "I can be any species, Lucien."

Shifting closer, Lucien slid his hand onto her silky back, provoking, "Show me."

With her heart thudding predatory compulsion urged her to take whatever she wanted. *Lucien was delicious.*

Fingering decorative pearls on her dress, Lucien seduced, "Drink those. I have your room number, I'll see you later."

So turned on she couldn't see straight, the mix of abilities began a tug of war for control as she drank the shots. *She'd obeyed, that was annoying.* Leaving the glass slippers as a song made her bouncy, she flounced to the crowded dance floor blatantly siphoning energy by running a hand along being's backs, blinded by magical euphoria.

16
BADASS MIC DROP

An old favourite song came on, Orin took Jenna in his arms, asking, "Hard to be away from Emery?"

"She doesn't do relationships, we're close friends," Jenna confessed with her head on his shoulder, way too drunk to be concerned about sending an ex mixed messages.

Orin chuckled in her ear, "Walking away with a woman was a badass mic drop. Two thumbs up for the shock and awe. I was impressed."

"I stopped trying to impress you decades ago," Jenna sparred as mauve light show orbs floated over couples.

With her warmth in his arms, Orin replied, "I thought I knew everything there was to know after a thousand years together. I had no idea you were into girls. You could have told me."

Pulling away to look into his eyes, Jenna taunted, "Booze making your memory foggy?"

"What?" Orin chuckled as they swayed, beneath

crystal chandeliers with romantic lighting. He flirted, "How did it happen, tell me everything."

Resting her head on his shoulder, Jenna disclosed, "Dear diary, while saving my ex-boyfriend's soul, I spent time with a sexy Shapeshifter who enjoyed switching things up."

"I missed that, the music is too loud," Orin answered, relishing the sensation of her wrapped in his arms.

Snuggling into him, Jenna closed her eyes, saying, "It's not important." Soothing lilac orbs of discotheque lighting made the ambience magical. Fluidly swaying as old lovers do, she whispered in his ear, "Are you planning to make young Molly's final wish come true?"

"It feels wrong, I can't explain why," Orin admitted.

Giggling, Jenna messed his hair, gushing, "I'm so proud of you. You're evolving."

"Don't tell anyone, they'll expect more out of me," Orin chuckled as they swayed.

Dancing next to the pair, Tiberius interjected, "I guess Lexy's out if Jenna's back in the game?"

"We're friends, go away," Orin muttered.

Pulling away to meet Orin's eyes, Jenna urged, "Ignore him, he's trying to stir shit up."

"I just wanted to say, no harm no foul. Lexy's moved on like neither of us exist," Tiberius provoked, grinning.

They stopped dancing. Unable to help it, Orin dared, "Be man enough to say what you mean without cryptic cracks."

"Prince Amadeus," Tiberius clarified, as the song ended.

Getting in Tiberius' face, Orin said, "Good for her. Did it hurt your feelings?"

A direct hit to the ego, Tiberius commented, "Funny."

Looking Triad's leader dead in the eyes, Ankh's Oracle shoved him over the edge, "Tiberius doesn't have feelings."

Yanking the pin out of a drunk confession grenade, Tiberius smirked, taunting, "It's better when it's recreational like your visits with Seth."

Orin came at Tiberius. Stepping between the pair, Jenna rationalised, "You've already punched a leader this week, Orin. I've got this." She hauled off and decked Tiberius. All eyes turned their way. A crowd of rowdy drunk immortals gathered.

Rubbing his jaw, Triad's leader revealed, "I would have preferred a kiss. Did you ever tell Orin I kissed you first or is that our little secret?" Jenna came out swinging. Laughing, Tiberius ducked and weaved. She booted him in the family jewels. He dropped to his knees as Aries Group guards came running.

Blocking her next attack, Orin reasoned, "You're going to get in trouble." Tossing Jenna over his shoulder as she squirmed and flailed, wanting to kill Tiberius.

On his knees in rising smoke, shielding his manly bits, Tiberius needled, "Everyone you care for wants a piece of me. Doesn't it concern you?"

Sending a wave of healing bliss through his ex with a touch, Orin sparred, "I'll worry when you can do that." He carried Jenna away, dangling over his shoulder, gasping.

Giggling, Patrick said, "That was awesome."

"Shut up, Patrick," Tiberius grumbled, storming away.

Mel stuck out her foot, and Tiberius landed on the floor. Enraged, he looked up to see who took him down. Mel innocently baited, "Sorry, my bad."

Brushing himself off, Tiberius playfully put up his

dukes, teasing, "Come on, let's go. You want some of me too?"

"Are you always an asshole?" Mel enquired, genuinely wanting to know. The crowd continued dancing.

Smiling, he disclosed, "Someone has to be the bad guy."

Offering Tiberius help up, Mel admitted, "You had me fooled, I believed you cared about her."

Letting his guard down by accepting the gesture, Tiberius confessed, "I do."

Confused, Mel asked, "Why hurt her on purpose?"

"I never claimed to be smart," Tiberius confessed. "It was supposed to be a joke. We knew you were coming."

"Why didn't you tell Lexy that?" Mel questioned as they strolled off the dance floor.

"She didn't want to hear it," Tiberius explained. "I don't blame her, I'm sure it caused drama with Grey."

"Understatement of the year, last I heard they were still fighting," Mel commented, snatching a drink off the tray.

"Thank you," Tiberius said, taking a glass of champagne.

Grinning, Mel paused before walking away, asking, "For what? I just tripped you."

"For listening," Tiberius replied. "Have a good night. Try not to trip me again."

Waving, Mel called out, "No promises!"

CARRYING THEIR CLAN'S MAGICALLY CHILLED Oracle,

Orin ran into Markus, chatting with heads of communities.

Ankh's leader questioned, "What's going on here?"

"I was going to punch Tiberius, she beat me to it," Orin replied, noticing the odd company their leader was keeping.

"Take the Oracle back to her room. We won't need you this evening," Markus assured, waving him away.

With a knit brow, Orin asked, "Are you sure?"

"Go! Get out of here before I change my mind," Markus chuckled, rejoining his conversation.

Adjusting his ex's weight, Orin replied, "Alright, see you in the morning." Emersed in another conversation, Markus didn't answer. Lugging Jenna into the elevator, Orin pressed their floor. Classical music played as the door slid shut and he giggled, recalling countless occasions where nights were cut short by his shenanigans. When they reached her room, he put her down and gave her a shot of healing energy. Jenna gave him the dirtiest look in her repertoire. Orin apologised, "The guards were coming to kick us out."

With raw emotional eyes, Jenna reprimanded, "You can't do that anymore."

"I'm sorry, old habits, I'll never do it again," Orin vowed, touching her shoulder.

"We can't be together," Jenna asserted with chestnut hair escaping her messy bun.

"You don't have to repeat the speech," Orin proclaimed. The passion in her eyes confused his resolve. Unable to help himself, he probed, "When did you kiss Tiberius?"

"I didn't kiss him. He tugged me onto his lap and kissed me, before we were together. It was a millennium ago, why would I bring it up?" Unlocking her door,

Jenna offered, "If we've been sent to our rooms, we could hang out."

Accepting her invitation, Orin wandered in. "I miss the Oracle perks," he said, sitting on her kingsize bed, reaching for the remote.

Jenna snatched it away, teasing, "My perks. I earned this remote."

"Hey, I'm a Healer. I have an important job too." Orin sparred as she sat by him and flicked through the schedule. "What do you feel like watching?"

He flirted, "I guess porn is out?"

Their eyes met as familiar closeness tempted them to do naughty things. With desire in her eyes, she whispered, "We shouldn't."

Grinning, Orin provoked, "That didn't feel like a hard no to a dirty movie. You shouldn't look at me like that anymore either, I might think you're still attracted to me."

Giving him a shove, Jenna ribbed, "That was never the issue. We can't do this, you should go."

"Why? What else do you have to do?" He looked at the clock on the nightstand, tempting, "It's late. We're in Vegas. What happens in Vegas…"

Interrupting mid-sentence, Jenna decreed, "Doesn't stay in Vegas. We're too drunk to hang out as friends, you should leave."

With a curious glint in his eyes, Orin got up and sighed, "Fine, I'll go watch dirty movies in my own room and think of you." Walking to the door, he glanced back, baiting, "Sure you don't want me to stay?"

Jenna tossed a pillow, laughing, "Get out of here. Don't hit any Brothers Of Prophecy."

Walking to his room, Orin glanced at his cell. There was a message from Frost, "Duty calls. That ass hat

Leonard is in Vegas. Lily and I left with Lucien's crew. Markus had me set Kayn off to end the night early so the Aries Group would have an excuse to shut the banquet down and join us. Take her out if she eats everyone at the ball." *Awkward, it was from thirty minutes ago. Why would Markus send us away? Maybe he was drunk?* Turning back to the elevator, he heard Zach's voice coming from Mel's room. *This was ridiculous, Markus had been asleep at the wheel for days.* Orin knocked on her door, Mel invited him in. Zach, Mel and Patrick were hanging out. Orin asked, "If we're all up here, who is watching Kayn?"

Coming over, Zach answered, "Markus told us to go."

Wandering in, Orin declared, "I guess Markus didn't let you know about his plan to set off Kayn to shut the banquet down early either?"

Mortified, Zach stammered, "What?" He sprinted out the door, followed by the rest.

17
WHAT DRAGONS DO

Kayn breezed past feeding with no filter as beings staggered and vanished in the smoke show. While filling her void with immortal energy, boundaries between powers faded. Ration ceased as the Dragon's overall vibe snuffed out residual guilt. A superhuman seductresses conduct was inconsequential. Carnal beings cared about nothing and no one. Immortals were playthings, unattended Dragons demolish toys with no Handler present to harness inhibitions. With nonexistent discretion as music pulsated, pheromones secreted from her pores, drastically altering the ballroom's dynamics. Writhing immortals worshipped dance partners in a titillating display. Always hungering for more, she joined grinding couples, fed off sensual energy and moved on like a hummingbird in a field of flowers consuming sweet nectar until it was spent. Certain flowers were delightfully fragrant, so she'd return for more sustenance until nearly everyone vanished into rising smoke. Moving onto her next snack, Kayn stumbled over a body and ended up in Tiberius' arms.

Trying to get through to her, Triad's leader allowed her to siphon energy, reprimanding, "You naughty thing, you've taken down every immortal at the ball. Where's Zach? Your Handler should be here."

Silencing Tiberius by stroking his face. He stumbled as his eyes went blank. Drained, the leader of Triad vanished into the waist-high sea of smoke. Kayn resumed dancing in amethyst light as sin disguising clouds rose around her. The music stopped. Mildly intrigued as healed beings of every immortal species emerged from the haze surrounding her, she waved, and everyone froze. Bored with everything, she left. Strutting barefoot through a lobby of petrified patrons, Kayn stole a couple's taxi and clapped her hands. Everyone sprang to life, she ordered, "Drive." Mindlessly, the driver took off. Touring the city, passing swarms of pedestrians with mortal auras, they took a beat to wait for a light, when she cramped. Kayn said, "Stop." Without asking for money, the driver pulled over, and she got out. With instinct as her guide, she strutted past a bouncer into a club. All eyes turned as she walked to the bar. Flesh prickled on the nape of her neck. *She was in a dangerous situation. How exciting.*

Sliding her a drink, the bartender explained, "This is from the gentlemen over there."

Lifting it up to the light, Kayn saw a powdery substance. *It was trying to drug her, how adorable. She was definitely going to eat that guy.* Pretending to drink, summoned him.

He held out his hand, introducing himself, "I'm Joe."

She shook his hand. *Plot twist, Joe smelled Lampir. This was going to be fun.*

"What perfume are you wearing?" Joe probed,

anxiously fingering his straw with a predatory glint in his eye.

She enjoyed the moments before a predator realised they were lower on the food chain. Grinning, she baited, "It's my natural scent, Joe."

"Finish that drink and dance with me," Joe seduced.

Smiling, Kayn said, "There's no need to drug me Lampir, I'm willing." Before Joe could flee, she touched his shoulder and commanded, "Stay." Picking up the sketchy drink, she asked, "What's in this?"

Mindlessly, he answered, "Ketamine."

"Hardcore. Ketamine won't drug me, Joe," Kayn replied, downing the drink. *She was so going to eat this guy.* Noticing Lampir feeding in dark corners, she got up and summoned Joe to follow. Finding a spot in the shadows, she offered him her wrist.

"This feels way too easy, what are you?" Joe asked, eyeing her wrist, not paying attention to her fingerless glove.

Smiling, Kayn tempted, "Try me." He sunk his teeth into her flesh. She shivered as pheromones released. Revelling in power as others were lured over like moths to a flame. With her healing ability broiling as they fed keeping her conscious, bliss-inducing venom created a euphoric web of pleasure. Entranced by magical pheromones, dozens were suckling her life essence as goosebumps prickled and the Conduit switched the direction of the current. The fangs released as the hoard limply slumped on top of her and she took a nap.

A voice called out, "Brighton!"

Party poopers. Groggily opening her eyes, under the pile of napping Lampir, Kayn smiled as bodies were shifted off her.

Scooping her into his arms, Kevin carried her out to

a limo, scolding, "You've caused an impressive amount of shit tonight, Brighton."

She didn't have much to say for herself as he placed her on the seat. *The limo was full of Triad.* Looking at their leader, Kayn enquired, "Where's Ankh?"

"The Aries Group gassed the banquet and gave everyone a time out. They sent us to find you for Lucien. I wonder if he'll still find you a delicacy worthy of his time after you've been fed on by riffraff?" Tiberius provoked, smiling.

Motioning Tiberius closer, Kayn ordered, "Sleep." Their leader went limp and passed out. *That was cool.*

Scowling, Stephanie threatened, "Try that shit on me. I'll snap your neck and ask questions later."

Meeting Stephanie's eyes, Kayn probed, "Still jealous?"

Mindlessly, Stephanie answered, "Yes."

This was fun.

"Enough, Brighton," Kevin chuckled, shaking his head.

Enough? Looking at her longtime nemesis, Kayn ordered, "Sleep." Stephanie slumped in her seat as they arrived at the hotel. Free to speak as they got out, their eyes met. Looking into Kevin's, she questioned, "You really came to get me so I can be fed on?"

"Yes, I'm supposed to bring you back to your room and wait with you," Kevin answered as they walked through the silent lobby.

She didn't want to be reminded of who she used to be tonight. She felt a twinge of apprehension as they got into the elevator. *She needed to stay vacant, Kevin was Dragon kryptonite.* "I don't have a key," Kayn said as they stepped out into the hall.

"You don't need one," Kevin placed his palm against the door, the light turned green.

As they walked into the room, her mind flashed to what Frost was doing. *She didn't want to think about that.* "You can leave, I'm not going anywhere," Kayn vowed. *It would be better if they weren't hanging out alone.*

"I'm not allowed to," he confessed. "This doesn't have to be weird, we were friend's for a long time."

Smiling, Kayn sat on the bed, admitting, "It still is."

"You're right, it is," Kevin chuckled, standing.

"I have no plans to seduce you, feel free to make yourself comfortable," she teased patting the bed, scooting over.

Sitting beside her, he baited, "What if I have plans to take advantage of your missing moral compass?"

"You'd never do that," Kayn replied, knowing it was true.

Grinning, he sparred, "I'm not the same person."

"I still see you in there," she disclosed.

Lounging on his back, Kevin turned to her, confessing, "I still see you."

Visions of childhood flickered through her mind with toothless grins and dandelion seeds floating in the air on a spring breeze until she closed her eyes, willing the sentiment away, whispering, "You shouldn't be here."

"What do you remember when you're with me?" Kevin asked, lying on his side, watching her response.

Exhaling, she confessed, "Everything beautiful we lost."

"Me too," he replied. "Did you make Frost apologise?"

Smooth, switching the subject. "Frost doesn't do anything he doesn't want to do," Kayn answered, smiling.

"Doesn't that concern you?" Kevin probed, waiting for a response.

With no need to sugarcoat it, she admitted, "Sometimes." Resisting the urge to take his hand, Kayn whispered, "Do you know how to use your abilities?"

"Not really," Kevin countered. "Do you honestly think I want to pop into your mind when you're with Frost?"

Shoving him, Kayn teased, "I witnessed plenty of your booty calls that first year in dreams, I know it sucks."

"How much more would it have sucked if you knew I was falling in love with someone else and you just had to sit there and watch?" Kevin enquired, inching his hand closer.

Smiling, she sparred, "I didn't sleep with Frost until after Testing when I knew we had no chance."

With a grin, he razzed, "You were already falling for him. I remember that sexy foot massage at the banquet."

"It's complicated," Kayn explained, embracing the cliche. "Most of that first year, you were all I thought about. I must have replayed our last goodbye in the in-between a thousand times."

"I didn't remember until it was too late to matter. More than anything, I wish there was a way to have our friendship back," he admitted, almost taking her hand.

She did too. He couldn't touch her.

"Are you okay with this?" Kevin asked, without moving his hand the final inch.

He felt guilty for staying here to make sure she fed Lucien. Pulling her hand away so he wouldn't be tempted to hold it, Kayn responded, "It's not unpleasant."

His cell buzzed. Reading the message, Kevin announced, "Duty calls. If you ever need me." He tapped his head.

She knew what he meant. As the door closed, Kayn went to the washroom and laughed as she saw her reflection. *She was a mess. There was blood on her ballgown. Cinderella never had these issues.* She touched up makeup but couldn't unzip her dress. Shrugging, Kayn checked out the minifridge. *Hanging out with Kevin calmed her. Knowing Frost wasn't behaving himself didn't stifle the knowledge that she may cross a line. She didn't have to feel anything if she didn't want to.* With limited options, she selected a mini gin. *It might be prudent to wipe the hard drive.* She took everything. Dumping her slate cleaning options on the bed, she cracked the seal of a bottle and froze as Lucien walked in.

Catching her with liquid courage in hand, Lucien teased, "You've had a busy evening, still up for visitors?"

Predatory reflex dulled nerves as Kayn sparred, "I wasn't aware it was a choice?"

Zorro masked Lucien insisted, "If this isn't something you're comfortable with, I'll hit pause. I understand this is new for you. I'd rather us have a good relationship moving forward than a bad one."

He'd given her an out but she had no reason to take it after allowing dozens of Lampir to have their fill. Offering her a choice made him seem more trustworthy.

Sauntering over, removing his black mask, Lucien asked, "Have a drink for me?" He politely removed his shoes.

He'd done his research. Lucien knew she was Canadian. Smiling, she motioned to her pile, saying, "Pick your poison."

"Match me drink for drink, I'll tell you anything you want to know about Lampir," he tempted, passing a mini whisky.

Laughing, Kayn admitted, "Whisky is not my friend."

Dangling a miniature bottle, Lucien stated, "Whisky

is nobody's friend, but it might make this less awkward."

Clinking tiny bottles, she drank hers and asked, "Why is the word Vampire offensive?"

Choking, Lucien replied, "It's culturally disrespectful, we prefer Lampir."

Crosslegged at the foot of the bed, Kayn grilled, "Do you sleep in a coffin?"

"Room darkening shades and a king-sized bed," Lucien disclosed, smiling as he passed her another shot.

After doing it, she questioned, "Sunlight?"

"Bloodlines play a roll in our tolerance," Lucien revealed. "Waterproof sunblock and feeding on the right blood types help susceptible lines. I can watch a sunset and go for a walk when it's overcast. Only riffraff and cross breeds burst into flames. They haven't been taught our skills. You guys deal with those situations."

Making it personal, Kayn probed, "Which blood type is your favourite?"

Enchanted by her lack of filter, Lucien praised, "Siren is the ultimate rapture, a delicacy to be savoured with sunlight tolerance, enhanced compulsion, stamina, and virility."

He was a personable guy, not at all like she'd pictured Vampires. Whoops, Lampir. "Is Lily alright with this?" Kayn enquired, knowing they had a thing.

Meeting her gaze with hypnotising golden-flecked brown eyes, he replied, "We've never been exclusive." Lucien got up, wandered to the sliding door and waved her over, saying, "Have you checked out the view?"

"I have," Kayn responded, following him onto the deck, revelling in the twinkling lights.

Leaning against the railing, Lucien said, "I spent a century in Vegas where the unusual is overlooked, there's nowhere like it."

"Where do you live?" Kayn enquired, looking his way.

"I travel North America policing hives," Lucien replied, ignoring the spectacular sights of the bustling city.

Curious, she questioned, "Have you ever been in love?"

Laughing, Lucien admitted, "Many times." Watching her, he probed, "How does a Siren relationship work? Fidelity must be a grey area."

Kayn confessed, "I've never been with anyone else."

"You're just a baby immortal," he teased, looking at her like she told him something wild. "It makes sense now."

She pressed, "What makes sense?"

"The speech about wading you into your duties," Lucien clarified. "How many trade for service jobs have you done?"

She admitted, "Only one. Frost needed me to understand what he does."

"Do you understand?" Lucien asked, intrigued.

Leaning against the railing, she said, "I think so. I highly doubt they'll be sending me on more jobs like that until I've learned control. I ate everyone."

Laughing, he praised, "You took out that Northern Hive testing aura vaccines, good work. I flagged that hive months ago." Raising a drink, Lucien saluted, "To the greater good."

Kayn lifted hers, repeating, "To the greater good." *It felt like she could trust him.* Meeting his deep-set brown eyes, she quizzed, "Are you using Lampir compulsion on me?"

"Not yet," Lucien answered with a genuine smile.

Self-preservation prodded her subconscious, cautioning her not to be naive. "Why not?" Kayn probed curiously.

Turning to her, he admitted, "I want you to know you're in control of what happens next."

With their eyes locked in a game of immortal chicken, she whispered, "Am I?"

"We can feed on each other or I can leave and catch you next time. It's your call," he proposed.

A rush of adrenaline let her know one of her powers was primed. Kayn warned, "I don't know which ability you'll trigger."

"You'll get what you need. I'll let it happen," he tempted, coming up behind her. "If you don't want to take another run at the feeding session we had in Mexico, I'll go."

What logical reason did she have for not doing it? She'd already been fed on this evening. Igniting her libido by sensually caressing her arm, Kayn shivered as the Siren stepped up to bat, daring her to take what she needed, repercussions be damned. *Frost was doing the same thing.* Relaxing against him like a bird in a cat's clutches entranced by its purr their chests rose and fell in unison, Kayn coyly said, "You'd just leave without getting what you came for?"

"I would," Lucien vowed, shifting her hair. She shivered and bit her lip as he undid the back of her dress. Lowering silk, unwrapping his gift, he kissed her shoulder, seducing, "If you'll grant me the honour."

With her stomach in a lusty knot, she took a page from his playbook, provoking, "Do it."

"It would be a pity to destroy this. Naughtily chuckling, Lucien tugged her gown to her waist, unclasped her bra, and seduced, "Take it off."

This was a dangerous game. They were on the deck. Ridiculously turned on, she slid it over her hips. It dropped, Kayn stepped out, with her pulse racing. Fangs sunk into her throat with pleasure so intense it ached. Enraptured, clutching his hair with her back against his chest, she whimpered as ecstasy emitted inhibition altering pheromones. Groaning, Lucien released his bite, she flopped facedown on the bed. *How did they get inside?* Blinded by need, she felt her healed neck and flipped over. Climbing up after her in his tux, Lucien sunk his teeth into her inner thigh like biting a peach as she floated on waves of euphoria. *She loved this.* Clutching the sheets, she squirmed as pleasure-inducing Lampir toxin flowed through her veins. Teeth sunk into her breast, curling her toes. *She was going to snap.*

"I'll lose sight of my friendship with Frost if you keep doing that to yourself," Lucien cautioned, pinning her arms. Entertained by her reckless behaviour, he chuckled, "You're a dangerous creature with those pheromones. You're healing as I'm feeding." His fangs sunk into her neck.

Basking in euphoria emotions vanished as the predatory being awoke from its slumber. Her pounding heart echoed as the current reversed. He flopped on top of her. *Whoops.* Smiling serenely, she shoved Lucien's dead weight aside and got up. *She wanted more. She could knock on doors and drain every immortal who answered. It wasn't permanent. There was no reason why she couldn't do it.* Someone knocked. *Delivery. Perfect.* Going to see who was unfortunate enough to drop by, she opened the door, the lights went out.

TWITCHING HER HANDS IN WARM SILKEN SAND, KAYN giggled. *She'd died way too many this week. Chances are she deserved this time out.* She sat up, smiling. *She was alone.* Magically flawless sand, sparkling in eternal sunshine, spanned the horizon. Waiting to be drawn back to the land of the living, she raked fingers through her eternal zen garden. *She might as well just stay here. There was only time for fun excursions when she travelled via tomb with her Clan.* When she didn't disintegrate in the usual amount of time, Kayn decided to experiment. *She was supposed to be able to go anywhere she wanted with full Guardian access. She'd always wanted to know what happened when mortals passed through. Did they all get to wander around the desert and build sandcastles, or was that just the ones associated with her path? If I was a mortal, where would I go?* The scenery flashed with light. She was standing before a golden door as luminescent orbs shot through, vanishing. *I guess she did have full Guardian access. Maybe she could just walk through it?* An invisible forcefield blocked her. Kayn looked at her palm with the Ankh symbol. *Guardian or not the brand prohibited entry. This must be the hall of souls.* She walked around it. *It looked like the immortal clean slate just went on and on. It was just a magical gold door that didn't appear to go anywhere. Well, this was anticlimactic.* Feeling a tickle, she watched her hand as she became sand floating away on a breeze.

Listening to humming tires, Kayn opened her eyes. *It was dark, she couldn't breathe. Ugh, she was in a trunk. Was this plastic?* Struggling out, she inhaled. *Much better. Whatever she did must have been gloriously epic. This wasn't the first time she'd woken up in someone's trunk, she knew the drill.* Shifting crinkly stuff out of her way, she felt objects in darkness, searching for a roadside assistance kit. *It was hot in here.* Clutching something wooden, she grimaced. *Not cool, it was an axe. When you wake up in a trunk wrapped in plastic with an axe, your day was about to go badly.* Feeling something else, she determined it was a shovel. *The bag must be lyme. Awesome, the driver planned to bury her. Being immortal, this situation was merely an inconvenience. She needed to remember what happened before she died. She'd been told to eat everyone at a ball. She had flashes of freezing time, stealing a cab and letting a bar full of Lampir feed on her. Triad found her. She made Tiberius and Stephanie go to sleep, that was funny. She G-rated hung out with Kevin, had a sexy time with Lucien, ate him and planned to eat more immortals but someone knocked on the door. She had no idea what happened after that. It was blank. They thought the trunk would hold her. That was cute.* She felt by the lights, punched one out, and peered out as a broken light tumbled away. *It was close to dawn. She felt exposed. Nice, she wasn't wearing a bra.* Half-naked, Kayn smashed out the other taillight. *Music was obnoxiously blaring. Awkward. She wasn't allowed to kill mortals.* Remembering how Kevin opened her room, she felt for exposed wires and gave it a telekinetic jolt of energy. *It didn't work. Come on, Kayn. You are an all-powerful being, you can't just let mortals kidnap you.* She screamed with her hands against the wires. The trunk flew open, the car sputtered, stalled, and continued slowly rolling. *Cool. That was easy.* She climbed out, leapt onto the pavement and walked around to see why nobody was scrambling to get out. The driver and passenger were sputtering up blood. It was running out of their eyes, noses and mouths. *Did she do this?* She opened the door, checking, "You alright?" *That was stupid. They weren't.* "I guess neither of you wants to explain why you've kidnapped me?"

One choked out, "Monster."

"Zealot for the win," Kayn sighed. "I was just at the hall of souls, it wasn't a big deal. I'm part Guardian, you're not headed there, after this." Patting a mortal down, she found a cell and perused messages. He led an uneventful life, there were no suspicious conversations, just pictures of his kids and domestic requests. *What was this?* She felt the man's dewy forehead. *He was hot. They were sick.* Foraging in the back, she found a towel, a crumpled shirt and shorts that smelled like chlorine. *It would do.* She put on stiff clothes, jogging through the possibilities in her mind. "You have a family, why would you kidnap a girl from a hotel in Vegas?" She grilled the near lifeless mortal.

He listlessly raised his head, mumbling, "Milk."

She wasn't going to get anywhere, they were almost gone. She didn't know anyone's number, there was no wifi or data. They couldn't be far out of Vegas. Her Clan would be following her signal after she died in her room. What if the shield from the banquet was still up? Nothing had been going right. These jobs were full of unanticipated plot twists. Their Oracle's premonitions had been ass backwards for weeks. It was normal to have surprises, but instinct was urging her to see something she was missing.

"Forgive," a dying man whispered, reaching out to her.

Aura's glowed as night's shadows lifted, bringing tranquil dawn. She didn't know why they'd taken her or what sinful deeds they'd planned, but in the light of this new day, their souls weren't tainted by nefarious final acts. *Perhaps mortal's lives weren't judged by one misdeed. Maybe, in the end, all that mattered was that their good outweighed their bad. He'd asked for forgiveness. She knew where these men were meant to go.* Kayn spoke to the dying mortals, "I can help." Searching for something to cut herself with, all she found was his keys. *There wasn't much time.* Taking off her earring, she clenched it in her fist. *No blood, not a drop. This was inconvenient timing for impenetrable skin. If she was supposed to save these men, she needed to mark their foreheads with her blood and repeat words assuring entry to the hall of souls. She remembered who she was.* Clasping her palms, looking at scarlet heavens, she willed an orb to appear with every ounce of her being. Feeling her palms heating, she parted them. *There was nothing.* She tried again. This time, as they separated the Ankh on her palm was shimmering with light. Guided by intuition, she pressed her radiant Ankh symbol on the man's forehead, assuring, "You are forgiven." His eyes rolled back, and he was gone. She did the same to the next as he departed. *It felt like she'd done the right thing.*

Feeling his jacket, she dug out the other guy's phone. *She wanted to see who she'd saved.* One cell was full of pictures with adorable kids and a wife with a gentle smile. All he'd been posting was game invites on social media. Scrolling down his page, Kayn stumbled upon hundreds of condolences for the loss of his family. *They'd died, he'd lost his family in an accident. Maybe he'd made bad choices during his grief, but he hadn't always been lost. He was the perfect prey for an evil entity, life dealt him a brutal hand. She knew what it was like to lose everyone.* Glad she'd adjusted his destination, Kayn began snooping through the other cell. It was all pictures of him posing with guns in his Mom's basement. *This tool was murder spree waiting to happen. This guy was a self-serving militant asshole. She'd made a mistake. Now what?* Leaning against the car, watching the crimson sunrise, she recalled a poem her Dad used to recite, *red sky at night sailor's delight. Red sky at morning sailors take warning. Well, she couldn't call 911. There wasn't wifi or data on either of these phones. What was she supposed to do? She might as well.* Looking up, Kayn said, "If you can hear me, Kevin, I woke up in the trunk of someone's car again and accidentally killed a few guys with something I picked up eating immortals at the banquet last night." Giggling, to herself. *If he was sleeping at the hotel, he might not hear anything.* Not a car drove by as hours passed. Sweltering in the desert's rays, Kayn was about to start texting random numbers when she saw an RV in the distance. As it approached, she grinned. *It was Ankh.*

Leaning out the window, Grey chuckled, "Problem?"

"I woke up in the trunk again and accidentally murdered my kidnappers," Kayn remarked, walking towards the RV, grinning. Grey vanished from the window. The door opened on the other side of the RV. Lexy and Grey wandered over.

Peering through the car window, Lexy probed, "Where did they kidnap you from?"

"Someone knocked on my hotel door and I woke up in the trunk," Kayn disclosed. *She wanted to go lay on her bunk and have a nap.*

"You really need to start looking through peep-holes," Lexy ribbed. Slapping Grey as he reached for the door, she taunted, "Do you feel like being lit on fire today?"

Grey chuckled, "I'll pass."

Joining the group on the deserted road, Killian teased, "Enjoying the sunshine? Nice outfit, way to keep it casual."

His energy was super tasty. "The alternative was nothing," Kayn sparred, grinning.

"You would have gotten a ride faster," Killian chuckled. Seeing the mortals in the car, he commented, "Impressively brutal. How did you do this?"

"No idea, it must have been someone I ate last night," Kayn admitted, smiling.

"Last night?" Killian questioned, looking at her curiously.

That was peculiar.

Lexy explained, "We'll drive these two off a cliff so the fire burns up whatever this is. There's a ravine back the way we came."

"I'll turn the RV around," Killian offered.

Already running over there, Grey shouted, "I can do it!"

They watched as Grey turned and began inching the RV back and forth. Struggling to keep a straight face, Lexy called out, "You sure you don't need help?"

Grey hollered back, "I've got it!"

"No he doesn't," Lexy mumbled, watching her Handler cautiously inching forward and backing up. With scarlet hair shining in sunshine, she sighed, "It's going to take a while."

Beaming, Killian declared, "He's impressively stubborn." Checking out the trunk, the burly immortal started howling.

Strolling over to see what he was laughing about, Lexy stated, "They were so going to bury you in the desert."

Viewing the trunk's rib-tickling contents with her friends, Kayn commented, "Waking up in a trunk wrapped in plastic is a red flag."

"Unfortunate run-ins with nefarious intentions is part of the package," Killian decreed checking out the collection of murder cover-up memorabilia. "An axe, a shovel and lyme. There are bullet holes in the plastic and lots of blood in this trunk. Being shot three or four times point-blank in the head would put any Healer down."

The reality of what she'd been through filtered in. Shoving it down, Kayn explained, "While I was trying to signal for help, I couldn't break my skin. It sure would be handy to know how these abilities worked."

Glancing over at Grey trying to turn, Killian muttered, "It might be faster to just go with you guys and take the decontamination fun that follows."

They were going to have to light her on fire. Fantastic.

The door slammed on the RV. Dean hopped out to see what they were doing. *It had been a while since she'd seen the newbie Ankh.*

Lexy yelled, "If you come over here, we'll have to light you on fire!" Saying nothing, Dean went back to the RV.

"They may not even know I'm missing with the spiritual blocker the Aries Group had at the ball," Kayn explained.

Giving Killian a look, Lexy switched the subject, "We'll chat while we dispose of these bodies. I'll ride with you."

That was ridiculous. "I'll follow you in the car, we can chat afterwards it's not necessary to light yourself on fire to have a conversation with me," Kayn teased, looking at her sister.

"Are you certain these men weren't magically compelled to dispose of your body, and infected with this virus to tie up loose ends? Maybe it wasn't you?" Lexy enquired, digging through the trunk's contents.

She wasn't certain of much. "I woke up in the trunk, smashed lights out and zapped the wires with a surge of energy to see if I could unlock it. The car slowed, I got out and these two were dying," Kayn repeated the events.

Big Sexy, sighed, "There's no way of knowing for sure, I guess Grey's lighting us all on fire."

"That'll be fun for him," Lexy said, slamming the trunk.

Leaning out the window, Grey yelled, "Get in."

Waving the RV away, Lexy called out, "We need to be decontaminated after touching stuff in the trunk. We'll meet you there!"

They lifted out the driver and sat him in the back. Killian volunteered, "You two chat, I'll drive."

Everyone got in. *Shoot the car might not run.* "Bad time to mention this but the car stalled," Kayn disclosed as the RV vanished in the distance.

"That would have been great to know before Grey drove away," Killian teased. "Cross your fingers." He turned the key, the engine hummed and they took off.

As unfamiliar scenery flashed by, Kayn noted, "We're not just outside of Vegas, are we?"

Glancing her way, Lexy asked, "How long do you think you were missing?"

"I'm usually only dead for twenty minutes. I never have much time in the in-between," Kayn replied, suspecting she was about to hear something unsettling.

"That ball in Vegas was nearly a week ago, you've been missing for five days. They've been frantically searching. We were on our way there to help. You really have no idea where you were?" Lexy enquired, unrolling the back window.

"I was just there," Kayn mumbled. *Her mind couldn't wrap around what they were saying.* "I answered the door, woke up in the in-between. I wasn't there for long."

"When your slate is wiped clean, it's usually a blessing," Lexy assured.

Where was she? It didn't feel possible. She was just at the ball. Frost and Zach were probably freaking out. Meeting her sister's gaze, Kayn asked, "Is Frost's number in your phone?"

Nodding, Lexy went to pass it to her. It started ringing. Looking at the number printing up, her sister smiled, saying, "Speak of the devil. One second, if I talk first, you'll have less explaining to do."

She heard Frost's voice, Lexy explained what was going on and handed her the phone. Nervous, Kayn reverted to humour, taunting, "Heard I got kidnapped in Vegas." *That was excessively dorky.*

Laughing, Frost confessed, "I'd give anything to hold you right now, Brighton."

"Ditto," Kayn replied. "Listen, in my mind, I ate Lucien, someone knocked on our door, and I woke up in the in-between. I'm still wrapping my mind around being missing for five days."

"Start looking through peepholes," Frost ribbed. "Where are you right now?"

Looking out the window as the vehicle slowed and pulled over, she disclosed, "We're about to push a burning car off a cliff and light ourselves on fire."

He probed, "Who is being lit on fire?"

"Me, Lexy and Killian. We all touched stuff in the car," she answered.

"We'll come to you guys, where are you?" he prompted.

Leaning closer to Lexy, she whispered, "Where are we? They're going to come to us."

Lexy answered, "Tell him to call Grey."

"Why? Where are we?" Kayn grilled without attempting to be stealth.

"Pass me the phone," Lexy instructed with her hand out.

Giving it to her, Kayn looked out the window. *Where were they?*

"Let's give her time to absorb the situation. I'll get Grey to call after we drive these guys off a cliff," Lexy explained. She answered, no, and handed the phone back, smiling.

Curious, Kayn questioned, "How was I kidnapped from the hotel without any of you knowing? Where was Zach?"

"All we have of your timeline is, Triad brought you back to the hotel after a Lampir murder spree at a club. You hung out with Kevin and followed through with what you were supposed to do with Lucien. Honestly, we assumed you shut off your emotions and fell down the Dragon rabbit hole in Vegas," Frost explained.

"Where did you end up?" Kayn questioned, intrigued.

Chuckling, Frost said, "Ask me anything you want when I can hold you in my arms. I'm going to say, no judgement, no fear and hang up now."

"No judgement, no fear," Kayn pledged, grateful for his low relationship expectations. He hung up. Smiling as her heart swelled, she closed her eyes. *In the beginning, she'd thought he was preparing her for his behaviour. He'd been prepping her for her own. He'd vowed to try to work through anything. Now, that she understood the gravity of his declaration, it meant so much more. She was a train wreck, and he'd vowed to love her anyway. Who does that?*

"Earth to Brighton." Killian announced, "Your love life is adorable and all, but we need to move a body and light ourselves on fire. I'd like to be healed before everyone else shows up and I need to compete for Haley's attention."

Getting out, Lexy commented, "She doesn't like him, it's sad to watch."

"Give it time, I grow on people," Killian chuckled as he got out, leaving the car running.

Guess this was happening. Climbing out, she wandered to the ledge to view the drop. "How are we doing this?" Kayn asked, watching as they lugged the body back to the driver's seat. Eight Ankh were a distance away watching. *This was a large group. Where was everyone sleeping?*

"We can do this ourselves," Lexy decreed, turning on the radio, she tossed Killian a lighter.

With overaccentuated sexy like he was in a mid-eighties music video, Killian strutted around the car waving a lighter singing along. Leaning in, he lit the driver's shirt on fire. Lexy sashayed over, doing the same thing to the other guy. Killian grabbed her hand and twirled her. Kayn laughed. *They were all certifiably insane.*

Wandering over, Grey instructed, "Get in the backseat and buckle up. We'll push this car over the edge and retrieve what's left of you."

"Get back!" Lexy cautioned. "We'll do it ourselves."

Grey reasoned, "Lex, that is needlessly slow."

Grinning at her Handler, Lexy lit herself on fire with no reaction as her flesh bubbled, not even a peep. Engulfed in flames, her charcoaled sibling dropped into the gravel.

Glancing her way, Killian declared, "That was brutal, let's get in the car."

The front seat was smouldering.

"It's time-sensitive, get in," Grey asserted, smiling.

They scrambled into the backseat, giggling. *They'd done this ass backwards.*

Pushing the car to the ledge, Grey yelled, "Seatbelts!"

Scalding fingers, putting belts on, Killian reached for her hand, nervously saying, "I hate this shit." Their stomach's lurched as they plummeted over the cliff.

Grey shouted, "God speed!"

They looked at each other, howling laughing. There was an explosion of light. Expecting warm, inviting sand, they were still inside the burning shell of the car holding hands. They'd been saved by the protective shield of blue light.

"Did you do this?" Killian enquired, in the backdrop of raging flames.

This was inconvenient. She'd saved them from being killed

in the fall. Kayn stated, "This is what happened when I lit the truck on fire."

"Turn it off, we need to be decontaminated," he ordered, shaking his head.

He didn't appear to know his skin was melting. Kayn probed, "Are you one of those people who'd rather not know if something horrible was happening?"

Killian dryly commented, "I'm melting too, aren't I?"

Holding his hand, smiling, Kayn declared, "If I were you, I wouldn't look. I'm not going to." *He had no skin left, his meat was cooking like a blackened hot dog over a campfire.* "On the bright side, we aren't in pain, and if I also have no skin left, we're sanitized."

"Let's get out, it'll be hilarious," he suggested. "Don't let go of my hand."

With their seatbelts burnt off, they carefully shimmied out as charcoaled meat and strolled away from the wreckage.

Looking up at the immortals watching in awe from their roadside perch, Killian bellowed, "Send a Healer down! We need skin!"

Unable to look at the toasted footlong dangling between his legs without laughing, Kayn hollered up, "And clothes!"

"Tell me it's still there?" Killian pled, being a classy guy looking nowhere but her eyes.

"If mine are, yours is," she taunted, with no intention of looking.

Mischievously, Killian baited, "That's concerning."

Damn it, he was trying to get her to look. Two could play at that game. "Have you always had three nipples?"

With surly eyes, he answered, "Always. I sure hope your appendages grow back. Frost will be so disappointed, they were nice."

Leaving fantasies of keeping it classy behind, Kayn

rid her sense of humour of its G-rating, "I hope half of your thingy is missing and that's not your real size. It's like a teeny tiny roasted marshmallow. I bet Haley is coming to heal us."

"That was impressively dark, bravo. You're almost healed and you have no boobs," Killian razzed, smiling.

Bold move. Gazing deep into his eyes, she compelled, "Am I healed."

"Not yet," he disclosed. His eyes widened as he accused, "Witchery in a battle of wits is cheating."

Grinning, Kayn ribbed, "Says Marshmallow. That's your new pet name."

"You wouldn't dare," Killian sparred, grinning.

Nodding, Kayn harassed, "No choice, It's happening."

"I bet you were a mean girl in school," he toyed, poking a tender spot.

"I was a nerdy jock with one friend besides my twin," she confessed, changing ploys. *Technically, she may have picked up the mean girl side absorbing the rest of her twin's soul.* Distracting him as he healed, Kayn revealed, "My boyfriend ended up being Tiberius' grandson."

Impressed, Killian commented, "That's a plot twist and a half. You were like Romeo and Juliette. How did you end up with Frost?"

"He slept with my ghost twin, I absorbed her soul. He ignored me for a year. We ate Twinkies. My ex slit my throat so I murdered all of his friends. The inevitable happened, it's complicated, but he gets me," she slammed. *She won, there was no way to beat that.*

"I've slept with your Mom," Killan mic dropped.

A chorus of laugher interrupted their battle of wits. They turned and saw Haley and Arrianna standing there.

Leaning in, Killian whispered, "Tell me you were lying your ass off about the marshmallow."

"Joking, it's impressive, but you wrecked your sexy by saying, you slept with my Mom," Kayn quietly taunted.

Tossing shorts at Killian's face, Arrianna commented, "Easily six marshmallows, we've been standing here for a while. How did you two stroll out of a burning vehicle hand in hand as charcoaled corpses and heal?"

Catching Haley staring at Killian's giant situation, Kayn grinned, answering, "My bad, no clue how I did that."

As they strolled away, Haley said, "We're going to find a campsite. We'll wait there for the others. You had everyone worried."

Oddly detached, Kayn questioned, "It doesn't look like bunks are available, where's everyone sleeping?"

Tucking shoulder-length pink hair behind her ear, Haley peered up, teasing, "After you've climbed this ravine in the sweltering heat, you'll pass out anywhere."

Kayn looked at her hands. *She'd protected Killian from pain and healed him, she was going to need to be fed energy if she planned to climb up the side of this canyon.* Everyone took off without her. *Suck it up, Brighton. You've got this.* Climbing after the others, she saw Lexy fully healed watching from the ledge at the top. As she grasped stone and pulled herself up. *She had no idea what she'd been doing for the last five days. The energy from the banquet was gone. That much, she knew from the will it took to keep climbing upwards when all she wanted to do is escape inwards. She wanted to shut her emotions down. It was difficult to ignore. Why?* Her sweaty hand slipped. *Crap!* Dangling one-handed from stone, Kayn secured her position by finding a jutting stone for her foot. *Maybe she should let herself fall and take the twenty-minute rest in the in-between?*

Leaning over the edge, Lexy hollered, "You all good?"

Not wanting to wimp out in front of the other Dragon, she grasped another rock and pulled herself up. "I'm fine, I just need a snack," Kayn shouted back as she fought the urge to grab Killian's ankle. *He was a tasty snack. She could use a hit of Big Sexy's strength right now.* With eating him as motivation, she climbed the rest of the ravine. He vanished over the top and reached to help her up, tugging her over the summit, they collapsed on their backs. Killian started giggling. Kayn looked his way and said, "What?"

"Thanks for not eating me mid-climb," Killian chuckled. "Knowing you wanted to helped me out big time in the motivation department."

"Damn inner dialogue," Kayn commented, staring up at a cloudless sky. Smiling as their eyes met, she whispered, "If it makes you feel better, I would have wanted to eat anyone."

With a halo of sunshine, Lexy held out her hand, saying, "Come on. Let's get you a drink."

Walking back, Arrianna asked, "How's Markus?"

"He's being a dick," Kayn decreed. *She was desensitised, she shouldn't be attempting to have deep conversations.* She backtracked, "I'm emotionally vacant right now."

Taking her aside, Arrianna whispered, "He ghosted me. I have no idea what's going on."

She'd gone from thinking Markus could do no wrong to being irritated by the sight of him in a matter of days. It was strange. She whispered back, "Midlife crisis?"

Giggling, Arrianna sparred, "He's like a thousand."

She should do something soothing so it looked like she

knew how to people. Patting Arrianna's shoulder, Kayn assured, "You'll fix it when you see each other."

Grinning, Arrianna whispered, "I'm an intuitionist and an empath, what's wrong?"

Slowing their pace behind the group, Kayn gave her the truth, "I'm hungry, I don't know where I am or where I've been for five days."

"We'll get you something to eat. Come on, I have candy stashed," Arrianna urged, waving her towards the RV.

That's not what she meant. She may eat someone. Killian opened the door for her, she walked in. Her senses were assaulted by heat, lack of personal space and the fact that everyone's energy looked delicious. *Sweet claustrophobia, this was a cramped space.*

Arrianna urged, "Scootch over on the bench."

She couldn't. It was like putting a starving human in front of a smorgasbord and saying, don't eat anything. Everyone smiled at her. *Look at those sweet, unassuming newbie faces, they'd never look at her like this again after she snapped and ate one.* She tried to bolt out. Killian blocked her in by sitting on the end. *Come on.* She asserted, "I need to go."

"Issues?" Killian whispered in her ear. Offering her his hand, he quietly tempted, "Go for it."

Was it just no Grey snacking? She couldn't remember. Her blood rushed. Kayn panicked as veins rose on her hands, "Go! Quick! I need to get out!"

He let her shimmy past. *They were moving. Shit! Crap!* She sprinted down the hall and dove into the bathroom. Looking in the mirror, she willed the zen state needed to make it to a campsite in a confined space with everyone. *She wasn't going to be able to sleep here. She couldn't trust herself. She might sleepwalk and eat everyone.* She sat, wrapped her arms around her legs and rocked. *She needed Zach.*

'Will I do?' Kevin's voice answered.

Relief washed over her. Without talking aloud, she smiled and thought, *you'll do.*

Kevin laughed, 'Ouch, that stung. Obviously, they found you. Where were you?'

Not a clue. I woke up in a trunk wrapped in plastic. I tried opening it the way you opened the hotel door and accidentally gave the guys planning to bury me in the desert a plague.

'How do you know they were going to bury you in the desert?' Kevin's amused voice responded in her mind.

I was wrapped in plastic with a shovel, lyme and an axe.

He laughed, 'Fair enough. Where are you right now?'

The crowded RV was making me murdery, so I locked myself in the bathroom.

'Ironically, I'm also in the bathroom. For future reference, you need to uncompel someone after compelling them to do something,' Kevin toyed.

Giggling, she thought, *how pissed was Tiberius on a scale of one to ten?*

Kevin responded, 'He was entertained, Stephanie was livid.'

That's not a scale of one to ten.

'Easy eleven,' he chuckled.

Smiling, she admitted, *I didn't mean to inconvenience her for longer than a car ride. Were you already in the washroom?*

'I was driving with Steph, I should get back to it, but I heard you. Grab Grey, he'll let you feed off of him,' Kevin suggested.

I promised Frost I'd avoid feeding off of Grey and he didn't seem impressed last time I fed off Killian. There's history, he hasn't gotten into, she explained.

'Did he ban you from feeding on me?' Kevin's voice

probed.

No, he didn't.

'He's a complicated guy,' Kevin chuckled in her mind. 'I have to go, someone knocked. Are you okay now?'

Ish, I'll be fine. I'll stay in here until someone makes me leave.

'Don't be a stranger, Brighton,' Kevin answered as he left the conversation.

You too, Smith. Whirling tires shifted to crackling gravel, she suspected they were stopping. There were a few loud knocks on the door.

Grey enquired, "You alright in there?"

She could be straight with him, "Feeling rather murdery right now, it's best to stay in here."

"Conduit issues?" Grey questioned from the other side of the door.

She admitted, "Conduit, Siren, Healer, whatever. I don't even know."

Trying the handle, Grey offered, "We're stopping to eat. Open the door, I'll feed whatever and we'll go for lunch."

Placing her hand against the door, resisting temptation, she sighed, "I can't, I promised, Frost."

"What's going on?" Killian prompted from the hall, "Tell her she's going to miss brunch."

Shit, seriously?

"She's ability hungry. Frost vetoed feeding from me. I'm a little insulted," Grey commented.

Killian said, "I'll do it. Let me in, you can have a quick snack before we eat."

Tempted was an understatement. Killian's energy was like drinking a case of energy drinks. It felt like she'd broken a lot of promises. Killian wasn't a hard no, but the conversation with Kevin had given her enough perspective to make good choices.

Laughing, Killian teased, "Your thoughts are super easy to hear. Did he veto both of us?"

"Why would he veto you?" Grey asked.

"He's threatened by unconventional sexy, I won't say a word. He'll never know. Open the door a crack, I'll slip my hand in there," Killian coaxed.

She might kill someone. Her stomach growled loudly.

"You'll scare children with that stomach of yours," Grey enticed. "We won't even tell you whose hand it is."

This was embarrassing. She couldn't promise Frost much, but this she could do. "Get anyone else," Kayn pled. *The Siren had a mind of its own. Staying away from temptation unless it was an emergency made the most sense.*

"What's going on?" Arrianna's voice came from the hall.

Grey answered, "Frost asked her not to eat us, and she's hungry."

"Save us a seat, I've got this," Arrianna said, knocking.

Humiliated, Kayn sheepishly let her in, "I'm trying to respect Frost's feelings while I'm aware of what I'm doing."

"I get it, I wouldn't want my significant other, feeding on Grey either," Arrianna replied. "Killian, I'd let slide. Healers need energy after giving energy to others, I know what it's like." She offered her hand.

Concerned she'd take to much, Kayn knit her brow, and cautioned, "I sure hope I don't kill you."

"Having a Pina Colada in the in-between, wouldn't be the worst thing that's happened this week," Arrianna taunted.

Accepting her hand, Kayn's core temperature rose, heat travelled down her arm with a euphoric shiver and reversed direction, draining energy until Arrianna wobbled. Yanking her hand away, Kayn steadied her by grabbing her shoulders and enquired, "Are you alright? I didn't take too much, did I?"

"Give me a second," Arrianna laughed.

Touching her, Kayn sent a bump of energy back, making her spine tickle, "Better?"

Giggling, Arrianna said, "What was that? I feel like I just drank a pot of coffee."

"No idea," Kayn laughed as they left the washroom. "I'm good now." Stepping out into the parking lot, it felt like entering another world as a tumbleweed rolled by in mid-morning heat. Walking past an empty fountain in crunchy gravel and rising dust, she clued in that everything was in a state of disrepair. Bells rang, announcing their entry.

Shimmying into a seat beside her sister, Kayn picked up the menu, flipping through it. Her sole intention, finding out where she was without asking for the tenth time.

Lexy whispered, "Grey following me like my shadow is the only reason it's never happened to me at a banquet."

She knew her sister was trying to start a conversation, but her mind still didn't want to buy that much missing time.

"You made yourself a target going postal at a ball," her sister whispered. "It happens, I get it."

What story did these guys hear? "Markus ordered me to do that," Kayn asserted, perusing her menu.

Overhearing their conversation, Killian said, "There's no way Markus ordered you to break every rule we have."

Meeting disbelief, Kayn put her menu down, explaining, "They found Leonard in Vegas. Markus ordered me to graze so the Aries Group would have an excuse to shut the ball down early. Afterwards, I was supposed to wait for Lucien in my room."

"So, what actually happened?" Astrid taunted, knowing there's no way it played out as planned.

I ate everyone at the ball, they got up and came after me. I may have used a new trick I'm not supposed to discuss to get away, stole a couple's cab and ended up at a club where I ate a hive of Lampir. Triad was sent to collect me and bring me back to my room for Lucien. I compelled Tiberius and Stephanie to sleep to shut them up, Kevin ushered me back to my room."

"Where was your Handler?" Grey questioned, upset.

Intrigued by their shocked expressions, Kayn disclosed, "Markus sent the rest of the Clan away and told them they had the night off. I was alone."

"He did what?" Stunned, Arrianna processed it. Looking around the table, she stated, "I knew something was wrong, but nobody would listen."

"Where was Jenna during all of this?" Grey probed.

"We were all dancing at the beginning of the night, I have no idea where she ended up," Kayn explained.

"Not a word about this conversation. I'm an empath, I'll feel the situation out," Arrianna said as their server showed up to take their order.

Lexy sweetly put her off, "We're going to need a minute."

After a drawn-out silence, Samid declared, "Who in the fuck is Leonard?"

"Language!" Killian reprimanded, scowling at the newbie like he was serious.

Kayn giggled behind her menu. *She liked Big Sexy.*

Cracking a shit disturbing grin, Killian chuckled, "I don't give a shit, only Markus thinks it's crass."

Detached without her Handler, Kayn met Astrid's eyes across the table, they smiled at each other. *They had a peculiar kindship. She'd gone into Immortal Testing with Zach and Melody. They'd lost each other in the massacre.*

After being killed and revived a thousand times, she was laying on unforgiving stone, ready to give up when an Ankh who'd been trapped in purgatory for decades found her. At her weakest moment, Astrid got her to stand up and keep trying. She'd introduced her to Haley, they caught up with her group and found the way out of Immortal Testing together. Their bond was forged in trauma. Astrid's eyes still triggered that urge to persevere. The thought of Haley being trapped in the Testing for decades with pink hair always made her smile.

Their server reappeared, Lexy ordered a chicken burger with hot sauce, fries, water and a beer. She ordered the same thing even though she wasn't a fan of beer and went back to trying to figure out where she was without asking. *At this point, it felt like a game. They were still in the southern states, she knew that much. If the others were driving from Vegas and were going to be here by this evening, they had to be in California or Arizona.* She looked at Molly and asked, "Are we in Arizona?"

"Yes, why?" Molly responded, mid chat with adorably pregnant Emma."

Making conversation, Kayn replied, "What did you guys do in Arizona?"

"Not much. Staying off the radar, waiting for the little one to be cooked," Molly disclosed as chocolate milk was placed in front of her.

It sucked to be treated like a child while being expected to make the sacrifices of an adult.

Dean gave Molly a side hug, whispering, "I'd give you my beer, but the waitress keeps looking over here."

"I won't be seventeen forever," Molly mumbled, stirring her chocolate milk."

Yes, you will. Someone kicked her under the table. *Whoops.*

In solidarity, Grey asked for chocolate milk.

Their waitress teased, "Whipped Cream?"

Grey naughtily flirted, "If you think I need some."

"Definitely," she agreed with a sexy smile, heading back to the kitchen.

Grey leapt up and took off after her. Catching up by the counter, he leaned against it, whispering in her ear. Killian commented, "That boy has the morals of an alley cat."

Choking on her sip of beer, Lexy raucously laughed.

Arrianna sparred, "Alley cats have higher standards."

Watching the waitress over-spraying whipped cream on his chocolate milk at the counter, Emma remarked, "Maybe he just loves whipping cream?"

Grinning, Killian whispered, "Young Emma, you are far too knocked up to be having impure thoughts about much older men."

"Gross," Emma mumbled, pouring tea with a smile.

Sometimes it was fun to sit like a fly on the wall listening to everyone else.

Returning to the table with a cream moustache, Grey sat, announcing, "Angel will be right out with our orders."

Shaking his head, Killian toyed, "Will you be taking off later with Angel?"

"We'll see what time everyone shows up," Grey replied, looking at the number she'd written on his hand.

She'd accidentally wash that off before she got a chance to use it.

Their waitress placed food in front of Emma, enquiring, "When are you due?"

Looking directly at Grey, Emma innocently asked, "It's two weeks, isn't it, honey?"

Covering his face, Killian teared up. Angel coldly

plunked Grey's plate on the table and left to get the next platter.

Amused by his expectant slanderer, Grey chuckled, "I thought you were on my team?"

Poised to eat a fry, Emma patted her belly, saying, "It was too funny to pass up."

Sipping his beer, Killian giggled, "At least she said it after you got your food." Their waitress came back with trays, put plates down and left without saying anything.

Molly seemed bummed out. Catching Molly's attention, Kayn assured, "We'll have a toast with pink flamingo wine glasses once we're settled into the campsite."

"I'm into it," Molly toasted with chocolate milk.

Raising her beer, Kayn had a drink while they carried on chatting. *I'm into it. She was cute.* As she listened to the newbies talking about simpler times, her mind travelled back to pink flamingo wine glasses in the RV and what it symbolised for her. *When the dust settled after her mortal attachments were severed, she had a final embrace with her lifelong friend in the in-between before their roads parted. She'd opened her eyes in a rose quartz tomb, facing an uncertain afterlife. Mid sinking into a pit of despair, she was introduced to the two strangers who would help shape her destiny. Mel was taken from Trinity and Zach was left behind by Triad. Grey broke the ice with cider in plastic pink flamingo glasses. He gave them a pep talk that bridged the gap, joining the trio. She'd tried to do it, but this group had tricky dynamics. Emma was a couch surfing pregnant psychic teen. Molly was working as a waitress when they kidnapped her. She had no idea what Dean's backstory was, and they'd been guilted into taking Amar's son Samid, who'd grown up entitled at a luxurious compound. If this group didn't bond, they wouldn't make it out of the Testing.*

"Earth to Kayn," Lexy prompted, passing her hot sauce.

Thanking her with a smile, Kayn dumped the rest into her chicken burger and took a bite. Hot sauce dripped down her chin as her brain sang, *hallelujah. She'd needed that in a crazy way.* Ravenously devouring a burger without taking the time to breathe, she was finished when everyone else was a few bites in. *Well, except for Lexy.*

"Nothing does that justice until you see it. Amar eats hot sauce like that, I wonder what it means," Killian said, passing Kayn napkins.

It couldn't be that bad. Kayn wiped her mouth. *Correction, she was like a messy toddler. Whoops.* She passed a heap of napkins to Lexy, who didn't question the need for it. *That was the level of badass, she aspired to be. I know I have a disgusting amount of hot sauce on my face. I'm aware I look like I've been eating people, I can own it.* Feisty after her spicy feast, Kayn shot Samid a smile. *Holy crap, the boy with the personality of spam smiled back, it must be a holiday.*

Nudging her, Lexy whispered, "Your inner commentary is crazy mean, feeling alright?"

Son of a... Damn it. No, she wasn't feeling alright. Holy shit, if she got drugged in a restaurant again, she was going to write a scathing review. Why was everyone looking at her like she had a drifter boogie dangling from her nostril? It was creeping her out. Nobody was moving. Did she accidentally freeze time again? The kitchen swung open and in walked an annoyingly familiar robust, tiny man. *Was she hallucinating? It was creepy Leonard from the night she woke up under a truck. I guess they didn't kill him in Vegas. Why in the hell was this idiot here?*

"Speechless?" The demon in a mortal shell tormented, flamboyantly twirling with his hands in the air.

Either everyone was frozen, or this was a crazy realistic nightmare. "You're not real," Kayn decreed, believing it.

He rifled a mug at her. She didn't try to stop it because it wasn't real. It smoked her face. With her hand over the injury, she accused, "Ouch, what is wrong with you?"

"Use my deity name!" The annoyed being commanded, with the authority of nobody gives a shit.

Oh, something was wrong with her. Plucking off this guy's legs like a psychopath plucks flies wings didn't seem like a bad idea. She was superhero immortal as shit and at least seventy five percent sure she could get away with it. Those were wicked badass odds. She didn't usually use those two words together. Why wasn't anyone moving? She struggled to move and couldn't. *How had it taken her this long to realise she couldn't move? She was a moron.*

"I'm sure your thoughts are deep, but I have a demon to summon and a riddle for you to solve Dragon," Leonard urged, waving his hands too close to her face.

"If you touch me, I'll bite your fingers and toes off like baby carrots, before killing you," Kayn vowed.

"If you kill me, I'll jump into that lovely waitress's body," Leonard stated. "Go ahead. I dare you to do it."

He didn't know she couldn't move. She started giggling.

Strutting away, he returned with a knife. *This was going to be degrading. There had to be a way out of this. Kevin! Hey Kevin! I can't move! Creepy Leonard is about to get up close and personal!*

'Not now, I'm on a date,' Kevin answered in her head.

So sorry I interrupted booty call time, Smith. Don't worry about me, I'll hang out with creepy Leonard. Go, get laid, and don't forget to kiss my ass the next time we see each other if he does cringe-worthy shit to me, Kayn countered, wincing as he came closer.

'Holy shit, Brighton, just eat the guy, you are a frigging Guardian Conduit, this isn't a tricky situation,' Kevin suggested, laughing.

Sending him scathing vibes, she broiled, *I can't move.*

Kevin commented, *'How does this keep happening to you?'*

Nobody else is moving either.

'You better not be interrupting my booty call for a bad dream,' he chuckled in her head.

Was he trying to piss her off? Wait, it wasn't rational to be this irritated. They'd moved on. They were trying to be friends from afar and enemies in person.

His voice chuckled, *'Is there anything you don't overthink?'*

Nothing. Not a thing.

'Steph just called me a dick and took off. Happy now? Compel him to do something, it'll give me a minute to help you get out of this.'

With a blade against her throat, Leonard sang, "My tasty, tasty pretty bird."

So gross. Curious, Kayn asked, "Why am I a pretty bird?"

Cutting her flesh, blood barely oozed before it healed. Leonard confessed, "Truthfully, you're not my usual calibre of obsession. Call this morbid curiosity."

Dick! She wanted to eat this guy. She needed to do it. But how?

Frustrated, he sliced her again. Scowling as she healed, he complained, "Stop doing that, I'm hungry."

"How are you here?" Kayn interrogated with a scathing glare. *She knew what she needed to do but didn't want to make him touch her.* Meeting his gaze, she lured him closer, "I remember your name."

"Do you, pretty bird?" He slipped into his routine like he hadn't just told her she wasn't his usual breed.

His pervie commentary wasn't clever enough to offend her. He was a sad, creepy man. She tempted, "Come closer, we can make a deal. I have to offer my blood. I'll give it to you, but I have questions first."

"I'll play," Leonard toyed, massaging her shoulders.

This was going to give her night terrors. Kayn asked, "Why is everyone frozen?"

"Where do you think you are?" He taunted with a smirk.

The pastel booths in the diner swirled. In a blink, Kayn was ankle-deep in manure at a farm. *Shit? Seriously? What was this?* Puzzled, she spun around as a murder of crows lifted off behind her, saying, "Kevin?"

"Who is Kevin?" Leonard taunted, stroking her cheek with his blade, slicing her skin.

She tried to knock his teeth out and only squirmed in place. "Why can't I move?" Kayn accused.

"I control that, and to be fair, I just gave you a full minute to attack me, and you didn't," Leonard chuckled. "You are a rabid freaky one, I get all tingly thinking about it. Do you ever give up?"

'Dragons never give up, kick his ass,' Kevin provoked in her head.

"You're having a nightmare, Sweetie. Wake up," Frost's voice urged, rubbing her back. *How did she get back to her bunk? The gap between the restaurant and setting up camp filled in. She had a nap.* Hugging her boyfriend, Kayn whispered, "I'm so glad you're here." *Something felt off.* Pulling away, it wasn't Frost, it was Leonard. She startled awake on her bunk with her heart racing. Despising multi-layered nightmares, Kayn got up and went the bathroom. *It was dark out. Whenever she died too many times in a short period, everything was off for a while.* She brushed her teeth and ran fingers through her curls. Semi-prepared to take on what remained of the evening, Kayn wandered out into a desert campground. Her friends were gathered by a crackling fire, roasting marshmallows, and sharing stories. *Walking into situations like this with familiar laughter felt like coming home. Travelling from disaster to tragedy with her Clan of immortal Nomads, she'd grown accustomed to chaos.*

Seeing her there, Grey prompted, "Grab a stick, hotdogs are on the picnic table."

Raised on Vancouver Island surrounded by mountains with dense forest, she felt exposed without towering trees guarding her perimeter. With an unobscured view of starry heavens and dinner on a stick, Kayn sat by the fire. Roasting her wiener in the blaze, she saw Markus' estranged girlfriend watching her. *Was that dream pieces of the puzzle to where she was or just her scrambled memory playing tricks?* Meeting Arrianna's gaze through a wall of flickering flames, Kayn asked, "When will they be here?"

"A flat tire altered their schedule. Long nap," Arrianna commented, with dancing flames reflecting in her shiny hair.

Smiling, Kayn answered, "I've lost track of how many times I've died this week."

Air high fiving her across the fire, Lexy declared, "I lost my sense of time, decades ago."

With seemingly endless rolling hills and short flowering cacti, it looked like they were the only people on the planet. *Whoops. She'd gapped out.* Pulling her burned wiener out of the flames, Kayn grinned as she thought of Killian's charcoaled manly bits. *It was amazing how much madness her mind let her stroll through in a twenty-four-hour period.* Uncomfortably pregnant, Emma was shifting in her chair. *That was going to happen any day now. She wanted to be here for it. Witnessing childbirth would be an unforgettable experience.* Eating burnt wiener, Kayn watched Killian putting out flaming marshmallows by swinging his stick, giggling.

"Ha, ha, I get it," Killian remarked with a smile.

Noticing Emma's discomfort, Grey offered her orange juice. As the evening of comradery and laughter progressed, Kayn realised offering Emma orange juice was Grey's only move, he had no other area of pregnancy expertise. *Orange juice didn't cure all pregnancy ills, but it was funny. She didn't know a lot about pregnancy but knew Braxton hicks false labour was a thing.* "Offer to rub her back if you want to help," Kayn hinted.

Waving, Grey suggested, "Drag a chair over here, Emma. I'll massage your back."

So close, Greydon. So frigging close.

Missing part of the conversation, Killian scowled at Grey, reprimanding, "Do you have no shame?"

Giving him a dirty look, Grey sighed, "Why would you go there? She's cramping, I'm trying to help."

They bickered back and forth like grumpy old men with sexy accents. Shaking her head, towing Emma's chair over to Grey, Kayn interrupted bitch fest, "I'm going for a jog. Do you have this now or do you need a few more minutes to get your shit together?"

Snapping out of it, Grey chuckled, "I've got this. Take a newbie with you, campers may tick you off."

Scanning the horizon, Kayn laughed, "What campers?"

"Rolling hills hide indiscretions," Dean announced. "I'd love to go for a jog with you."

Downing what remained in her water bottle, Kayn took an elastic off her wrist, and put her hair up, baiting, "Keep up." Leaving Dean in her dust as she sprinted away.

"Wait, cardio beast!" he hollered, pursuing her.

Hearing Dean's footsteps behind her, she slowed a hair allowing him to run at her side, sparring, "There's no easy level with me."

Laughing, "For anything, I heard." He took off ahead of her.

Oh, you stinker. She paced herself on the even sandy gravel trail, chilled until he tired and pushed past, cackling as they came upon tents hidden by rolling hills. *I'll be damned he was right.* Dean picked up his pace as they sprinted by. He took off down a hill. Losing her footing in loose gravel, she flail-toppled to the bottom of the embankment. Facedown in sandy gravel, Kayn mumbled, "Every damn time, I'm having a cool moment." *Immortality didn't change her luck a speck.*

With glittering heavens in the backdrop, Dean gushed, "Awe, you're an accident-prone superhero." Helping her up, he took a napkin out of his pocket, insisting, "Let me do it."

It felt like their roles were reversed. "Thanks," Kayn sighed.

Handing her a napkin, Dean suggested, "Keep it in your pocket."

Realistically, she was only a few years older. The training, surviving Immortal Testing and nonstop duties without a second to breathe for six months only felt like decades. "I won't trip again," she vowed. Grinning while stretching her legs, Kayn cracked her neck, enquiring, "I don't know much about your mortal life."

Strolling under night's heavenly display, Dean shared his story, "I was snagged by a tech firm right out of high school, but their funding for my project tanked. I needed cash fast for my prototype. I was stripping at an upscale club with a closeted boyfriend when we were sideswiped into oncoming traffic. My Mom died, I was granted a second chance as a sacrificial lamb, you know the Guardian spiel."

Blown away, Kayn dug deeper, "No other family?"

"Nobody," Dean disclosed. "Maybe it's easier that

way?" They climbed an embankment with a hidden valley. Standing at the top, he declared, "Now we know where the showers are."

"These are way too far away to be for our campsite," Kayn said, viewing the sleepy town. Taking a seat on the hill, enjoying the tranquil desert sky.

Sitting beside her, Dean ribbed, "Your boyfriend is crazy hot, how's that going?"

"I have no idea, I vanished for five days," Kayn admitted, noticing a mosquito feasting on her arm, she squeezed the flesh on either side and watched it implode.

Smiling, Dean commented, "Insta bloodsucker revenge."

It was nice to hang out with someone who didn't expect anything out of her. The interesting hot black guy in their Clan was clearly into dudes. It wasn't good to get attached to the newbies going into Testing. She might not be able to help herself in Dean's case. He was fantastic on many levels. The ease of their personalities was reminiscent of her years with Kevin before the horrors of the afterlife. It was a similar sense of tranquillity. "We should run back for our shower stuff," she suggested. Careful with her footing, she let him lead the way. When they arrived, they were playing crazy eights.

Raucously laughing, Killian announced, "Last card!"

Noticing her there, Lexy stated, "Back already?"

"We found the showers," Kayn explained, walking past. Peering into the backroom, she asked, "Does anyone want to come with us?"

Grey leapt up, saying, "We'll be fighting over whose turn it is in the morning, I'll go now."

Handing Kayn a bag, Lexy urged, "Keep using my stuff."

Backpacks in tow, they sprinted into the night.

Following the trails, Grey bailed in the same place, tumbling down the embankment. In agony, he groaned, "I broke my ankle."

Her symbol warmed, flashing in the dark. *She didn't have her glove. Why hadn't she noticed?* Inspecting Grey's injury, Kayn teased, "I think we should cut it off."

Protectively shielding it, Grey butt jogged away, giggling, "Don't make me laugh, you jerk, it hurts."

It would take two seconds to heal him. Kayn's symbol strobed again, lighting up the night sky as Lexy and Arrianna showed up at the top of the hill.

"Damn it Greydon, we thought it was serious," Arrianna razzed as they shimmied down.

Relieved, Lexy sat next to Grey, saying, "This is a perfect opportunity to have an inescapable chat with my Handler. We'll catch up."

Glowering as they prepared to walk away, Grey declared, "If you let her play this game with me, I'm going to be pissed at all of you!"

"Go, he's being overdramatic. It's far past time we talked our shit out," Lexy stated, shooing them away.

They left him there. Arrianna came along, saying, "I'm going to use your stuff, Lex."

As they walked away, Grey shouted, "You guys are giant assholes!"

Grinning, Arrianna whispered, "His jealousy bullshit is exhausting."

As their argument escalated, Dean glanced back asking, "Why is he acting like she cheated if they aren't together?"

Without divulging her sister's secrets, Kayn explained, "Handlers and Dragons have complicated dynamics."

Zach left her there, and bad things happened. Dwelling on it wasn't going to alter anything. It wasn't his fault. Orders were written in stone. It was the only aspect of her afterlife where grey areas didn't exist.

With a new lease on the afterlife after showering, Kayn wandered out into eerie silence. *Where did everyone go? She was alone. It didn't make sense.* She knocked, waited for a response, and peered into the men's washroom. *The lights were off.* In a blink, she was standing on a darkened road with a streetlight flickering at the end of the block. A beastly creature emerged from the shadows dragging a sickle. *What do we have here?* It was coming for her, scraping a farm tool on cement. *She'd just walked out of the bathroom. This wasn't real.* Her duplicate sprinted by clutching a knife, body checked the monster and shrieked like a feral maniac rage stabbing it. *This was new. Was it a memory or a vision? She'd been shanking the sickle wielding beast for way longer than any sane person would. She couldn't step into a thought to stop herself from doing something she'd already done, could she?* Her doppelganger made eye contact with her. It got up drenched in blood. *Feral her was coming to kill rational her. Seems legit. Was she supposed to reason with herself? Could she summon up power and battle herself? Was this a wizard challenge?* In a flash, she was back in the shower rinsing her hair. *That was trippy.* Startled by a noise, Kayn spun with fists clenched, prepared to throw down. Joy surpassed everything as she realised it was Frost and leapt into his arms.

Embracing naked in the stall, Frost promised, "I'm never leaving you alone at a ball again."

Pheromones were coming from his alluring everything. "I'd avoid ordering me to eat everyone at the next ball," she taunted in his arms.

Gazing into her eyes, he seduced, "Still mine?"

Hovering her lips over his, Kayn enticed, "Still mine?"

"Always," Frost pledged, naughtily caressing her breast, voyeuristically watching as his hand heated.

Every hair prickled in response as volatile lust filled the steamy tile cubicle. Desire ached, swelling like a wave to the surface, gaining momentum to crash upon a shore, releasing a gust of Siren euphoria. With raw untethered emotion, lips merged, slippery torsos entangled like sensual puzzles as tongues cavorted, and slippery soapy hands slid over curves. Primally triggered, he savagely took her, in a blur of moans and toe-curling crescendos.

Holding her up after buckling her knees, Frost gasped, "Hope we're far enough away, Arrianna will be pissed if she gets dosed by pheromones before having it out with Markus. Have you talked to her?"

"Girl solidarity aside, she's not angry, just concerned. I know everything is subject to interpretation, but ..."

"But?" Frost asked. "Don't send it with flowers, what do you think?"

She hadn't thought it out this far. Unfiltered deductions are a go. She prompted, "Could Markus be possessed?"

Entertaining the idea, he slipped on underwear, teasing, "I'm not sure breakup induced bad behaviour warrants an exorcism."

"He ordered me to eat a ballroom full of immortals." She questioned, "Does that seem rational?"

With their eyes locked, he stroked her wet hair, ribbing, "Irrational choices happen during breakups."

His form-fitting black underwear made her want to stay in the bathroom all night.

Hugging her, Frost changed the subject, daring, "Let's walk back in our underwear."

Groping his behind, Kayn taunted, "We won't make it to the campsite."

Wriggling away, collecting his things, he baited, "I hope we don't," provoking her with a towel swat.

Grabbing her bag, wearing only underwear, she followed him outside. Holding hands, they went for a half-naked stroll through the desert under twinkling stars. *Every cell in her body wanted him. She needed immersion therapy. Frost and her in bed for a month. All day, every day, until it stopped being all she could think of. She'd sleep in the sand with rattlesnakes to spend the night in his arms.*

"I'll sleep under the stars with you anywhere, Brighton," Frost seduced, taking her in his arms under the desert moon.

Giggling, she stated, "We haven't made it far."

"You could charge admission for your inner dialogue," he teased. "It seems counterproductive to change your train of thought, but they'll have questions when we get back. If there are any revelations that sting, I'd prefer to know before it's public knowledge."

With arms laced around his neck, Kayn admitted, "You had the gist of it when we spoke on the phone. I may have stolen a cab for a side excursion to a club where I ate a bunch of Lampir. Triad brought me back to the hotel. I had a G-rated visit with Kevin. After Lucien, someone knocked on the door and I woke up in the in-between. It felt like I was only there for twenty minutes before I turned to dust and woke up in someone's trunk."

"That's it?" Frost probed, looking into her eyes.

Should she mention the daydreams?

"Was I in these daydreams?" He flirtatiously answered.

Her laughable unfiltered commentary made her an open

book. She switched the subject, "How did your night go? Did you catch Leonard?"

Gaging her response, Frost divulged, "We all woke up in compromising positions, none of us recalls finding Leonard."

Intrigued, she enquired, "Lampir compulsion?"

Grinning, Frost answered, "Lampir can't compel each other. Skipping the details of your time with Lucien wasn't necessary. Lampir toxin was involved, it's a Siren thing. No judgement, no fear. You can't control what you do under the influence of magic."

She'd done sketchy things riding the magical Conduit Dragon, but she'd also consciously respected his wishes whenever she'd been capable of doing so. The impulse to succumb to a lusty encounter won. Brazenly kissing Frost under a desert sky, tormenting him with her tongue until his shallow groan lit her libido on fire, it was like dividing oceans as mouth's parted. She confessed, "When you snuck up behind me in the shower, I was having a flashback or premonition of myself, stone-cold Dragon feral, running at a giant ogre looking beast dragging a sickle down the middle of the street. I tackled it and stabbed it until I shredded it, then got up and ran at myself."

"That's so hot," he chuckled, tossing his underwear.

He was certifiable. She'd never been able to resist a dare. "I'll get sand in uncomfortable places," Kayn flirted. He sprang to attention, and she caught her breath. *What sand? She couldn't effectively say no to him. He was dirty sex crack, he'd given her a pleasure addiction.*

Lying on his back, he lured, "You'll only get sand on your knees."

"Where anyone can see us," Kayn seduced, removing her panties. Dangling lacy underwear from her finger, she toyed, "Should I drop these?"

Naughtily stroking her calf, he taunted, "You won't need panties for days."

Quenching her thirst for chaos, she tossed her panties. Inhibitions vanished in a hedonistic blur as she rode until a tornado of euphoria took her under a twinkling ceiling of stars. Crying out as their union imploded, they lay gasping. A chorus of wolves responded. They looked at each other and howled. *Just in case they thought it wasn't going to be awkward when they made it back to the campsite.* She attempted to move.

Clutching her hips, Frost suggested, "Maybe we should check out your theory about doing it all night? See if we can get it out of our system?"

With joy shining in their eyes, her lips tenderly met his as they vanished into an endless lovemaking session.

Stirring in his arms as the sun peered over the horizon, she opened her eyes, panicking. *Crap, it was morning. Where was her underwear?* Shaking him, Kayn rushed, "Babe, wake up, it's dawn. Get up, we're naked in a public place. I can't find my underwear."

Grinning like a lethargic cat, Frost mumbled, "Five more minutes, babe."

Where were they? She didn't see the bathrooms. Last night was a hedonistic blur of wolf calls and unfiltered naughty games. Kissing his lips, Kayn persisted, "We don't have five minutes, everyone will want showers. I'm dirty."

Opening his eyes, he tugged her to him, kissed her and chuckled, "Impressively dirty."

Lost in sensual kisses, it took everything she had to pull away and get up, prompting, "Last night was outstanding. Where is our underwear?"

Up in a flash, retracing their steps, Frost laughed, "We grabbed our bags to go have another shower but didn't make it far."

About to run back to look, they heard voices. *Crap!*

They took off in the opposite direction, giggling. *There was nowhere to hide, they were at the bottom of a slope. Shit!*

"It's too late, get behind me. Grab anything out of that bag and toss it to me," Frost giggled, blocking her from view as she dug through contents.

Tossing him something, Kayn scrambled into shorts and a shirt.

Holding a red t-shirt over his junk as Killian, Grey and Lexy appeared at the top of the hill, Frost waved and called out, "Good morning!"

Cackling, Kayn passed shorts and suggested, "Your turn, get behind me and put these on."

Standing there, as the others came down the hill, Kayn waved and sang, "Good morning." *This was ridiculous.*

Snatching her backpack, Lexy teased, "We figured we'd stumble upon wolf instigators on our way to the showers."

Discreetly passing her sandy panties, Killian leaned in, whispering, "I'm assuming these are yours."

Her underwear. Fantastic. Ten shades of burgundy, Kayn mumbled, "Thanks." As their friends continued the trek to the showers, Kayn giggled, "That wasn't embarrassing."

Holding her waist, Frost kissed her, taunting, "Well, now we know."

Now we know, what?

Swaying, almost dancing under a breathtaking sunrise, he confessed, "Having sex all night only makes me want you more, but I'm certain, Lexy will veto us sharing a shower."

"We'll sneak away later," Kayn vowed as their lips met. Hearing more voices, they stopped making out and sprinted to the washroom.

Shoving on the door, Frost said, "I'll wait for you."

"I'll wait for you," Kayn promised, vanishing into the washroom. Her cocky stance faltered as her sister harassed, "You left my underwear in the desert."

Wincing, Kayn turned on the shower. Stepping under the spray, apologising, "Sorry." Wetting her hair, thinking about their incredible night, she needed to say it, "I love him."

Smiling, Lexy responded, "I know."

Keeping sister bonding flowing, Kayn asked, "Did you work things out with Grey?"

"As long as I stay away from Tiberius," Lexy divulged, rinsing her hair with a shit disturbing glint in her eyes.

That dirty devil was up to something. With curiosity egging her on, Kayn delved deeper into her sibling's psyche, "Are you going to?"

Under the spray, Lexy revealed, "I spent all night talking with Grey. We've worked everything out. I'll always love him more than anything. We can't be together physically, without him forgetting, so we've set ground rules. He has people he doesn't want me to be with. I have a few on my list. It was all dealt with, but this morning, Mel told me Tiberius has feelings for me. He's a horrible idea, I should honour our agreement and stay away."

"I recall you saying, Frost was a horrible idea before the Testing," Kayn answered. "Look at us now?"

Laughing, Lexy countered, "I haven't altered my opinion, Frost's a horrible idea. Surviving Immortal Testing changed you. Now, you're also a bad idea so it works."

Impressed, Kayn commented, "That comeback was epic, well done." Turning off the spray, her mind flashed back to their shower. *Nope, sister bonding time.*

Walking to the sink, Lexy remarked, "Our comic

timing may be priceless, but I still want to strangle our seed sowing sperm donor, I won't be going out of my way to thank him." Tossing Kayn undergarments, shorts, and a tank top, they dressed in front of the mirror.

Curious, Kayn asked, "Is Orin on Grey's hard no list?"

Brushing her crimson locks, Lexy smiled and said, "He's all good with Orin, but I'm fairly certain I've wrecked that." Lexy passed the brush.

Smiling, Kayn brushed her damp curls, giggling, "Maybe that's why Grey left him on your to-do list?"

Packing her bag, Lexy grinned and joked, "Odds are slim he still wants to hook his caboose to my train wreck."

"I'm surprised Frost hooked his caboose to mine," Kayn ribbed, about to put blush on.

Snatching the rouge away, Lexy teased, "You won't need blush. You guys set off a choir of wolves all night. For future reference screams echo here."

Pressing her lips together mortified, Kayn asked, "Was it really that loud?"

Grinning, Lexy harassed, "We used it as a drinking game and did a shot each time the wolves joined you. Everyone at our campsite is dead on their feet hungover."

"You're joking," Kayn stated, knowing it was plausible.

"Nope," Lexy replied, slowly shaking her head. "Most of us were impressed if that helps."

They walked out. Frost, Grey and Killian were pitching rocks like bored kids. Sexual tension flickered like electricity in the air as they wandered back to the campsite. *All she could think about was being in his arms.* Everyone started one-upping each other, disclosing hilarious things they'd done. *She'd done something Lexy would appreciate.* Kayn commented, "After the banquet, I compelled Tiberius and Stephanie to sleep when they were being lippy in a limo and left without undoing it," Kayn admitted, smiling.

Walking beside her, Grey said, "Nice."

It was the first time in a long while Grey wasn't set off by the mere mention of Tiberius. Maybe everything was going to go back to how it used to be?

With his arm around her, Frost whispered, "That damp tank top is giving me impure thoughts."

"No towel." Without thinking, Kayn whispered, "I'm so wet."

Abruptly stopping, Frost snatched her into his embrace, teasing, "Really?"

Everyone else kept walking. Grey glanced back, smiling. Clicking, Kayn laughed, "That's not what I meant."

"If chafing is the issue, I've got something to put between your legs," he provoked, nuzzling her neck.

"We've kept everyone up all night, we should behave," Kayn backtracked, watching the group walking away. Her libido whispered, *run back to the bathroom. No, come on, Brighton. Get it together.* She changed the subject, "Who did Zach end up with?"

Caressing her face, gazing into her eyes, Frost disclosed, "You'll have to ask him yourself. Zach feels like he let you down. I've had my chance to apologise, we should give your Handler the opportunity so he can stop stressing." Kissing her, he pulled away and switched gears, "You neglected to mention naked time with Killian."

She did, didn't she? Kayn wove the not so sexy tale in her most titillating come hither tone, "It was so hot, we went off the cliff and burned in a car until we were charcoal."

"Sounds hot," Frost giggled, nibbling on her ear.

Hugging him, she shut her eyes and groaned, "Emersion therapy didn't work at all."

"Not a hair," Frost decreed, grinning. Stepping away to stretch his hamstrings, he challenged, "I'll race you."

Cackling, Kayn took off, manoeuvring rocky terrain like a pro, nearly losing her footing running up a hill with Frost hot on her tail. Skidding to a stop as they caught up with the others, laughing, she taunted, "Good try."

Out of breath, Frost gasped, "I let you win."

She shoved him, he almost toppled over. He tried to grab her, she dodged the attempt, giggling. Keeping up with the others, Kayn provoked, "Anytime you want to be beaten again, let me know."

"Isn't love grand?" Killian said, patting Frost's shoulder.

Whenever someone else brought up the topic of love, joy dulled in Frost's eyes. With zero experience in the relationship department, it felt like she was trying to read between lines written in a language she barely understood. It made her leery of overusing the word. She'd loved him last night, recklessly, passionately, with every fibre of her being. If he stopped recoiling from the word itself, she wouldn't be afraid to say it. Maybe the hollow ache in her chest was warning her they weren't in the same place?

As they strolled rolling hills with sandy gravel shifting underfoot, Lexy responded to her thoughts, "Fear is normal, it's terrifying to have something to lose."

Smiling at her sister, Kayn commenced watching Frost's backside. They were gathered drinking coffee at picnic tables as they approached. *This was going to be embarrassing.*

Zach jogged over and hugged her, apologising, "I'm the worst Handler."

Anxiety dissolved to zen in his embrace, all was forgiven in a millisecond. "We aren't supposed to question authority. I know you were told to leave," Kayn consoled. "Where's Markus?" *She'd missed Arrianna's post ghosting absentee boyfriend reunion.*

"He dropped us off and got a room," Zach quietly filled her in.

Holy shit. Feeling horrible, her eyes met with Arrianna's. It was obvious she'd been crying all night, there was firm resolve in her expression. *She was trying to be strong.*

Touching Arrianna's shoulder, Grey assured, "He won't be able to escape a conversation with you forever."

Whacking her Handler, Lexy whispered, "Rethink that sentence."

Clicking in, Grey backtracked, "I meant, he'll be here today to set us up with our next job. We're all in the same place." Looking, he asked, "Where are my newbies?"

Coming out of the RV with a mountain of waffles on a plate in one hand, and syrup in the other, Astrid teased, "The newbies are sitting right there," pointing at another picnic table. "Emma is a zillion months pregnant, it's hot, so she's napping." Placing a plate on each table, she laughed, "How hungover are you?" Smiling at Arrianna, Astrid advised, "Tequila is not your friend. Eat a waffle."

Grimacing, Arrianna picked up a waffle, mumbling, "No promises it's staying down," chomping into a dry one.

"I'll hold your hair if you end up praying to the porcelain god," Grey assured, eating his waffle dry in solidarity.

Naturally pretty with sleek blonde hair and a golden tan, Arrianna mumbled, "I may need you."

Nearly due, expectant Emma waddled out of the RV, the new Ankh shifted to make room for her at their table. Grey got up, poured her a glass of orange juice, and placed it in front of her, saying, "Folic acid for the baby."

"Thank you," Emma replied, smiling.

With her Handler's attention elsewhere, Lexy offered, "I'll deck him, everyone else got to hit a leader this week."

She'd get away with it. Meeting Lexy's eyes, Kayn provoked, "I double-dog dare you to do it."

"Stop egging her on. Neither of you is hitting Markus," Grey reprimanded, returning to his seat, pointing at Kayn.

Touching her chest, feigning shock, Kayn baited, "Well, I wasn't even thinking about doing it myself." *Now she wanted to. She could get away with it.*

Tossing a waffle at Kayn's Handler, Grey scolded, "Pay attention!"

Scowling, Zach said, "What did you do?"

Innocently, Kayn answered, "One of us should hit him." *Why not? Maybe it would shake sense into him. He was an ass.*

Shaking his head, Zach pled, "Give me an hour before you start shit, Brighton. I'm so hungover, I can barely see. How do you have energy for anything?"

Laughter erupted as the picnic table of newbie Ankh began howling like wolves. Reminding the foursome, she was top of the immortal food chain, Kayn commented, "By all means, keep digging your graves.

I'll have an opportunity to work out my aggression after Emma gives birth, chasing you around the in-between with an axe for a few weeks." In the snap of a finger, it was quiet enough to hear a pin drop.

Grinning, Lexy stated, "Nice. That made my day."

"We should hunt them down and kill them like we're in a slasher movie. Have you ever thought up a chainsaw as a weapon in the in-between?" Kayn suggested like they were making plans to go to the beach.

"Um, no, but we're so doing that," Lexy decreed, winking at newbie Dean, who'd paused mid waffle bite, listening.

Grinning, they Dragon sister high-fived. Their Handler's shook their heads. *Oh, yeah. Her boyfriend was here.* Frost was holding his forehead with his elbow balanced on the table like he had a headache. *Maybe she should stop?* Arrianna was grinning. *They'd taken her mind off her drama.*

Unaffected by lippy shenanigans, Zach remarked, "Done torturing the children, Brighton?"

"For now," Kayn saucily replied, snatching a lukewarm golden waffle off the plate, amused by the silence.

Smiling at Arrianna, Lexy instigated, "Do you want me to hit Markus? I'll do it."

"No, he looked past me like I wasn't even there and drove away last night," Arrianna explained. "If leaving me with an ounce of dignity was a stretch, why give him the time of day?"

"That's the spirit, gorgeous. Only an idiot would cheat on you," Killian declared, raising his coffee, winking at Grey.

Grey was Arrianna's last boyfriend. He cheated on her with Lily.

Instead of being pissed at Killian for calling him out

on misdeeds, Grey turned to Arrianna and admitted, "I'll always regret hurting you, Markus will too."

Working things out with Lexy brought Guru Grey back.

With perfect tension breaking timing, Lily emerged from the RV like a gorgeous ray of Arabian princess sunshine with a plate of bacon for each table, urging, "Eat up." Shimmying onto the bench by Killian, she met Frost's gaze and asked, "Have you eaten?"

"What do you need me to do?" Frost enquired, finishing his coffee."

"Please wake up, Orin. He's still sleeping," Lily answered, fixing herself a plate.

Grabbing bacon as he got up, Frost sauntered over to Markus' crew's RV and went in. Gapped out, watching the door grazing on bacon, Kayn heard someone say Markus is coming.

Getting up, Arrianna volunteered, "I'll go clean up."

Cutting waffles, as her father's rental car approached, Lily said, "I can't believe they broke up. They seemed so happy."

"He left on a job like everything was perfect and ghosted her. There was no argument," Kayn filled her in.

With blind trust in her father, Lily defended him, "He wouldn't do that."

"Are you sure," Kayn asked, watching the vehicle pull up and park. Jenna got out, slammed the door, and stormed into the RV without speaking to anyone. *Nobody mentioned Jenna going with Markus to the hotel.*

Swaggering over, Markus snatched a handful of bacon and ignorantly decreed, "Jenna's a handful."

Confusion filled Lily's eyes as she clarified, "How so?"

"She showed up at my hotel room in the middle of the night and came onto me," Markus gossiped, smirking as he reached for the empty syrup. "Is there more?"

Smiling blankly, Lily replied, "I'll be right back... Dad. I need to use the washroom." She got up and went after Jenna.

Everyone else had to see this, it couldn't be just her.

WHEN FROST CAME IN, Orin looked up, stating, "Sorry, I'm not going out there."

"Lexy?" Frost probed as he sat across the table.

Chuckling, Orin shook his head and disclosed, "No."

"Spit it out then," Frost baited, smiling.

Stalling, Orin switched subjects, "Judging by the all-night wolves' serenade, your reunion with Kayn went well."

"Quit wasting my time, tell me why you're hiding in here, eating Corn Pops," Frost asserted, smiling.

"We're testing a theory. Jenna will be back soon," Orin replied, eating a spoonful of cereal.

Sipping lukewarm java, Frost asked, "Is that coffee fresh?"

Enraged, Jenna stormed in, slammed the door, muffled her face with a dishtowel and screamed. Massaging bruised wrists, she calmed enough to speak, "That's not Markus. He tried luring me to his room, there's no way."

Rushing over, Orin checked her wrists, declaring, "I'm going to kill him." He reached for the door.

Grabbing his arm, Jenna commanded, "Stop. I've pieced together my visions. He can't know we've figured it out. He's outside with the others, nobody can react."

They froze as someone came in. Closing the door quietly, Lily stated, "That's not my father. What do you know?"

Peering out the window, Frost whispered, "He's going into the other RV. Tell us everything."

Defeated, Jenna sat at the table, saying, "Somehow, he's been switched, cloned, maybe possessed? Where's Emery? I can't explain why, but we need her."

"She was with the other group, she should be here," Lily whispered, tearing up.

Taking Lily in his arms, Frost consoled, "We'll find him."

"Until we've had a chance to speak privately to everyone full Ankh, do everything Bad Markus says no matter what," Jenna asserted. "He can't suspect anything. If this is a Clone or a Shapeshifter, Good Markus is being held somewhere and needs our help. If this version of Markus vanishes, we'll have nothing to barter with. No proof."

"If we don't want anyone to call him out, we have to make sure everyone understands why they can't. Bad Markus is with Arrianna right now," Orin explained, watching out the window.

Their Oracle Jenna urged, "Arrianna's intuition is strong, she'll be useful. Quietly, take everyone with enough seniority to question his motives for a walk."

Mel wandered out of the bunk area, groggily saying, "I'm way too hungover for this shit."

"Sorry, I forgot you were back there," Orin apologised, peeking out the window. "Emery just came out of the other RV. She's coming over."

The door opened as Emery walked in. Everyone went silent. She walked over, planted a kiss on Jenna's lips and addressed the room, "I'm guessing everyone knows that's not Markus trying to sleep with Arrianna?"

"Nope," Mel commented. "Not doing this today." She spun on a dime and took off to the washroom, muttering, "I've suspected it for days, I'll let you guys catch up. Let me know when you figure out a plan."

Watching Orin's lippy hungover offspring stagger away, Emery chuckled, "I like her."

"What do you think? Is he possessed or cloned?" Jenna enquired, looking at Emery.

Pouring a coffee, Emery decreed, "You can't possess or clone immortals who belong to Tri-Clan. In theory, another immortal being can bounce a soul out into Crypt storage and temporarily highjack a body if they are the same tier soul. It won't hold longer than two, maybe three weeks."

"Weird information to know," Frost toyed, suspiciously.

With a grin, Emery divulged, "I have special friendships with Third-Tier who have loose lips after a few drinks. The Crypt containing the soul belonging to the inhabited body is usually close by."

"How close," Jenna probed. "A Crypt can't be difficult to find."

Smiling, Emery revealed, "Not a full-size Crypt. It could be the size of a pendant on a necklace, small enough to be on one's person. Arrianna might be able to find it. In my experience, Third-Tier rarely say no to being propositioned by a pretty anything."

Letting it sink in, Frost announced, "Orin, take a group and get the newbies out of here for the day. I'll go stop it." He walked past everyone at the picnic tables without looking and went into the RV.

18
DECONSTRUCTING MARKUS

*H*ightailing it into the RV as Markus pulled up to avoid the awkward conversation, Arrianna rushed down the hall to the washroom and shut the door, needing space between her and the person who stomped her heart. Leaning against the sink, her mind replayed their love story, frame by beautiful frame. Stolen from Trinity, she'd begun her journey in Ankh despising Markus for taking her. Trinity's leader Thorne was a selfless, superhero guy, he'd been easy to follow. She had friends and a boyfriend she genuinely cared about in Trinity. One second, she was starting her afterlife in the strongest Clan, and the next, she was in a diner with Ankh. There were two other newbies, a feral redhead who'd been living in the wilderness for years, and a cute blonde guy with a surfer vibe and an amazing accent. They'd cleaned up the redhead and combed her matted hair, but she seemed mentally unwell. Watching the nonverbal cabin girl eat was equal parts sad and entertaining.

In the months that followed, she grew to adore both.

Training for Immortal Testing, they strengthened their bond and gained Lexy's trust, giving her greater purpose. Tired of her hatred, Markus promised she could go back to Trinity before her eighteenth birthday if she didn't want to stay. When the time came, she couldn't bring herself to leave, and the trio survived Testing together with their feral champion.

Eventually, her friendship with Grey evolved into more, and they were happy for a long time. She understood Lexy and Grey's Dragon Handler bond, she loved Lexy too. Their relationship ended abruptly when Grey cheated with Lily. Looking back, she knew there was little anyone could do to stop themselves from falling into bed with a Siren, secreting pheromones. She'd been so hurt; she left her best friends to do jobs with Markus' crew.

A small-framed guy, the authority in Markus' voice made him six feet tall. He was attractive, sweet, and found her stubborn distaste for him entertaining. As their friendship blossomed, she began paying attention to the little things. Good to everyone, even when furious, he saw the other side of every situation. A calming influence, Markus could use compulsion to get people to do his bidding, but rarely did, allowing everyone the freedom to be who they were. He wasn't the obvious choice in an RV full of sexy immortals.

When that flicker of curiosity blossomed into a crush, she wanted more, but Markus was dead set on keeping their friendship platonic. For months, she spent a bizarre amount of time, luring him into sexy situations where she was only wearing a towel or scantily clad. He knew she was trying to seduce him. A decent guy who didn't want to take advantage of her, Markus turned a blind eye to every flirtation, until she jimmied a window open and broke into his cabana one fated night in

Mexico. He must have thought she was insane. She climbed into his bed naked. He woke up, laughing, "I give up. You are so crazy, get over here." That first night was the most beautiful experience of her afterlife. Merely saying making love with Markus was incredible, didn't do it justice. Body and soul, they meshed in a way she'd never known. Exquisitely tangled in his arms in the aftermath, Markus confessed his feelings and explained why he kept walking away. He feared it would hurt his relationship with Grey. He needed to be an unbiased party to lead Ankh properly. Lily was his daughter, that was complicated enough. After being together, there was no way to deny what they were.

Markus was an amazing boyfriend. He'd never cheated, she'd be willing to wager immortality on it. He was devoted to her, and in turn, he was her whole world. They loved each other like it was forever. They weren't apart often, and when they were, he texted all day. She'd never doubted his feelings, not for a heartbeat, and then one day, he disappeared.

She found out they broke up in a text from someone else. Shell shocked, she knew something must be wrong with him. There was no way he'd do this to her. Not a chance. When Markus looked right through her and went to a hotel instead of staying, she knew it was happening. For the first time, Arrianna wished she could shut her emotions down like Lexy. Having friends around helped, as did the comedy of wolves howling in response to Kayn and Frost's lusty escapades. The bottle of tequila came out, they turned it into a drinking game, and the rest of the night faded to black.

She'd woken up too hungover to think. She must have looked badass acting like he didn't deserve the time of day, but right now, knowing he was outside, her heart ached like an empty pit in her soul. *She planned to switch groups to avoid Markus for as long as possible. She didn't want to see him. She couldn't. Not until she'd gotten over it enough to feel like ration might step in.* Arrianna walked out of the washroom to find Markus standing in the hall between the bunks. Neither one moved. Markus stepped towards her. She panicked and slapped him across the face so hard her hand stung.

Rubbing his cheek, Markus grinned and taunted, "Good morning... Arrianna?"

That was strange. Confused, Arrianna decreed, "I need you to leave."

"What if I don't want to?" Markus dared, with a naughty glint in his eye. She tried to smack him again. Grabbing her wrist, his eyes softened as he admitted, "I deserved that. I let you hit me once, you don't get to keep doing it." Without relaxing his grip on her wrist, his gaze lewdly travelled from her feet to her flushed cheeks as the love of her afterlife, seduced, "You are far too sexy when you're angry."

"You don't get to touch me anymore, Markus," Arrianna cautioned, recognizing his touch but not his tone of voice. Squirming, she demanded, "Let go!"

Gazing into her eyes, his demeanour softened. He toyed, "Promise not to hit me again?"

"Fine," Arrianna replied, with her heart thudding.

Releasing his grasp, he sat, patted the bunk, and tempted, "Sit with me for a few minutes."

Sitting beside him, she allowed him to take her hand out of habit. Caught between how she felt a week ago, and where they were now, Arrianna questioned, "When you kissed me goodbye last week, we were great. I deserve an explanation."

"I don't have one for you," Markus confessed, watching their joined hands.

Staring at their entwined fingers with her heart

aching, Arrianna whispered, "You can't just walk away from a love like ours." Searching for the magic that moved her soul as her eyes met his, she implored, "What happened?"

"I didn't anticipate you," he said, squeezing her hand. "I should have texted back."

I should have texted back? I didn't anticipate you? He wasn't making sense. Overcome by the urge to kiss sense into him, she tenderly kissed his lips, seductively deepening it until she experienced a familiar rush of emotion. As they parted, she was certain he'd felt it too. *Something was off, but she couldn't pinpoint what it was.*

Moved by their connection, Markus whispered her name, "Arrianna," as he kissed her again, deepening the intimacy.

Someone came into the RV. Arrianna leapt away. *What was wrong with her? He hadn't explained anything.*

"No fraternizing in the RV kids," Frost teased, peeking behind the curtain.

Irritated by his interruption, Markus ordered, "Leave us."

Ignoring his command, Frost said, "I was just coming over to make sure Arrianna knew she was right. Jenna found the gift for Markus in the other RV. Go, grab it. I need my bag, and then, I'll get everyone out of here for a few hours so you lovebirds can be alone."

"I hurt you, why get me a gift?" Markus asked, curious.

Always on the ball, Frost answered, "Your birthday was last week."

"I see, I'll wait, go get it," Markus prompted, grinning.

Smiling, Arrianna strolled out. Tears swelled as she left. *They didn't celebrate birthdays.* On her way, a sob shuddered. *Be strong.* She took a breath and entered the other RV. Everyone was here, except for new Ankh and untested newbies. As Lexy and Grey embraced her, tears escaped. Blinking signs of weakness away, Arrianna addressed the group, "Explain." They gave her a rundown of how they'd concluded, Markus was inhabited by a Third-Tier soul.

Their Oracle, Jenna stepped in, "This version of Markus has been setting us up for failure. He's doing something to stifle my ability. Everyone should have caught on when he ordered Kayn to take out high ranking immortal community members in front of the Aries Group, but we were all drunk and stupid. There's nobody to blame but ourselves. His soul must be contained in a pendant or jewellery close to the inhabited body. You need to steal it."

This wasn't happening. He still loved her. Who had she kissed? A mix of relief and fear washed over her.

Cupping her face, Lexy prompted, "There's no time to breakdown, you have to do this. Does he have any jewellery he always wears?"

With tears in her eyes, Arrianna disclosed, "He doesn't wear rings or a necklace, but he has piercings one nipple and his..."

Unfazed, Jenna probed, "You'll get him drunk. It's still his body, can you do this?"

"Back that up... What?" Grey blurted out, shocked.

Grasping what she needed to do, Arrianna confessed, "I don't know how I'm going to get those off. I need a gift."

Intrigued, Emery declared, "For what?"

As resolve set in, Arrianna explained, "Frost interrupted us saying, Jenna found his birthday gift."

They all scrambled around the RV looking for something gift-worthy. Passing her weird things until Arrianna asserted, "Come on people, I need a reason for coming over here."

Strutting out of the back, Emery tossed Arrianna lingerie and decreed, "This will do, change over there."

Clutching her shoulders, Jenna coached, "It's his body. Find where his soul is being stored and get it to us. We'll be waiting."

Passing bottles of alcohol, Emery gave her a quick pep talk, "Third-Tier have a high tolerance, take these. Now, get back over there and get him drunk enough to pass out so you can get that piercing off his Tally Wacker."

Scrunching her face, Lily complained, "I'm traumatised."

Tossing her a bracelet, Jenna explained, "You'll need to hide your thoughts."

She had to find Markus. It was his body. Strutting through the campsite, Arrianna took a deep breath as she went in.

Frost stated, "Nobody will disturb you," quietly leaving.

Pulling back the curtain, Bad Markus was lounging on a bunk awaiting her return. Giving him the bottles, Arrianna instructed, "Wait in the backroom." Dangling lingerie like a lure, she sauntered into the washroom to change. Closing the door, she exhaled. *He still loved her. She was right. She couldn't overthink it.* She put on the lingerie. Viewing her sizzling hot reflection, Arrianna thought of the last time she wore it. *She wasn't going to have time to get him drunk if she walked in like this.* Putting shorts and a tank top on over it, she cleared her mind of doubt, used a spritz of perfume, and went into where he was lounging on multicoloured pillows in front of the TV.

He greeted her, saying, "Where's my surprise?"

Taking a swig from the bottle of whisky, watching her intently.

Sitting next to her lover's highjacked body, she held out her hand. Not really Markus passed the bottle. *Her stomach wasn't going to like this.* "We're going to play a birthday game. If you're a good boy, I'll let you unwrap it." Stretching her smooth tanned legs over his, Arrianna pretended to take a long swig from the bottle, only having a sip.

Stroking her legs, Bad Markus toyed, "I have a few games I'd like to play with you."

His hand slid up her thigh. Placing a hand over his, she reprimanded, "Naughty thing, I haven't told you the rules."

Reaching for a T-shirt covered breast, he complained, "I don't like rules."

Swatting his hand so hard it stung, she corrected, "I'm in control of everything or I'll leave you here with that painful bulge in your shorts."

Smirking, he chuckled, "Alright, you're in charge. Tell me what you want me to do?"

She gave him the bottle, prompting, "Drink this. If you're a good boy, I'll let you peek at your present." With devious eyes, he did as she'd instructed, chugging the bottle. When he attempted to get up and follow, Arrianna booted him down with her foot, coldly reprimanding, "I didn't say you could move. Drink up, I'm going to get something we need. Stay." Feeling him watching, she sauntered away, gathering her thoughts. *How was she going to do this? Zip ties would be handy, maybe rope?* Searching cupboards for restraints, she couldn't find anything. *She'd have to think outside the box.* She found tequila. *She was going to puke if she tried to drink any of this after last night.* Wandering back, she slipped into the washroom and grabbed a curling iron, planning to use the cord.

Greeting her with an amused grin, he chuckled, "Kinky, are we burning me or tying me up?"

Getting him drunk was going to take all day. "Does it matter?" Arrianna coldly seduced, removing her shorts.

"Not really," Bad Markus taunted, wriggling his bottoms off, with lusty devious eyes.

Stripping off her shirt, Arrianna tossed it at his face and prompted, "Your turn."

Smelling her shirt like a freak, he looked up, took in her lacy see-through G-string lingerie, exhaled, and admitted, "I should have texted you back."

"Yes, you should have, but you didn't," she accused. He reached for her ankle. Whapping him with the cord, she scolded, "I haven't given you permission to touch me. Do I need to tie you up?"

"You should," he agreed, enticed.

Plot twist, he was all for it. Running the curling iron cord between her fingers, Arrianna warned, "You know the rules, touch me, and I'll leave you here."

"I'm not blind, you're turned on too," he taunted, gazing at her erect peaks, straining through the lace.

She was... her body was reacting to the visual. "Don't move a muscle," she asserted. Straddling his lap, his bulge twitched. With her lacy breasts in his face, Arrianna whispered, "That counts as moving a muscle." She bound his hands with the cord behind his back, tightened it and seductively licked his chest, checking his nipple piercing, disguising it as foreplay.

Groaning loudly, as she slid her hand into his underwear and cupped his groin, Bad Markus chuckled, "I'm going to go off before we've done anything if you keep this up."

With her lacy chest against his, she whispered, "I

haven't given you permission to speak." He twitched in the palm of her hand. She grabbed the bottle of whisky and took a swig to stifle the familiar ache. Needing freedom to search and a closer look, she had an idea. She blindfolded him with her shirt and tore away his underwear. Tenderly kissing his thigh, she hovered her mouth to check out his piercing. *There was nothing out of the ordinary. He needed to go nighty night so she could check his pockets. She had an idea.* Continuing the naughty game, Arrianna straddled him with lace as the only barrier between her and his ridged instrument of pleasure. Grinding against him, she taunted, "You should have called me back." *The titillating friction was doing it for her.* Rocking her hips, she commanded, "Never do it again."

"Never, I won't, keep going," Bad Markus begged with a pained expression.

Pleasure imploded, Arrianna stifled her reaction as he groaned. Confident he'd do anything she said, she whispered in his ear, "Baby, I need healing energy."

Gasping, Bad Markus chuckled, "You can have anything you want."

Placing her hands on his chest, she drained his energy. He slumped over on the pillows, Arrianna scrambled around searching pockets. *Damn it, there was nothing suspicious. Nothing new. What now?* Leaping up, she darted down the hall, opened the door and frantically waved. Grey dashed out of the other RV, she let him in.

Taking in her lingerie and flushing cheeks, Grey toyed, "Hi Arrianna."

"I took enough energy to knock him out. I don't know how long I have. There's nothing out of the ordinary," she quietly explained as he followed her down the hall.

Taking in the kinky majesty of their leader blindfolded, naked, and bound with piercings, Grey whispered, "Did you check his ass?"

"No," Arrianna asserted, "You do it."

Scowling, Grey whispered, "You're his girlfriend."

She'd barely grazed his rear when blindfolded Markus stirred, mumbling, "That's nice. Do that."

Shit! She put her hands on his chest, drained more, and he went limp. Looking up at Grey, she implored, "What am I supposed to do?"

"I'd wash my hands," Grey chuckled.

They went to the washroom, he pressed the pump soap, saying, "I've got your back."

Shaking her head, she mumbled, "I barely touched him."

"I was joking. I can't believe you tried to check," Grey giggled, evading a swat.

Shooting him a dirty look, she whispered, "Why did they send you over?"

"I lost rock, paper, scissors," Grey confessed, grinning. "Also, I've seen you naked before." He waved his hands in her direction. Pointing to the backroom, he admitted, "That shit is going to haunt me for decades."

"Be serious Grey, what are we going to do?" Arrianna whispered.

"Quick, take out his piercings before he wakes up, I'll give them to Jenna. Tell him we need the bunks. Get a room, see what he takes with him," Grey whispered. "Make sure he's out. Do it now, I'll wait."

With her hands on his chest, Arrianna drained his energy. Bad Markus slumped over on the pillows as she searched his pockets. "I can't lose him," she stated, placing piercings into the Kleenex in Grey's hand.

Wrapping it up, Grey answered, "You won't. Keep

him with us. Use whatever means necessary. Emery offered to do it if you can't."

No, Emery wasn't touching her boyfriend's body. "Can't we just force him to tell us where Markus is?" Arrianna whispered at the door.

"We don't know how high up it goes. You'll get a room and keep him distracted while they search through personal items. We'll figure it out," Grey whispered, squeezing her shoulder. He went to leave, turned back and said, "Arrianna, you don't have to do this. Emery will take your place. I'd take your place if I could."

Smiling, Arrianna replied, "I've got this. Get out of here."

19
DISTRACTIONS AND REACTIONS

*H*ungover, they drove into the closest town, playing tourist for the remainder of the morning. Keeping the topic of Bad Markus mute, they enjoyed a touch of normalcy babysitting newbies. Kayn managed to fight off her Canadian reflex to apologise for threatening to chase Dean through the woods with a chainsaw, knowing what her duties entailed. *Why make friends with victims of a future murder spree?* They tried on clothes and only picked up unperishable supplies. After going to a snake emporium with all kinds of creepy-crawly creatures, they stopped for lunch. A clock on the wall played a tune she recognised announcing a new hour. Zach snatched one of her fries. Scowling at her Handler, Kayn laughed, "Why didn't you order fries?"

Pouting, Zach replied, "My onion rings were soggy."

"Have mine," Dean offered, shoving his plate over. "I want to be buffed before this infamous Testing people keep referring to but won't explain."

Snagging a fry, Zach chuckled, "We're not allowed to say much. As soon as the baby comes, you'll be worked to the bone." Looking at Emma, he asked, "Feeling alright, hun?"

"Happy to be drinking a milkshake, instead of orange juice," Emma commented, rolling her eyes.

Smiling, Kayn exclaimed, "Guru Grey means well."

"Guru Grey, that's funny," Killian laughed boisterously. "Still hungry, Sami?"

Samid replied, "Bored stiff. Why couldn't we stay at the campsite and hang out with everyone else?"

"Administrative difficulties," Zach answered, eating one of Dean's fries.

Snickering, Kayn sparred, "Management problems."

"Why not just tell us what's going on? We're Ankh too," Molly asked, drinking her shake, eyeing up Orin.

"When are you due, Emma?" Orin switched the subject, watching the pregnant girl drinking a shake balanced on her tummy.

"Honestly, I don't even know what day of the week it is," Emma mumbled, stirring her shake.

Astrid's cell rang. She walked away from the table to talk. *She wasn't sure how this Markus scenario was going to play out, but she had a feeling she was going to be separated from Frost.* Watching Astrid pacing outside the front door running a hand through her short blonde hair, it was obviously bad news. *Of course.* Playing with her straw as Astrid came back, Kayn looked up and said, "We're taking off, aren't we?"

"After they're done searching the RV," Astrid disclosed, visibly concerned.

"How bad is it?" Killian probed.

"We'll talk about it in the car. Pack up your food," Astrid instructed.

Giving her a half hug, Zach teased, "It won't be forever, you'll be able to sleep tonight."

Samid chuckled, "So will the wolves."

Smacking the back of his head, Killian scolded, "Don't be a dick, Sami. She's going to miss her friend with benefits."

Finishing the remnants of her shake with a noisy slurp, Haley clarified, "Boyfriend."

"That blows my mind," Killian chuckled, putting their wrappers on the tray.

As he put their trash in the garbage, Astrid whispered, "Ignore him. He's missing his trolling buddy."

Trolling. That was funny. She wasn't ready to let him go, even for a day. This was the afterlife she'd signed up for though. They drove back to the campground listening to the newbie's debating random situations.

With dancing chestnut eyes, Molly bantered, "If someone gets rid of the ghost and it comes back is that repossession?"

"In theory," Zach laughed.

Curious, Dean flirted, "Hey, sexy Viking guy, can you get repossessed?"

Grinning, Killian answered, "If you're stupid."

"How so," Dean bantered.

"Avoid people who only have pupils," Killian chuckled.

Molly laughed, "That's in every horror movie, are you telling me that's real?"

"It is," Emma confirmed, gazing out the window.

Playfully poking her, Molly badgered, "How would you know?"

Emma responded, "I'm Clairvoyant and Psychic, having visions of future events comes with afterlife spoilers."

Testing her, Samid pestered, "Are you having a boy or a girl?"

Emma stated as fact, "A girl."

Samid pressed, "What are you going to name her?"

"Don't," Killian reprimanded, giving him a look.

"I'm not naming her. She's not going to be mine," Emma admitted with strength far beyond her years.

Catching on, Sami apologised, "Sorry, I wasn't thinking."

"It's just how it is," Emma answered, smiling sweetly.

Placing a hand on her shoulder, Molly decreed, "You're doing a selfless thing, it's heroic."

She couldn't help but feel endeared to the likeable misfit. Little Molly, a lively waitress with doe eyes was the five's first job alone after Testing. Zach had just been shoved into an unwanted role as her Handler. As a Conduit, the Siren was the only ability she'd figured out how to trigger. They were supposed to kidnap a girl who survived Correction. When Trinity showed up, there was nowhere to hide, so they made out in the stairwell. They were so bad at their jobs the leader of Trinity showed up at their hotel room to stop them from embarrassing themselves. Like naïve simpletons, they went for dinner with Trinity. Triad drugged everyone, but Lexy and Grey saved the day. She'd woken up on her bunk driving down the highway with the waitress locked in the bathroom of their RV. Lexy sent her back there with Zach to mark her Ankh. When they unlocked the door, Molly attacked Zach with a plunger. She giggled every time she thought about it. She felt responsible for Molly, she'd branded her Ankh.

Killian cave manned, from the backseat, "Unicorn girl, my cell is charging, pass it back here." When there was no response, he went full Neanderthal, whistling and shouting, "Unicorn girl, cellphone!"

Everyone was looking at each other with wide eyes. *He was purposely trying to irritate Haley.*

"Slam on the breaks, he's not wearing his seatbelt,"

Haley muttered, playing the game.

Even Sami seemed shocked. Was this his idea of flirting? Maybe he didn't know what decade he was in?

Driving, Astrid laughed, "Viking boy, let me save you some time, she's never going to respond to Unicorn Girl."

"You call me Viking boy, what's the difference?" Killian toyed, invading Haley's bubble by kicking the back of her seat.

It was like a kid throwing sand at their playground crush.

Turning back, Haley said, "Seriously?"

"He's got me there," Astrid commented, as tires jumped a pothole, bouncing everyone in their seats.

Haley looked back and smiled, shaking her head.

Grinning, Killian ribbed, "Unicorn Girl likes me."

"I assure you, she does not," Haley bantered, pitching his phone at him.

"Don't you want to put your number in it first?" The burly Adonis, baited. When there was no response, Killian nudged Zach, saying, "Do you have her number handy?"

"She'll kill me in my sleep, I can't," Zach whispered.

Glancing back, squinting, Haley enquired, "Why me?"

Peering up from his phone, Killian giggled.

Her phone vibrated, Haley read the message, grinning. She tossed an empty coffee cup at Killian, demanding, "Who gave it to you?"

Chuckling as they parked, Killian replied, "That's a clear violation of bro code."

Leaning over to peek at Haley's texts, Astrid whispered, "He finds you fascinating."

Getting out, Haley mumbled, "He finds a spool of thread fascinating."

Shimmying out of the backseat, Killian said, "She's

so mean to me."

Haley swatted Grey's butt as she walked past. He leapt and giggled when he saw who smacked him. He called after her, "Love you too, Haley!"

Beaming, Lexy scolded, "What did you do?"

With an arm around her waist, Grey kissed Lexy's cheek, giggling, "It doesn't matter. She'll only have that number for five minutes."

Wandering up to Lexy and Grey, Orin commented, "I hope I get to stay with you guys."

She spent most of her time observing like a scientist, deciphering the reason for everything. She didn't need mindless TV anymore. You don't go looking for drama when it's your afterlife theme. She was a player in an immortal game on the Ankh channel. Frost was moving seats out of the RV with Jenna and Lily. *There was her sexy boyfriend.* Kayn sauntered over, asking, "Is there a reason we're not all helping?"

Looking her way, Lexy explained, "We were getting in the way. There's a method to their madness."

"I'm too sexy, it's distracting," Grey chuckled, adding his two cents.

"Seems legit," Kayn teased, watching Frost's perspiration glistening in the sun. *Somebody is too sexy for sure. She didn't want to leave him.*

"Why are we removing seats?" Killian enquired, watching the trio work.

Lexy answered, "They're checking for bugs and tracking devices. Markus has been switched out with a Third-Tier, that's all we know. Arrianna and Bad Markus got a room. Jenna, Frost and Lily have the room next door."

She knew they were splitting them up. Damn it. Every time they spent the night together, her libido was off the hook cranked up for weeks.

"I've seen too much today," Grey said. "We can't leave until they're sure we're not being tracked. How's Emma?"

Watching Frost shirtless in sunshine like an eyecatching beacon, Kayn replied, "Ready to be done with pregnancy."

"Did you make sure she had orange juice?" Grey grilled, watching Emma waddling after the others like an adorable downtrodden duck.

Astrid wandered past, saying, "She drank ten glasses of orange juice, Daddy Grey." Catching the unintended double meaning, Astrid glanced back, laughing, "That might stick."

Before she went into Immortal Testing, everyone seemed perfect. She knew better now. The Ankh were mismatched tragic fools. Comically disorganised, their jobs rarely went as planned, but they handled plot twists like champs. They played hard, loved harder and were magically flawed. The perfect family to spend eternity with.

Frost jogged over, gave her a giant sweaty bear hug and seduced, "I'll need a shower before I go."

Wrapped in his arms, inhaling his addictive scent, Kayn provoked, "You'd better, I have needs."

Sticking her head out of the RV, Jenna shouted, "Killian! Take over for Frost!"

"Race you there," Frost taunted, taking off like Jenna's words were gunshot at a horse race.

Everything about him turned her on. Sprinting after him, Kayn quickly caught up. With their footsteps turning up dust, they raced, each one pushing ahead for only a second before the other gunned it. Booking it up a hill at full speed, she glanced back and down she went rolling ass over tea kettle down the hill. On her back, laughing. His grinning face moved over the blue sky in dazzling sunshine, making it look like he had a glowing halo.

"You are an intoxicatingly beautiful accident-prone hot mess. I'm so into you, it makes me crazy," Frost confessed, tenderly kissing her. Pulling away, he asked, "Are you okay?"

Tugging him on top of her, Kayn's heart soared. It felt like she was still falling as their lips met. In a beat of their hearts, they were breathlessly lost, seducing each other with their tongues and hands. Mid wild public make-out session, she rolled him over, pinned him beneath her and enticed, "Right here? This early in the afternoon? What if someone needs to use the washroom?"

Dreamily gazing into her eyes with sun shining behind her crooked halo, Frost dared, "I'm not worried about it."

Recklessly, stripping off clothing, laughing. They were a combustible pair with an intense need to push each other's buttons. Ration and modesty were just words used by boring people, and they were the only ones in the universe when they were in each other's arms. Merging under a sweltering sun, each savage thrust intensified euphoria until whimpers of passion were muffled by a breathless kiss. With her nerve endings humming, wanting nothing more than to stay like this forever, Kayn whispered, "We definitely need a shower now."

Jiggling as he giggled beneath her, she pulled away to look into his eyes. Biting her lip as her lust fried mind searched for words. *He rocked her world. It was lame but true.*

"We won't be apart for long," Frost promised with the intensity of their union evident in his eyes.

Lovingly, caressing his shiny dark hair, she sighed,

"Now, you've jinxed it, don't forget about me."

"Never," Frost vowed, with devotion in his gaze. "We're going to get busted by someone. We're pushing our luck."

"Race you there," Kayn said, leaping up and scrambling into her clothes. *He took off before her. Damn it.* She chased him down. Laughing as they reached the washrooms, they each yanked on a door.

Denied entry by locks, she laughed, "Nooo!"

"I'll have a shower when I get to the hotel," he sighed.

Playfully whacking him, Kayn scolded, "We may be on the road driving for days."

Chuckling, Frost bantered, "I didn't push you down that hill."

True. She was already dirty when things got out of hand. Kayn commented, "Maybe someone is in there?"

"Who?" Frost naughtily questioned, pinning her against the building. Untucking her hair from her shirt, he nuzzled her neck, whispering, "I want you in my bed for days."

Grinning so hard her cheeks hurt, she closed her eyes as he slid his hands under her tank top, caressing her breasts, nibbling on her ear. *She wanted to confess everything in her heart. If Frost interrogated her for anything, she was toast. She loved him.* As her Siren nerves frazzled, Kayn grabbed a fistful of his hair, forcing him to look at her, provoking, "Are you all talk?" Before she took a breath, his lips aggressively met hers as they made out like lust starved heathen's in a dark closet, scratching her back against the building. With a twinge of pain, her Healing ability revved its engine, heating her flesh. A stranger came out of the washroom and shimmied past. *Oh, thank god.* They darted in, locking the door.

"Are you all talk?" Frost taunted, stripping off his

shorts, vanishing into a stall.

Being with him really was a crazy amount of cardio. Taking her top off, flinging her shorts and undergarments, she joined him, seducing, "You were saying?" Stepping into his slippery embrace, he forcefully spun her around, so her hands were against the wall. *Public bathroom pump soap always made her itchy.* She couldn't will the words from her lips as hands journeyed over slopes into valleys. Sudsy hands slid between her legs from behind, she gasped as her knees buckled. Talking her through it, Frost whispered wicked goals, rapidly rubbing until she was whimpering his name, pleading with him. He took her so close to the edge the sensation was beginning to swell, then backed her away like an asshole as she clawed the walls. Livid, Kayn spun to face him, he lifted her, and in a few thrusts, she was surging with inside-twisting euphoria, clinging to him, crying out as he gave it his all against the wall. After numerous toe-curling crescendos, Frost groaned with violent final thrusts, swearing.

She clenched and moaned, "Don't stop."

Digging his nails into her backside, gasping for breath, he cautioned, "Don't move, not a muscle, I'll fall."

She wanted more. She did it again.

Chuckling, Frost whispered in her ear, "Next time we're going to be in a bed."

The words slid off her tongue, "I love you."

With his hot breath on her neck, he persevered, knowing she needed it, without answering until she finished. They slipped and fell. He chuckled, "I warned you."

Catching her breath, Kayn laughed, "You could have just said the words."

Caressing her damp hair, he admitted, "Tearing

down the walls protecting my heart when it's not based on ration is a process. You scare the shit out of me, Brighton."

She didn't know how to play these games. He scared her too. "Let me understand this, you pick and choose when we say the words? One day we say it, and the next, someone mentions the word and you shutdown. If you love me back have the balls to say it," she decreed, getting up to gather her things.

"Do you really want to get into an argument right now? Does that seem wise?" He sarcastically remarked, following her, tugging on shorts.

Now, she was pissed. Boldly facing him, Kayn said, "When I put myself out there and say the words, you need to say it back. I'm trying to be understanding, but you're not making all the rules. Let me love you or stop wasting my time and walk away." *What was she doing?* She stormed out without looking back. *He wasn't following her.* Trudging back to the campsite, aware she'd overreacted, she wanted to apologise but wasn't sure if it was just easier than standing her ground. Her head was pounding. Her ears started ringing, and she dropped to her knees, shrieking.

AT THE CAMPSITE, THEY WERE putting everything back into the RV getting ready to go, when Zach, turned and ran away. Everyone else followed as Kayn's screaming echoed through the desert.

Pacing back and forth angrily as they approached, Frost said, "Relax, it's an Enlightening. I'm only angry at myself, I should have known something was wrong when she picked a fight and stormed off."

Glaring, Zach accused, "What did you say?"

"It's what I didn't say," Frost mumbled. Looking at her Handler, he explained, "I'm an idiot."

"Leave these two with her. It's evolution pain. Let's go, nothing to see here," Grey ushered everyone away.

As the other's wandered off, looking back worried, Zach prompted, "You might as well tell me."

"I love her so much it hurts," Frost confessed, "Fear creeps in and stops me from saying it back sometimes. She took off, I didn't go after her."

Watching her writhing in agony, Zach whispered, "Your situation can't be easy, but hers isn't either. How do I fix it? Am I supposed to try?"

"Let it happen, it'll run its course. There's no way to skip past this, everyone has to go through it," Frost responded. Guiltily watching her seizing in the sand, he caved, "If it goes on too long, your immortal and her Handler, you can try."

Jenna walked up, urging, "Emery and Mel are back. We need to go. Zach will talk to her. You can text her later. We shouldn't leave Arrianna alone."

Hesitating, Frost touched Zach's shoulder and said, "Tell her I'm sorry. Make sure she knows I'll do better."

Understanding what he was saying, Zach answered, "Go, take care of Arrianna. I've got this." Wishing he had a lawn chair as they walked away, he watched her writhing in agony until his heart couldn't take it anymore.

Hours lapsed before Killian showed up. Zach got up to stretch his legs. The burly immortal passed a book. "This might help you pass the time. Hungry?"

"Starving, thanks for this," Zach stated, waving the book. "I was about to do something stupid."

Grinning, Killian chuckled, "Do tell."

Watching her squirm, Zach disclosed, "Instinct wants me to touch her."

Wincing, Killian cautioned, "Trust me, you don't want to do that." His phone buzzed, Big Sexy texted someone back.

Zach probed, "Frost?"

"You haven't been texting him back," Killian chuckled.

"My cell is in the RV," Zach sparred.

"Have you just been sitting here alone for hours?" Killian asked, "Why didn't you say anything?"

Zach ribbed, "My telekinesis is choppy in these parts."

"You could have gone back to get your phone?" Killian countered.

"I didn't want her to wake up alone," Zach replied. "If you bring my cell and a snack, I'll text Frost. What's going on over there?"

The burly immortal disclosed, "They're having dinner at a restaurant pretending Markus is really Markus."

Her shrieking and squirming amped up a few octaves. A blast of energy knocked both men off their feet, rippling away under sand like an earthquake tremor. Thousands of snakes slithered out of the cracked desert floor. "I hope this is a hallucination," Zach stammered, scrambling backwards, kicking away swarming reptiles. Fangs sunk into his ankle, he shrieked, "Get it off! Help!"

Terrified, Killian yanked the snake off like a hero and whipped it away. Scurrying out of harm's way, Zach tripped over Kayn and commenced screaming, thrashing with her. With the pair flailing, slithering reptiles slid between their limbs until they vanished beneath a slithering mass, Killian carefully backed away, "Hard no. I'll get help!" He sprinted to the campsite with a mass of snakes in pursuit, frantically screaming, "Snakes! Help me! Do something!"

Roasting hotdogs over a campfire as the massive frantic immortal bombarded them, losing his shit, Grey casually said, "This is new."

Twirling, tugging imaginary snakes off his body, Killian was panicking, "They're biting me! Eating us! No! Please!"

Grey calmly rationalised, "Buddy, calm down. It's okay, you're hallucinating. There's nothing on you, man."

Creeping up, Lexy snapped frantic immortal's neck and decreed, "Well, that was enough of that. Guess we'd better check on Kayn's Enlightening."

Grey commented, "I hate snakes, take Orin."

Getting up, Orin laughed, "I'll go."

"Can I come?" Molly eagerly offered, taking her stick out of the fire.

Amused by Molly's infatuation, Lexy went with Orin, saying, "You should stay. We don't know what that was, I'll go."

Orin yelled, "You guys put Killian in the RV and protect Grey from imaginary snakes!"

"You suck!" Grey called out as they walked away. Getting up, he sighed, "Come on, kids. Grab a limb, let's get the big guy inside. He'll be down until they come back to heal him."

Once they were out of earshot, Orin flirted, "Pulling the awkward, ex booty call Band-Aid off by volunteering to come with me?"

"Maybe a little," Lexy countered, strolling away with her crimson hair shimmering in sunlight. Smiling, she enquired, "Are we good?"

Grinning, Orin replied, "We're good."

In comfortable silence, they followed heavy prints until they approached the area where they left Kayn. They were gone. "Do you feel that," Lexy asked, with her lips moving, but not an insect's buzz or crackle of steps in gravelly sand registered in isolating silence. The hair on her arms rose as unnerving icy wind passed through her. A wave of nausea hit as ill-omened shadows snuffed out the sun and azure sky.

The temperature descended as rapid breaths pirouetted, Orin mouthed the words, "What is this?"

With not a star, nor a moon in darkness, turmoil ceased. Merging with dark places, the Dragon gazed into the onyx nothing with zen solidarity. Observing Orin yelling into his phone with the volume off and then… nothing.

Shadows extended until the desert was swallowed by darkness. Orin lost sight of Lexy in the vacuous muted void. Grasping the plausible scenarios, everything was in slow-mo. *Alone in the nefarious surroundings, it felt like a nightmare. Maybe it was? He was asleep on his bunk.* Something creepily caressed his hair. *No, no, he wasn't doing this.* Ducking, Orin tried bolting away with furry things pushing against his legs inhibiting movement. *These weren't snakes. Kittens? He needed to believe they were kittens.* Wading through the knee-high fuzzy herd with burning calves, his palm heated. *No, he didn't need a visual.* His Ankh symbol strobed, revealing enormous furry spiders as far as the eye could see. He talked himself down, *spider's sense fear. Be calm, be mellow. You are intelligent. You do not need to lose your shit.* The brand on his hand flashed another image as arachnid fangs sunk into his thigh. He tore spiders off with full-body heebie geebies and nowhere to run. *He was bleeding.* The urge to shriek hysterically was overpowering logic. *He was going to have to fight, he wasn't ready.* His legs heated as they healed, but not fast enough to avoid riling up the writhing hoard, fangs sunk into his flesh, hairy legs crawled up his skin as the ravenous eight-legged monstrosities mercilessly attacked. Fending off spiders with spine-chilling visuals each time his symbol flashed, the herd of arachnid's swapped eating him for saving him for later as sticky web bound his body. Struggling, Orin was rapidly spun into a cocoon. Once his legs were encased, they gave him a yank, and he toppled over. *They were going to stab him and liquefy his insides. He hated spiders. This was going to suck. He really didn't want to do this today.* Squirming, he froze. *He shouldn't make himself more appealing by being feisty. Lexy was down the Dragon of the night rabbit hole, she wasn't going to notice he was in trouble until he was killed, triggering longer strobes of her symbol. The Dragon's priority would be Grey. What if they were all encased by spiders? He might be furthest down the* list. *Grey, then newbies, Killian was already dead that lucky bastard. Damn it, he was an immortal.* Grasping his unfortunate predicament, Orin chuckled. *There was no purpose in awaiting impalement. Nobody was coming to save him.* Each time his symbol went off, spider shadows loomed ominously behind a white web veil. *He might lose it. He was going to have to bust out of this.* Opting to go out fighting, he punched through the cocoon and writhed his way out with relentless fangs punching into his flesh. Sweltering hot as his healing ability fought the good fight, it imploded, in the next strobe of his symbol, he saw a path. Released a battle cry, Orin ran through the herd waving his arms broiling hot until the lights went out.

BACK AT THE CAMPSITE, THEY'D finished putting the massive immortal on a bottom bunk and were all standing there as the RV dimmed.

Reaching for the cord, Dean gave it a tug and said, "The light's burnt out."

A wave of nausea washed over Grey as the temperature rapidly dropped. *There was no time. He couldn't do it by himself.* Grabbing a bag of salt out of the closet, Grey tossed it to Dean, barking out orders, "Get wet, cover yourselves in salt, Emma first. Nobody leaves the bathroom." Armed with his own bag of salt and a knife, Grey leapt out of the RV into frigid darkness. Stabbing the bag, he encircled the RV giving the newbies spiritual protection and went back in. Standing on the other side of the bathroom door, Grey asserted, "Lock the door.

Stay in here, no matter what anyone says, even me. They can imitate our voices. They will try to trick you. Your symbols will warm and flash as each of us goes down just like it did for Killian. We have this. Ignore the urge to help. We're immortal, death is temporary. Protect the baby, stay in here no matter what."

On the bunk across from Killian, Grey tried texting the others but there as no signal. *It didn't feel like they were safe with only him as the line of defence.* Clutching a knife in the darkness, with his heart palpitating, he went in the closet and dumped a barrier of salt in front of the bathroom door. Running to the kitchen sink, he turned on the water. It made a creaky noise as it started running. Planning to splash it on himself, he cupped his hands under the tap. His palms filled with a thick warm substance. *He smelled pennies. His hands were full of blood. He hadn't circled the RV with salt fast enough. They weren't protected. It wasn't safe inside.* Pacing in darkness, he took off the bracelet, stifling his pyrokinesis and went outside.

In a flash of light, he was back at his mortal family's rural home in Scotland. The six-year-old version of himself came out of the house with a toothless grin. *He barely recalled the time before they moved to Australia.*

His mother's voice hollered, "Greydon Zoa Riley, don't you dare leave the property!"

Momma. Mortal memories lured his consciousness away. *He needed to see his mom.* Smelling dinner as he went into his house, the beauty of a carefree childhood filled his senses. From the pictures with people he didn't recognise in the hall to the sensation of the rug beneath his feet, everything felt vaguely familiar. As he walked into the kitchen with yellow curtains and sunflower wallpaper, his mother carried on with dinner preparations. The rotary phone on the wall rang.

His mom turned and answered with her usual joke, "Riley summer home. Some are home and some are not."

Something about this place felt off. In the open cupboard were dishes with a pattern he didn't recognise. *Not much came to Australia. Including his mother's red hair. She'd always been blonde, hadn't she?* His heart reminisced as she chatted with easy humour until she looked out the window. He followed her line of sight to his six-year-old self, lighting the woodpile on fire with his mind. She dropped the phone, leaving the caller dangling as she ran out the backdoor.

His six-year-old self got up sobbing, "I'm sorry, Momma. I didn't mean to."

Kicking the smoking log away from the pile, she threw dirt on it. "Give me the matches," his mother commanded, frisking him for what he'd started the fire with.

Blubbering, his childhood self wept, "I don't got any."

Kneeling, compassionately looking into his eyes his mom corrected, "I don't have any."

Looking up guiltily, his young self repeated, "I don't have any."

"Play inside where I can keep an eye you until dinner is ready, I left Aunt Everly on the phone," his mom stated.

Following his younger self inside, he wanted to hear his mother's conversation. *He didn't remember Aunt Everly.*

Hanging up as he came in, his mom prompted, "Go play with your sisters. I'll call you when dinner's ready, sweetie. I'm nightshift tonight. Auntie will be watching you."

Sisters? He had an infant sister at sixteen when he joined

Ankh. She'd survived his Correction. He'd been forced to finish the job when she was a teenager. This must be a dream. Confident it wasn't real, and curious about the rest of the house, Grey followed his childhood self upstairs to a room he didn't remember with bunk beds and a single bed. *This had to be a dream.*

A girl of eight or nine ran into the room giggling with a paper in her hand, chased by a teenage girl, scolding, "Give it back!" Snatching it off her, the older one stuck her head out the door, yelling, "I need my own room!"

What was this? It flashed forward to bedtime. His mother kissed the younger girl on the forehead, whispering, "Sweet dreams till sunbeams find you, Wendy Marie." She did the same to his younger self. Giving the girl on the top bunk a pat, his mom reminded, "No middle of the night phone calls Carol Ann, you're grounded."

"Whatever," the teenager answered, pulling covers over her head.

Time lapsed as he went downstairs. Aunt Everly was on the couch, engrossed in a book. Someone knocked on the door. She got up, mumbling, "Carol Ann, if that boy is here, your mother is going to kill you."

Shivers ran up his spine as Aunt Everly's hand reached for the doorknob. Shaking her head, she panicked, "No, no." A rifle boomed. His aunt looked down at the circle of red spreading on her nightgown and flopped in the doorway.

In a heartbeat, he was his six-year-old self, being picked up with dozy eyes and dangling legs, Carol Ann hid him in the closet, whispering, "Not a peep, Greydon."

The door in their room closed. It was eerily quiet. Carol Ann screamed. A shot rang out. Covering his mouth with her hand, Wendy Marie moved a plank and forced him into a small space. Concealing his hiding spot with the board, she whispered, "Not a peep, Greydon."

He recognised voices, but his sleepy mind couldn't grasp it. The closet creaked open.

Wendy Marie started crying, "Don't hurt me, don't."

"Well, hello little girl," a male voice said. "Where is your brother?"

With a shaky voice, Wendy Marie lied, "He's not here. He slept at a friend's house."

The gun clicked. *Momma.* Covering his ears as his sister pled for her life, Grey rocked, hugging his knees to his chest with eyes squeezed shut. A shot rang out. His eyes met with the shooters through the hole in the wall.

"There you are," the man taunted, reaching in.

He scrambled between boards. The stranger caught his ankle and hauled him out. Clawing at wood, he was dragged by his sister, carried past the other in the hall squirming, and dropped at the top of the stairs. Fear-induced flames shot from his hands, engulfing his captors. He slid down a railing as a shot hit the wall, he ran down a country road until he stumbled, and everything went dark.

It flashed to the here and now. *He felt it in his bones. They were here. They'd come for the baby.* "I'm not a child anymore," He decreed as crimson flames shot from his hands, igniting his assailant. *There was no volume on the screaming.* Protecting the door, he ignited everything trying to gain entry until he was drained of energy. Lightheaded, Grey staggered back into the RV, felt pain in his back and went down.

20

NO REST FOR THE WICKED

*L*imply plummeting into the in-between, vaguely aware of the pressure of decent, Kayn's mind sparked. Blinking, she burst through damp clouds towards the rapidly approaching clean slate desert. *What? Where? Oh, shit. Her limbs wouldn't work. She couldn't stop. This was going to suck.* Closing her eyes, she splatted on the sand. *The explosion of pain wasn't stopping. Come on. She was still conscious. This was inconvenient.* She heard Zach screaming. A loud thud followed by a cloud of sand sprayed everywhere like a baptism of ineptitude. *He missed her. That was good. Naptime.* She closed her eyes.

"There's no rest for the wicked," Killian's voice baited.

He had her there. Squinting in the sunshine, Kayn rolled over. Staring at a multihued blue sky with fluffy clouds, she saw Killian looming above in a halo of sunlight, smiling.

"What in the hell was that? You landed like a

Newb," Big Sexy teased offering her a hand up with his hair majestically flowing in the breeze.

Standing in the in-between with her perception rattled, Kayn wiggled her toes in the silky sand, stating, "Guess we're dead? I don't remember anything, it's blank."

"We've been here for a while," Killian revealed.

"We've?" Kayn probed, noticing nearly every full Ankh at the campsite. *What happened?*

"That was brutal," Zach groaned, facedown in the sand.

Crouched by her Handler, Kayn teased, "Rise and shine."

"I need a minute, or twenty," Zach laughed. Looking up, he noticed Killian, saying, "What are you doing here?"

"I was chased by imaginary snakes. Lexy snapped my neck," Killian admitted as they joined the others.

Seems legit. That was usually the reason she ended up here. Lexy wasn't here yet. Her sister was such a badass. Kayn asked, "Lexy's still alive."

Vacantly pitching sand, Grey mumbled, "Of course."

"What happened? Spill, I'd like to know what I'm waking up too. I'm only dead for a short time," Kayn rushed.

"You were having an Enlightening, thousands of snakes attacked us. Zach tripped over you, joining the madness. I ran for help," Killian decreed. "That's all I know."

Orin admitted, "Spiders ate me, it was unpleasant."

Joining the conversation, Astrid disclosed, "Our symbols went off. When we showed up, Lexy was chasing a lizard around the desert like a ravenous animal, Grey was lighting things on fire, and there was a singed corpse on the ground. We called for back up and tried talking Grey down."

"Clearly, it didn't go well," Haley added, smiling.

Normally, Grey would have felt horrible and apologised. "What happened?" Kayn probed, gauging Grey's reaction.

Solemnly, Grey shared, "We moved to Australia when I was ten. I've only ever had foggy memories of my childhood in Scotland. Now, I know I had older sisters and another life. I didn't just have a Correction as a teenager. They came for me as a child. My sisters sacrificed themselves to keep me safe. Remembering erased mortal trauma, set me off."

Wishing Lexy was here, Kayn took his hand as her sister would and met his teary eyes, asking, "Are you sure it wasn't a hallucination?"

As they gathered, Grey blankly shared, "In the middle of the night, my teenage sister hid me in the closet with a sister who wasn't much older and told us to be quiet. They shot her in the upstairs hall. The sister I was hiding with put me in a cubby in the back of the closet. She lied about where I was, and they shot her. The bullet went through the wall, and they found me. I set their murderer's on fire at six-years-old and ran down a country road until I passed out."

Mortal memories were sacred, somebody erased his. Embracing Grey, Kayn whispered, "I'm sorry that happened to you."

In her arms, Grey teased, "Why be sorry? You didn't do it."

"It's a Canadian thing," Kayn ribbed, holding him tighter, happy his sense of humour reared its head to ease the pain.

As each Ankh took turns hugging him, she witnessed the beauty of a marriage of souls. All was forgiven as each did their part to soothe his pain, reminding him, he wasn't alone. In the afterlife, mortal memories snuck up on you. They all understood this. At times, she thought it would be easier to forget those beautiful simpler times. The parents she adored still haunted her in crowds. She'd swear it was one of them, and in a breath, she'd be needing that lost connection like oxygen. She'd lost many people along the way. Her carefree brother Matty who'd died courageously had been tiered up and reincarnated. Her father's friend Jenkins, who stepped up after the loss of her parents so Matty could keep going to university. Her deceased twin was with her always, and for this, she'd been forced to let go of preconceived notions of who she was. Evolution had a price…Everything.

Rustling Grey's hair, Astrid baited, "I'm not much of a hugger." A beer appeared in her hands, she passed it to him.

Laughing, Grey raised the honey ale and sighed, "This is deeply touching, Astrid. I wasn't sure you liked me."

Impervious to his charms, Astrid ribbed, "I guess you're alright."

With a stranglehold bear hug, Killian chuckled, "I don't like you." Releasing Grey, the endearing giant, playfully side socked him, ribbing, "You're mediocre at best."

Seeing where this in-between reunion was headed, Kayn thought up a Pina Colada with a yellow bamboo decorative umbrella and saluted, "To friendship." Everyone envisioned a cocktail and clinked beverages as white light blinded the group. Shielding her eyes, squinting in the glare, Kayn smiled as she saw Azariah strolling towards Ankh trailing angelic luminescence. *This was the most amazing magical place.*

"Kayn, Zachariah, come with me," Azariah prompted, summoning the Handler Dragon duo. With a swoosh of her hand, they were standing in a cornfield.

It was a touch warmer. A soothing gust caressed her skin. Zach was eagerly husking corn. Kayn stated, "This must be about my Handler."

Parting corn like seas, the angelic entity glanced back, saying, "Yes, intuitive girl, this detour is for Zachariah."

Her eyes darted to Zach contently eating raw corn, Kayn probed, "What did you do?"

"Nothing that I know of," Zach answered, pitching his finished cob into the field.

Turning to face the duo, with a divinely floating gossamer gown, Azariah corrected, "Technically, something was done to you. Whether it's good or bad is in young Zachariah's hands. His nature leads me to believe he can handle this adjustment in his role."

Maybe he got his wish and wasn't her Handler anymore? The thought stung, so she looked for a beautiful distraction. Watching a ladybug meandering on a stalk. *Hello, imagination induced happy thing. She wanted to hold it.* The worshipped childhood treasure flitted into her outstretched palm. Spellbound as the ladybug ventured a ticklish path to her pointer finger and flew away, vanishing into the swirling blue sky, Kayn grinned.

"Child! Pay attention!" Azariah reprimanded, smiling.

She'd gapped out watching a ladybug like she was five. "I'm listening," Kayn assured, feeling like a space cadet.

"There was an incident where Zachariah jumped out of a moving vehicle. When you healed him, that tingle in your spine created a pathway. You've duplicated and transferred an ability to your Handler. The Enlightening Zachariah had at the cabin afterwards was his brain expanding to meet the ability's functional needs," Azariah patiently explained.

He was eating raw corn again, she was tempted.

Stoked about having an ability, Zach ceased gnawing on a cob long enough to say, "I was beginning to think I wasn't ever going to get one."

Happy he was thrilled, Kayn nudged him, teasing, "I'll take my thank you in the form of a foot massage."

Entertained by their juvenile repartee, Azariah revealed, "Before you get too excited, when you tripped into Kayn's Enlightening it's highly probable you were granted more abilities. You'll need to be entombed as your brain expands. Trust me, a multi-ability expansion is a level of excruciating you'd prefer to avoid. Emery will be acting as Handler proxy until Zachariah's growth has been dealt with. Obviously, the attachment won't be there, but Emery is powerful enough to subdue you until Zach returns."

She wasn't even sure she liked Emery. Kayn suggested, "Can't Frost do it?"

"For reasons I'm not at liberty to disclose, no," Azariah answered, watching Zach eating corn like nothing big was happening. Grinning, their Guardian explained, "Your Clan has been infiltrated. Your part in gifting young Zachariah powers must be kept quiet. If you keep doing this, word will spread. If you ever feel a tingling in your spine while healing someone, stop. Promise me."

Distracted by the urge to try raw corn before they left, Kayn plucked off a cob, replying, "No healing anyone if it tickles, got it." She took a bite. *It was tasty.*

Shaking her head, the angelic being, prompted, "Promise me."

What? Looking up from her treat, Kayn replied, "Sure, I promise."

"Heaven help us," Azariah waved for them to come with her, laughing. "Come on, one-track minded snackers. It'll be way less magical if you leave from here. Let's get back to the others. I'll explain Zachariah's tomb time out. He won't be gone long."

There was a luminescent explosion of white light as they returned to the desert where her Clan was sprawled enjoying slushy drinks in the sunshine. *It's a hard knock afterlife.* Before Kayn could join, she felt a tingle. *It was time to go.* She ceased watching the others play to ritually look at her hand as she disintegrated into sand, souring away on a light breeze in the in-between.

IN ONE BREATH, KAYN WAS SOMEWHERE MAGICAL, AND IN the next, she was in a dark place unable to breathe. She figured her situation out rather fast inhaling sand. *She'd been buried in the desert. There's Karma for you.* She forced a hand up, hitting rock or clay. *That wasn't up.* Shifting her shoulders, struggling, it felt like her legs were in cement. *Shit, she was going to pass out. It was a first for her, she didn't know what to do. Damn it.* She recalled Grey covering her eyes, giving her a speech in the surf, at the beginning of her immortal journey. *Pay attention, think. With her chest burning and head pounding, there wasn't enough time for deep thoughts, she needed air. Oxygen was her biggest necessity.* Squirming, she reached the other way, feeling the victory of movement. Wiggling her fingers as the headache ceased. Her eyelids felt weighted, everything went black.

· · ·

On her stomach in luxurious sand, Kayn opened her eyes and met everyone's impressed expressions. *Shit, she died again. This was embarrassing.*

"Well, that has to be a record," Grey chuckled, contently creating a sand sculpture masterpiece. "Is there a fight going on? What happened?"

Breathing deeply, Kayn calmed down enough to reply, "I haven't been buried alive before, give me a minute."

Grinning, Killian butt-scooted over and offered to help, "Are you in sand or dirt?"

"Sand," Kayn answered. "I went the wrong way. I only had enough time to get one hand out before I died."

"Sometimes, you have to take a few runs at it. Sand is heavy as cement when you're disoriented," Killian explained. "You'll wake up with a hand free, but you have less than five minutes to figure it out. Strength is my ability. The second run at it, I usually burst out. You have a crazy mix in you. You can do it."

Astrid joined the conversation, "Bring Grey's ability up. Make glass and bust out."

Shaking his head, Grey cautioned, "Heating sand you're stuck in, to 1700 Celsius for seven to ten minutes is a no chance scenario."

"Sexy the sand away, Siren," her Handler taunted, petting her hair.

Whenever someone patted her head like that she felt like a golden retriever. An occasionally rabid Old Yeller. Not fully rabid, just during special events like bar mitzvahs and graduations. As a sacrificial lamb for the greater good, she was put down like Old Yeller a lot.

Responding to her inner dialogue, Zach baited, "Golden retrievers are adorable, don't be so hard on yourself."

She'd give him a pass, just this once. Without enough time to think of a plan, Kayn felt a tingle and cursed, "See you in a few minutes, assholes." They were laughing as she turned to sand and floated away as a powdery heavenly afterthought becoming one with the in-between.

JOLTING TO LIFE IN A SANDY GRAVE, KAYN FELT SOMETHING moist moving by her exposed fingers. *Was that breathing? Damn it, something was breathing on her. If a coyote ate her fingers, she was going to lose it.* Wiggling her digits, she only shifted her arm. *Shoo, shoo.* It bit her wrist. Flailing, she couldn't shake it off. *Maybe it would play with her before it ate her?* The headache dulled and disappeared. *Time to reset the game. Oh, the irony.* She blacked out beneath desert sand.

ON HER TUMMY, IN THE SANDY WOMB-LIKE WARMTH OF THE in-between, Kayn sprung from death in the mortal world to life in the realm where Tri-Clan's come to play. Irritated, Kayn proclaimed, "A desert creature is eating my hand. I will maim the next one of you who cracks a joke. Get me out of this."

Ignoring her cautionary suggestion, Killian harassed, "I say she goes a few more rounds with the sand."

Did sexy Viking guy just slam her? What in the hell big aqua? Everyone looked pissed. She'd done something. She was afraid to ask.

With a playful shove, Zach disclosed, "After a tiff with your boyfriend, you released nightmare-inducing psychedelic toxins. We murdered each other."

She didn't even know what to say. That was impressive. Kayn laughed so hard, she fell backwards.

Tossing a handful of sand at her, Astrid teased, "If your boy toy pisses you off enough to kill everyone at a campsite, it's a waving red flag. We're not the cast of an eighty's horror movie."

With kind eyes, Grey chuckled, "I owe her one. Brighton knows she's forgiven."

Beneath infinite swirling shades of eternal cerulean sky, sprawling on her back, Kayn danced a finger through dips and swirls as she wrote his name, confessing her sins to the mesmerizing azure. In blissful warmth, she opted to enjoy her final moments in heaven without worrying about the possibility of hell. A tingling through her being as she moved from one plain to the next, left only delicate floating grains.

SQUINTING IN THE GLARE, KAYN OPENED HER EYES. *Ding, ding, ding, round three. Plot twist, who dug her out? Feral Lexy's face was uncomfortably close. She was covered in blood. Who was she eating? Hope it wasn't her.* She peered at her chest. *It felt like she was in one piece.* She checked her fingers, breathing a sigh of relief. Kayn whispered, "Thank you for digging me out." Lexy took off as she sat up. *There was the hole she'd been dragged out of.* She reached in, felt for Zach, and dug on either side of her hole until she found her Handler's body. Tugging him out, she used her shirt to clean off his face. Brushing his hair with her fingers, Kayn smiled. *She needed to put him in a tomb. How was she going to do that? She could ask Lexy.* Watching her sister chasing desert wildlife, she got up covered in sand and saw people approaching with their identities blurred by the sun's glare. *Please be Ankh, she'd died way too many times today.* Mel, Emery and Jenna's faces came into focus. *Oh, thank you. She just couldn't.*

"How are you feeling, Brighton?" Mel enquired,

passing her a bottle of water. Kneeling to check Zach's pulse, she said, "He's dead, we have time."

Time? They motioned for her to come along. She glanced back, saying, "Zach needs to be entombed."

"We know. We're waking Grey first. He needs to reign in Lexy. The newbies won't come out until he says it's okay," Jenna explained with a secretive grin.

Frost didn't come to say goodbye. She shouldn't overthink it.

Answering her thoughts, Jenna whispered, "Frost's not going anywhere, but Mel could use healing back up."

Smiling, Kayn knelt by Mel, placing her hands on Grey's bullet-riddled torso. Yanking them away, she stated, "Before we bring him back, who shot him?"

They searched the area, no gun in sight. Kayn suggested, "Grab him another shirt. If he asks, someone snapped his neck. Trust me on this, I'll explain later."

Their Oracle prompted, "Explain now, so I'm not caught off guard."

"He had a flashback of an earlier Correction in Scotland at six-years-old, where older siblings and an aunt he didn't know he had were shot," Kayn disclosed, wanting to soften the blow.

Their Oracle didn't conceal her emotions fast enough, Kayn saw the truth in Jenna's eyes. *It was true.* She probed, "Did it really happen? I thought they had to wait until they were sixteen?"

"The children were all sired by a Second-Tier. They came under the guise of Correcting his of age sibling. In cases like their's the genetic line is collateral damage," Jenna admitted. "Grey's sire made a deal to protect his surviving family. He avoided entombment by agreeing to have everyone's minds wiped, including his. Grey and his mother were given a new life in Australia. The memories of his father were planted, a substitute called for a while, then contact tapered off."

She thought her story was crazy. "Are you going to tell him this?" Kayn asked, awaiting the answer.

"It's out, I'd have to erase the conversation you had in the in-between to keep it a secret, and honestly, there's no time. Things rarely remain buried forever," Jenna answered, nervously looking up at the sun's placement in the sky.

As they changed Grey's shirt and shorts, Kayn replied, "Hope it doesn't wreck his Guru Grey vibe."

"Your crew needs to be long gone before dark," Jenna rushed. "We'll exhume Grey's childhood and pray the ripple effect has been dulled by passage of time."

They went to work healing, moving onto the charcoaled mystery corpse as Jenna waited for Grey to open his eyes. As the singed blackened body returned to original form, they realised it was Mel's father.

Stretching as he sat up, Orin declared, "Who did that to the tires?"

They all looked at the slashed tires. Kayn offered, "I did this, I should do it. Should I steal tires from the other RV?"

Strutting over, Emery remarked, "Heads up, kid," tossing Kayn a rose quartz stone. "Put this somewhere safe, it's your Handler. I've got the tires."

She must have meant it's your Handler's. Shoving it into her pocket, Kayn watched Emery saunter away from a fixed tire. Her eyes darted to the other RV. *That was fast.* She watched as her temporary Handler replacement pointed at a back tire. It magically sealed and inflated. *That was cool.* With a skip in her step, the immortal she barely knew, vanished at the back of the RV. Grey sprinted past chasing Lexy. *Her afterlife was wild. It was easier to not question anything.* Kayn started walking back to Zach.

"Where do you think you're going? We need to leave," Emery scolded, catching up to her.

Continuing her walk back to Zach, Kayn answered, "I'm not leaving my Handler's body in the desert."

"It's been taken care of, no worries. We're ready to go," Emery urged. "Trust me."

Following her back to the RV, Kayn rolled her eyes and saucily baited, "I don't even know you." *The engine was purring, they really were ready to go.*

Grinning at her rebellion, Emery said, "Jenna trusts me."

Good for Jenna. Mentioning sleeping with her boyfriend was lots of cardio wasn't a fantastic first impression. Even though she was aware it was jealousy making her wary, with how she'd left things with Frost, it was going to be difficult to diffuse.

Wandering over to their Oracle, Emery flirted, "See you soon," seductively kissing Jenna before getting into the RV.

They had great chemistry. Kayn teased, "If you admit you are more than casual, I'll try to like her."

Brushing sand off Kayn, their Oracle laughed, "Powerful beings are slaves to magical impulse. Crossing paths is fun. No expectations, no drama." Jenna instructed, "Give your hair a shake. It may be days of driving before we can stop to shower. Go to the bathroom and stand in the stall when you take your clothes off, so you don't get sand everywhere. Use wet wipes to clean up. Ask someone to grab your clothes."

As Kayn went in, she felt her pockets. *Shit, she already lost Zach's stone.* As she leaned back out, Jenna tossed his rose quartz to her, shaking her head.

After a naked moist towelette shower stall adventure

in a moving RV, Kayn wiped her face, swabbed her ears, and put on clean clothes. Sitting on the closed toilet, she put her hair in a ponytail. Someone knocked. *Time to face the music.* She reached over and opened the door.

Standing there smiling, Mel explained, "I traded places with my Dad."

Awe, she referred to Orin as Dad.

Passing her the phone, Mel stated, "I'll be out there when you're done talking to Frost."

Nervously staring at her cell, leaving Frost hanging as she prepared herself, Kayn whispered, "Hi."

"I should have said it, I don't know why I freeze up like that. I'm crazy in love with you, Brighton. I feel like an idiot. Forgive me?" Frost apologised, awaiting her response.

She wanted to be with him, whatever it took even if it wasn't easy. "I didn't mean to pick a fight, I love you," Kayn replied, wishing they'd had a chance to make up before parting ways. Lightening up the call, she teased, "I'm sorry I got pissed off and killed all of your friends."

Giggling, Frost provoked, "Maybe next time we get in a fight, I'll kill everyone?"

"It's only fair," she countered, laughing. "I was buried in the desert. That was a first, I just spent half an hour trying to clean myself up. I need a shower so bad. Where are you right now?"

"I'm sharing a room with Orin, he went out. I'm just sprawled in bed wishing you were here," he baited. "Now, you've got me thinking about naughty showers."

Reminiscing the incredible night they'd shared before the silly argument, Kayn sighed, "I'm hiding in the bathroom, avoiding my apology tour."

"What are you wearing?" Frost's sultry voice enticed.

Grinning, she whispered, "Shorts and a tank top. What are you wearing?"

"Nothing, I just had a shower. I'm lying here naked," he flirted, chuckling.

Picturing the titillating visual, Kayn quietly taunted, "Did you call me to apologise naked?"

"Oh, I did," Frost seduced. "I plan to call you every time I'm alone naked."

Alone...Don't overthink it. Unable to resist pointing out what he'd let slip, Kayn ribbed, "Maybe, I'll call you every time I'm naked, alone."

Laughing, he scolded, "If you were here, I'd turn you over my knee and spank you for trying to start another argument."

"If I were there, I'd let you and enjoy it," Kayn toyed, longing to spend the night in his arms. Ridiculously turned on, she tempted, "Put on your clothes and come find me. I bet you can catch us. We can't be that far away. I'm sure we'll be stopping at a gas station or rest stop. Come and get it."

He groaned. Quiet for a beat, Frost vowed, "You won't be able to walk for a week when I catch up with you."

Someone knocked on the door. "Be right out," she said. *Fantastic.* Giggling, Kayn whispered, "You jerk. Now, I have to go out there turned on."

He chuckled, "Are you nervous about the apology tour?"

"No," she confessed, grinning from ear to ear.

Laughing, Frost teased, "Then my work here is done. Call me next time you're alone."

Damn it. Blushing, Kayn opened the door to find Grey standing there.

Grinning, Grey harassed, "Your pheromones are

magical and all, but we need to keep our heads on straight."

Embarrassed, Kayn began her apology tour, "Sorry about everything."

"If there's ever a choice, I prefer Siren pheromones over nightmare-inducing hallucinogens," Grey ribbed, following her past the bunks.

Killian was on her usual bunk. He was awfully still. Glancing back at Grey, Kayn asked, "Is Killian dead?"

A lightbulb turned on, Grey laughed, "That's why I came to get you. Sorry, I was sidetracked by pheromones. Emery is driving, Mel's exhausted and Lexy is post feral asleep. Can you do it?"

"Sure, is everyone mad at me?" Kayn enquired, placing her palms on Killian, concentrating.

Touching her shoulder, Grey slurred, "I was never mad at choo," and passed out in the hall.

Whoops, she must have used his energy. Well, he was on her side for a second there.

From the top bunk, Lexy mumbled, "Is Grey drunk?"

Smiling as Big Sexy's eyes opened, Kayn answered, "He touched my shoulder while I was healing Killian."

Peering over the edge of her bunk to see Grey out cold in the hall, Lexy laughed, "He does things without thinking. I'll get him." She leapt down and gave Grey a jolt of energy. As he came too, Lexy stroked his hair, saying, "You can't touch Healers when they're healing people, you goof."

"Hey Lex," Grey replied, with adoration in his eyes.

Watching their connection, her thoughts drifted to Zach having a cocktail on a white sand beach enjoying his mental vacation. *She hoped that's what he was doing. It was better if she imagined it that way. Thinking of him in pain made her heart ache.* They hit a pothole. Scrambling to grab the bunk above her, Kayn stopped herself from falling on Killian, giggling. Lexy landed on Grey with their lips a breath apart.

Getting up, Killian towed Kayn away, suggesting, "Come on, Brighton. Let's have coffee and leave these two alone. They've got a lot to talk about."

Balancing in a moving RV with steadily humming tires, music playing and the easy ambience of the others playing crazy eights at the table, it felt like everything was normal.

With a grin, Dean declared, "Last card," laying it down.

"Last card," Astrid chuckled, placing hers on the table.

Of course, the coffee was made. Pouring Big Sexy coffee, Kayn passed it to him, urging, "Find a seat." *She'd heard voices in the backroom. Dean was the only newbie playing cards.* Pouring one for herself, she enquired, "Is anyone up there with Emery?"

"She doesn't need backup," Astrid stated, slamming her cards down, obnoxiously cheering.

Killian peeked at Haley's cards as he sat next to her. "Stop cheating," Haley scolded, elbowing him.

Shoving her back, Killian teased, "Horn down unicorn, I'm not even playing."

That was cute. She went to see if Emery wanted coffee. *Holy shit, she was asleep.* "Emery!" Kayn panicked, diving for the steering wheel.

Swatting her hands away, Emery mumbled, "What?"

"You were asleep," Kayn asserted, calming herself.

Rolling her eyes, Emery let go of the steering wheel and flippantly decreed, "It was on autopilot, it was driving itself."

In the passenger seat with wide eyes, Kayn commented, "That's not how autopilot works."

Changing the subject, Emery enquired, "Work things out with Frost?"

"We're good. Do you want coffee?" Kayn asked, passing her the one she'd made for herself.

Smiling, Emery took it saying, "Thank you."

"I'm going to grab another one for myself," Kayn said, shimmying out. Looking back, she questioned, "Would you like a snack?"

"Sure, I'd love one," Emery responded.

Wide-eyed with frazzled nerve induced arrhythmia, Kayn gave Astrid the stink eye, surf balancing to the coffeepot.

Reaching for powdered creamer, Astrid pushed it closer, whispering, "What was that look about?"

Under her breath, Kayn whispered, "Emery was asleep at the wheel."

"It's magic," Astrid quietly revealed. "I freaked the first time too."

Shaking her head, Kayn chuckled, "I could have used a heads up. Is there anything else she does I should know about?"

"She's crazy magical. You name it, she can do it," Astrid disclosed with a secretive smile, perched on the counter.

"She's my proxy Handler until Zach's done his growth spurt," Kayn whispered, pushing the lid on her coffee down. A song she enjoyed came on. *She has good taste in music.* Kayn enquired, "Where are we off to next?"

Jumping off the counter, Astrid revealed, "We're going to a Coven in Mexico to hide Emma."

Right, dropping off the pregnant girl at a Coven. Why not? Nothing surprised her anymore. Smiling, Kayn whispered, "Guess I'll go try to bond with my temporary Handler." Bringing a box of cookies, she made her way back to her seat. Taking a few, she passed Emery the box. Eating snacks, listening to music, they sang along whenever the mood struck. Everyone at the table joined in, belting out tunes as they toured the southern route. Easy unfiltered conversation flowed as day turned to night, with friends perching on the edge of her seat hanging out until their backup singers called it quits and went to bed.

Drifting off to the lullaby of humming tires, Kayn dreamt of intoxicating innocence as a joy enamoured child twirling in a summer meadow, releasing dandelion parachutes into a sunshine sky. Braiding buttercup stems with the boy who played a role in every level of her evolution, and the twin whose fated demise fulfilled her being. Nobody was a hero or a victim. Unspoiled by darkness, they had nothing to fear. Monsters only existed in frightening stories and wishes made blowing on dandelions always came true. In each mystical frame, Kevin was by her side as friendship matured to love, and when they kissed, it felt like destiny. In a twist of fate, they were clinging to each other saying goodbye in the in-between. Assimilating to roles in rival Clans for a year, they were reunited a week before Immortal Testing, and in his final act of love, he'd done the unthinkable to guarantee her survival by triggering her evolution. In the aftermath, who they were ceased to exist, but their connection remained as an ache in her soul reminding her of the path sacrificed, and sometimes in dreams, she slipped back into familiar arms and danced as they were meant to. Memories secured his loosening hold, and even though she'd moved on, a part of her was his. *Perhaps, this was how it was for everyone? Weakened connections ignited by the slightest touch or acknowledgement. Gone, but always lingering like an unfulfilled promise.*

Hours passed by before she stirred. Sleeping for longer than intended, Kayn looked at the clock on the dash. *It was three fifteen AM.* Hungry, she yawned and said, "Tell me we're stopping for breakfast?"

"We can't, they missed a tracking device," Emery replied. "Were being followed by a sedan two vehicles back. A friend slipped into my thoughts to warn me. Look in the mirror on your side."

She saw a trailing line of lights. It was too dark to see much else. "Jenna?" Kayn probed, hoping for entertaining juice on their affair.

"Actually, it wasn't Jenna this time," Emery disclosed, keeping tabs on her mirror "Triad is our closest backup, they are hours away, and we're almost out of gas, any ideas?"

Her eyes darted to the glowing fuel light. *Shit, they were in trouble.* Kayn whispered, "How long have we been driving on empty?"

"Too long," Emery answered. "I took a nap and noticed it when I woke up. When it runs out, I may be able to keep us going for a while, but we have decisions to make."

"Whose shift is it driving the car? Where are they?" Kayn enquired, looking back at the empty table.

"No idea, I wasn't paying attention," Emery stated.

Jumping up, Kayn volunteered, "I'll find out and wake the others." In the wee hours of the morning, humming tires in the quiet RV was soothing even though shit was about to hit the fan. Shaking everyone on bunks awake, she made a mental list of who was inside. Peering into the backroom at the newbie Ankh sound asleep on pillows, Kayn asserted, "Everyone up! We've got a problem!" *Someone was crying in the bathroom.* Kayn knocked on the door.

Emma's strained voice answered, "It's unlocked."

Kayn peeked in. The floor was covered in water with a red tinge. *Seriously? Now? Of course, it was happening right now. Further proof the afterlife had no easy setting.* Heavily perspiring, Emma was panting, holding her stomach crying, in agony. Shoving down the hopeless situation, Kayn soothed, "I'll be right back." Calmly closing the door, she leaned against it gathering her wits. *The game changed. She'd planned to tell whoever was driving the vehicle to ram their tail. Now, they needed the car to get Emma away. What they needed was a miracle.* Looking down the hall, she prepared herself. *She needed someone capable of seeing the bright side of things. Please be in here, Grey.* Entering the kitchen area where everyone gathered, relief washed over her. *Astrid and Haley were the last shift in the car.* Summoning up rarely required authority, Kayn announced, "We missed a tracking device when we searched the RV. The gas tank is empty, and we're being tailed. Swallowing nerves, Kayn grasped Grey's arm and froze like a deer in headlights, thinking of a way to toss in Emma's labour without freaking everyone out.

Meeting her eyes, Grey touched her hand, prompting "If it's time-sensitive, spit it out."

Kayn quietly disclosed, "Emma's water broke. She's in the washroom." Grey raced to her aid as everyone lost their shit. From the driver's seat, Emery howled laughing.

Keeping well-intentioned newbies at bay blocking the hall, Mel commanded, "Stay put. Act like adults, Kayn isn't finished."

Sitting on the counter, swaying her legs without a care in the world, Lexy chuckled, "This is awesome."

"No adults in here," Samid insolently mumbled.

Swatting the teen, Killian scolded, "Manners Sami,

you're immortal, I'm allowed to kick your ass for being a dick."

The kid was an ass, but right. There were no responsible adults in this RV. Giving adulting a shot, Kayn addressed the group, "Our closest backup is a few hours away. We need to take out the car two behind us and get gas while Emma delivers a baby, any ideas?"

Grinning, Lexy jumped off the counter. Looking at the roof, she clapped her hands, instructing, "Newbies to the closet for demon blades. Get on the left side of the RV." They took off. "Mel, circle the RV with salt as soon as we stop, you guard Emma with the newbies. Killian, thirty years ago, south of Montreal." Lexy ran away.

Chuckling, Killian unlatched an escape hatch on the roof, yelling, "Emery, we've got this! Lights off! Veer onto the first backroad you see with no turn signal! They'll drive by, it'll buy us a minute to get a few of us on the roof!"

They were about to do crazy shit. They were on speakerphone with the other car, everyone was laughing.

Shaking her head, Emery sighed, "You guys are so much fun."

Killian repeated impressively insane instructions to the other vehicle. The car ahead gunned it and vanished as they turned off their lights.

"We'll have twenty seconds before the lights of the next car," Lexy explained, reappearing beside her.

Emery's voice called out, "It's a straight turn off, pray we don't tip this beast."

This was exciting. The reality of what was at stake sunk in as Emma cried out in agony.

Lexy lured Kayn into the kitchen, saying, "Want to do something crazy?"

Always. "Do you have to ask?" Kayn sparred, grinning as Lexy passed a blade. She slipped it in her top.

"Up and out, the second we made it around the corner," Lexy instructed, meeting Kayn's eyes.

Sticking his head out, Killian shouted, "Everyone on the left!"

Everything was dead silent, except for whirling tires as they stepped over to the left side.

Emery's voice loudly instructed, "Lights off!"

Everything went dark. Killian counted down, "Five, four, three, two, one... Now!"

They veered to the right, with the tires off the ground. *They were flipping.* Killian dove to the left with everyone else as they bounced back on all four tires and burned off the highway down a sideroad.

Dangling from the escape hatch, her sister provoked, "Coming?"

Yes! Kayn jumped up and pulled herself out.

Tugging her through onto the roof, Lexy asserted, "Flush with the RV, until we're out of sight."

They laid there watching lights pass in the distance with the humming of tires on the road. The third set of headlights passed without slowing as they lost sight of the highway. Peering in, Lexy yelled, "Pass me that spiked strip."

Handing it up, Killian stated, "We're only postponing the inevitable if we don't find out how they're tracking us."

"Get everyone to dig through their personal belongings, pockets, purses, wallets," Lexy suggested. Getting up as they stopped. Haley and Astrid were parked, taking jugs of gas out of their trunk. "There's more in our side compartment," Lexy yelled. They sprinted into action, refilling the RV. Her sister leapt off and jogged down the road, hollering, "Give me a minute!" Positioning the strip, she sprinted back and climbed up the ladder.

On her back gazing up at a spectacular starry night sky as they cruised down the road into nowhere, Kayn asked, "Why are we on top of the RV?"

"Sneak attack strategy," Lexy said, joining her watching stars as they rumbled down the road with Emma's labour as back noise and a full tank.

Kevin's voice piped into her thoughts, *'We took a short cut. We'll be less than an hour. Find somewhere unpopulated to fight and split up. You don't have enough time to deliver naturally.'*

I'm on top of the RV looking at stars. We left a rumble strip on the sideroad we turned down, Kayn answered, happy to hear his voice.

'I'm not joking. Someone has to take that baby, separate from the group and run,' Kevin forewarned. *'Should I talk to Emery?'*

She's the one driving. Once again, I'm on top of a moving vehicle. Kayn saucily toyed in her mind, grinning at the moon.

'They've realised they lost you and turned back, tell Lexy,' His voice prompted.

Looking her sister's way, Kayn repeated, "Kevin says, they've realised they lost us and turned around. Someone needs to take the baby and run."

"She's in labour, there's nothing to take anywhere," Lexy replied. Her expression shifted as she clicked, "Does he want me to cut it out?"

'Grey has to do it,' Kevin responded, firmly.

Hesitating for a beat before relaying his response, Kayn echoed, "He says, Grey has to do it."

Shaking her head, Lexy got up, firmly decreeing, "No, I won't ask him to do that. I'll do it."

'Lexy's going to be preoccupied,' Kevin warned.

Shit, she felt that. Nauseous, Kayn cautioned, "Something dark is coming."

Roof surfing with wind blowing her crimson hair like flames, Lexy hollered, "I know, I'm trying to get a lift!"

In her mind, Kevin shouted, *'Duck!'*

Kayn flattened against the hood.

With a loud whoosh, a beastly pterodactyl with scales and talons snatched Lexy off the roof. Laughing, she yelled, "I've got this!"

Holy shit. Wrapping her mind around it, Kayn stuck her head in the RV, shouting, "A lizard pterodactyl stole Lexy!" Emery stomped on the breaks, Kayn fell through the hatch. Dangling into the kitchen with a blur of everyone shoving past and Emma's heightened screaming. Mel ran out with a bag of salt. Music blared, making their location obvious.

Laughing, Killian said, "Nobody steals Lexy and keeps her." Shoving Kayn back out, the big guy tossed her a bag of salt, instructing, "Cut it open with your blade, cover the roof."

Sprinkling salt on the top of the RV, her stomach turned. *Shit.*

Kevin's voice screamed, *'Down!'*

Dropping on her belly in salt as a scaly-winged, demonic predator swooped, missing her by a hair. Adrenaline rushed through Kayn's veins as her heart echoed in her ears. *This was awesome!*

Appearing on the ladder, Emery yelled, 'I'm taking your place." Kayn got up as her proxy Handler instructed, "Mel, Killian and I are defence. Grey knows what he needs to do."

Walking to the RV with twigs and random flora in scarlet bedhead unscathed, Lexy decreed, "Let's go, Dragons are offence. I'll take you out if your proxy Handler's a dud."

"No worries," Emery assured, patting Kayn's head like a puppy.

Wow. Leaping off the roof, Kayn walked over to Lexy. Extended pitchy shrieks froze her steps. She looked back at the RV. Compassion tightened in her chest as her memory retrieved the excruciating sensory of being sliced open.

Kevin's voice whispered in her mind, *'I have to.'*

In a flash, Kayn was in Immortal Testing. Kevin grabbed her from behind, whispering those words as he slit her throat with the visual of blood spurting into sand. The simmer of betrayal broiled to vengeance, reliving the devastation that left a gaping unhealable wound in her soul, giving birth to a Dragon. All unnecessary concerns dissipated into the void. The two Dragons sprinted away and separated, each taking a side of the road.

21
BEAUTIFUL THINGS

*T*here weren't many things Greydon hadn't experienced. His been there done it list was rather epic as Lexy's Handler, but right now, his usually upbeat persona was stifled by recent revelations. *The alterations to his past were so fresh, he hadn't had an opportunity to bare his soul to Lexy. They'd been going through a rough patch, but he wished she was here. Him delivering a baby was madness. Emma's pregnancy intrigued him. How had a seemingly with-it girl been duped into a hookup resulting in pregnancy? She came across rational but being impregnated by a stranger was avoidable.* Sitting with the teen, he tried distraction, "How long have you been able to see things?"

Breathing through contractions, Emma growled, "What things?"

"The future, ghosts, whatever it is you do?" He probed. She released a tortured wail, cramping and he froze. *It felt like he should be doing something to help. Maybe this was how everyone felt?*

As agony tapered, Emma gasped, "For as long as I can remember."

Lexy popped her head into the washroom, tossed Grey a blade and said, "Thirty years ago south of Montreal."

As the door closed, Grey laughed. Shaking his head, he explained, "We're turning off with no warning to lose a tail. Worst-case scenario, we tip the motorhome."

Panting through a contraction, Emma mumbled, "What tail? Are we being chased while I'm in labour?"

"We have this, no worries," Grey soothed, sweetly taking her hand. "I'm here with you until the end." Squashing his hand like a hazelnut in a nutcracker, Emma spasmed, and they simultaneously cried out as someone yelled something neither one caught. The lights went out as the RV swerved. They were jostled to one side, driving on two wheels. Emma crushed his hand with no mercy as all four tires bounced on the road. He wanted to yank his hand away but didn't. In momentary silence, Grey questioned, "If you knew what was coming, why didn't you avoid Correction?"

"How long do you rationally avoid what's inevitable?" Emma gasped, wincing as the next torturous wave surged, releasing a wail of anguish, squeezing his hand like a vice.

There had to be someone else more capable of doing this. Before thinking, he said, "Why didn't you avoid getting pregnant?"

With perspiration damp hair, Emma confessed, "I was dying either way. Why wouldn't I have a one-night stand with a stranger? I didn't know the child in my visions was mine. It's like putting together a jigsaw puzzle if events play out figuratively. You can't fit the pieces together until you've seen the bigger picture."

Caressing her wet hair, Grey suggested, "Maybe it's

time to take off your pants?" Catching the double meaning, after the words slipped out.

"I've been told that will help move things along, but I'll pass," Emma teased, laughing as the next contraction began, squeezing his hand until he squirmed, relaxing as pain dulled.

Opting to keep her laughing, he pretended to be serious, "I'll take one for the team if it'll help." Shoving him, Emma screamed as relentless excruciating waves surged. *He wanted to help.* In the middle of a hand squashing spasm, Grey asked, "Do you want orange juice?"

Enraged, Emma lost it, "You son of a bitch, I don't want any fucking orange juice!" Tackling Grey like a savage beast maniacally strangling him.

Clawing at her hands, he croaked, "Joke, a joke."

Releasing his throat, Emma pointed, threatening, "If you ever even mention orange juice again, I'll kick your ass to next Tuesday," wailing as the next spasm hit.

Feeling like an asshole for upsetting her, Grey took her hand so she could exact orange juice joke revenge and cried with her as she squashed it. She released his throbbing hand, but the relief was short-lived. Her eyes rolled back, so only whites were visible. *She was having a vision.*

Defeated as her eyes normalised, Emma looked up, and under her breath, she pled, "I can't do that. I can't." A swell passed without her trying to reach for his hand.

Wary, Grey assured, "You do whatever you need to do."

As a convulsion passed, she closed her eyes for a beat. Mustering up courage, Emma confessed, "You're going to need help."

Without clarification, Grey got up, peered out the

door and saw Killian. Waving the big guy over, he said, "We need help."

At the door, Killian rushed, "They need me out there."

Swallowing fear, Emma picked up the blade on the floor, passed it to Grey and prompted, "There's no time. Pin me down and cut out the baby."

What? Freezing in place, Grey whispered, "You're almost done. We'll do this naturally."

With tears in her eyes, Emma stated, "No time. Do it."

He couldn't. Panicking, Grey met Killian's eyes and pled, "You have to help, I can't do this."

Kneeling, Killian teased, "First things first, why are your pants on?" Helping Emma get her pants off, he questioned, "How far apart are her contractions?" Killian roughly felt her abdomen, repeating, "How far?"

Brutally contracting, Emma cried out. Grey replied, "I don't know."

Checking, Killian peered up, stating, "She's not dilated enough, it may take another day." Stroking Emma's hair, he gazed into her eyes, saying, "Are you sure there's no time?"

Doubling over in agony, Emma prompted, "Do it."

Passing her a rolled-up facecloth, Killian instructed, "Bite down on it, with any luck you'll pass out." He showed Grey where to cut, tracing his finger two inches above her pubic area, instructing, "A light incision with the pressure of slicing a banana, don't think about it."

Blinded by tears, Grey whispered, "I'm sorry, I'm sorry," slicing into her. Emma expelled a gut-wrenching wail. Killian took the knife to do the tricky part. As he cut the next layer with her pitchy shrieking. Grey embraced Emma ignoring the heat of his mark, soothing, "Pass out. I promise we'll make sure your baby's safe, pass out." As the infant released its first crackling cries, she went limp in his arms. Devasted by the part he played, he numbly sat there.

"Take off your shirt," Killian instructed. On autopilot, Grey did it. Passing the infant, Killian said, "Hold the baby against your heart, it's important. I'll be back in a minute."

Awestruck, Grey cradled the newborn. Even covered in goo, she was the most incredible thing he'd ever seen with pursed suckling lips searching for sustenance. *He'd spent his afterlife in search of beautiful things. This was the pinnacle; he'd never top it.* New life squirming against his chest was impossible to beat. Grinning with his heart ready to burst, Grey whispered, "I don't have what you're looking for wee one." His eyes drifted from the newborn to Emma's sacrifice. *This beauty felt stolen.* He held the infant suckling on its fist to Emma's face so the child could sense her and brought it back to his heart. Caressing a delicate cherub cheek, he pledged, "You're going to grow up to be brave and stubborn just like your Mom. I'll make sure you know her." *After your sixteenth year, when we meet again.* Grey kissed the newborn's head. Sensing a presence, he peered up. *It was time to let her go. He wasn't sure he could.*

Haley crouched, urging, "I need to take her, we have to go."

Holding her to his chest, Grey's vision blurred with tears as he gave her up and watched Haley walk away. His eyes returned to Emma on the floor with an open stomach. He didn't need to feel for a pulse, he'd sensed it as she slipped away. *She was gone.* Covering her with a towel, he moved her body into the shower and numbly cleaned up the blood. *For immortals, death was temporary but tending to her was his obligation. He'd experienced what she would always long for. She'd only hold her newborn daughter against her heart in dreams. His part in this would be forever etched in her nightmares. She'd never look at him the same, but she was more too. Before this night, she was just a girl who'd taken a few wrong turns, but he saw her now. She was brave and selfless. He'd believe her capable of anything. There had to be no hint of what took place when she healed. That much he could do.* Grey heard someone and looked up.

Solemnly, Killian explained, "This is the only road. We have to keep it blocked until Triad shows up."

"Thank you for what you did," Grey whispered, standing up with Emma's shell cradled in his arms.

Grabbing the bloody knife, Killian said, "Don't mention it. I'll bleach this so there's no breadcrumbs leading to the child's identity."

Placing Emma's body on pillows in the backroom, Grey peered out the window. *It was a new day.* He exhaled, walking down the hall to the kitchen. *He was grateful for the big guy's help but didn't want to be friends. Emery and Killian would go back to the other continent and he'd be left with holes where bonds used to be.* Grey confessed, "I can't remember what happened at the end of the story?"

"Which one?" Killian taunted, rinsing off the blade.

Grey countered, "South of Montreal."

"Your girlfriend leapt off the roof of a moving RV onto the car tailing us," Killian regaled, with a knowing grin.

"It's not like that," Grey replied, noticing the lack of chaos. *The fight hadn't made it here, they were holding their ground.*

Waving the knife, Killian said, "I wouldn't advise going out there without a weapon."

Taking the blade, Grey prompted, "What's the plan?"

"I'd know if I wasn't yanked from duty to cut a baby out," Killian sparred, opening the door. "The salt line hasn't been disturbed. Your baby momma is safe, kid."

"She's not my..." Grey paused his denial, seeing Killian's grin. *Ass. Kid? He wasn't a newb.*

The pair emerged into breathtaking crimson dawn as the sun rose above a picturesque mountain with the commotion of their Clan fighting down the road. Molly was motionless with her back to them. Grey called out, "Let's go!" She didn't move a muscle as they approached. Killian poked Molly's shoulder. Solid, she tipped, hitting the road with a thud. Looking into unblinking petrified eyes, Grey asked, "Any idea what did this?"

"A lizard pterodactyl snatched Lexy off the roof earlier," Killian disclosed, casually walking into battle.

Most of Abaddon's party favours were nocturnal. A carload of demon-possessed mortals; how bad could it be? "Try to keep up old man," Grey challenged, jogging away. Clutching his weapon, Viking guy, chased him, laughing. As they sprinted around a bend, their Clan was battling Abaddon shells. *This wasn't an even fight at all.* There were vehicles stopped on the road and bodies everywhere. Dean and Sami were still on their feet. Mel was fighting off a group and Emery was enjoying herself way too much. Joining the battle, Killian pitched a shell into the hoard with impressive airtime.

Fighting his way through the herd to back up Mel, Grey shouted, "This isn't one carload!"

Exhausted, Mel kicked one away and slashed another's throat, yelling, "They keep coming! I can't keep this up much longer. We need the Dragons out here not in the bushes."

Scanning for Lexy's crimson hair in his peripheral vision, fending off assailants, his attention was split into too many directions. *The baby and Emma's unattended body weren't his job. Lexy was his sole duty. He had to focus.* A truck pulled over down the road. *It was Triad.* As Tiberius joined the battle jealousy tugged his heart home. *He hated that guy.* Fighting harder in his rival's presence, he gave it his all, hoping they'd leave before it was time to bring Lexy out of her emotionless abyss. *Knowing he was irrationally jealous, didn't stave off the desire to pummel Tiberius into a pile of mush.* A flash of red hair caught his attention. Distracted, a blade sunk into his back. *Damn it.* Choking, sputtering up blood, Grey staggered forward and went down. Struggling to lift himself up, he was kicked in the stomach. Someone stomped on his back as his head hummed. With seconds to live, he saw Lexy no holds barred slaying everyone. *Good, bad, Triad, Ankh. Oh, no. Shit.* His vision flickered and the lights went out.

22

PREDATORY REFLEX

In the Dragon state, choices were predatory reflex. With no functional moral compass nor sense of consequence, there was only a dark obsession to vanquish everything her lizard brain set its sights on. An inborn impulse to avoid shiny things was Ankh's salvation if they ventured into a Dragon's layer. With instinct as co-pilot, urges altered in the blink of an eye. Hostile voice's triggered animosity as the fragrance of copper fed enraging snippets of past demises. Swooshing steps in foliage, led her feet as she manoeuvred terrain with tiger-like agility, ruthlessly tracking and pouncing on prey. Each time a weapon grazed her, she'd sneak a vitality snack, calming energy cravings by consuming swirling onyx clouds before they vanished into the earth. As the hum of euphoria ceased, vaguely recognizable voices would filter through the emotionless fog luring her back to the fight.

Crouched like a feral beast, pack acuity sensed the other Dragon across the road. As weakest links fled, her crimson-haired predatory counterpart vanished in pursuit. Guarding territory, observing sparkly things, she lingered until another breached her domain. Systematically tracking, tackling, and subduing snacks until her Ankh symbol heated, drawing her back. Emerging with a vengeance to thin the herd of Clan irritants, she gutted each depravity close to the injured and chased those endeavouring to flee. Relentlessly locked onto prey, she pounced on malevolent beings, plunging blades into their chests vanquishing entities. Unable to resist, she'd quench the Conduit's thirst by drawing smoky essence into her being through her pores, preventing a malicious being's ascent into purgatory. With the volatile Conduit next to the whim enabling Dragon on her mental throne, Ankh's battle scraps ceased to satisfy cravings. The line between shiny and dark entities blurred, and for a glorious time, she morphed into the beast tip-top of the immortal food chain, devouring anything her lizard brain fancied, vanquishing all who dared question her reign. Snapping teeth, scratching, her power was zapped by a glowing fist. The Conduit vanished, pissing off the Dragon whose wrath shrieked like a Siren in fables. A thing with a golden hue sent her soaring through the air mutely enraged with her back snapping and crackling as she tumbled to a stop concealed by brush. Forced to be still as healing magic repaired injuries, she rested her eyes.

Interrupting her mending, something spoke, "Kayn."

Squinting, as a shiny thing disrupted greenery, disturbing her healing burrow. *No.* She swatted it, hissing. It laughed, reaching in. Scratching it, she inched away as it kept trying.

"If you won't let me touch you, I have to come in," a faintly recognizable voice explained. It was shimmering way too much for her patience level, so she closed her eyes and curled into a ball, disregarding it. As she drifted off into a dream, it snuggled with her, and that was okay.

Staring at small bare feet in unkempt grass strewn with buttercups, clover and dandelions, Kevin's childhood voice, yelled, "I found one! How long am I lucky for?"

They were her feet.

Chloe marched over, saying, "You always say you found one, it never is." She tried to snatch it.

Kevin accidentally dropped it into the untamed lawn. On all fours frantically searching, he said, "Why can't you ever let me have one thing?"

"You dropped it all by yourself," young Chloe scoffed, with windswept blonde curls and crossed summer tanned arms, judging his search for the coveted four-leaf prize.

She felt bad for him, she always did. "I saw it. He had a four-leaf clover," Kayn fibbed, backing up her friend.

"You'd say that even if he didn't. You always lie," Chloe sparred prancing away, singing, "I don't even care."

That was mean. She wasn't a liar. She just wanted to help. Kayn sat by him, whispering, "She's gone, you can stop looking."

He got up, mumbling, "I really had one you know."

"I know," she replied, handing him a purple clover.

"I'd put this in your shoe but you're not wearing any," he giggled.

Sprawling on her back in the grass, she instructed, "Put it between my toes. I'll keep it there all day."

"You're so weird," Kevin ribbed, grabbing for her

foot. "Ewww, disgusting, your feet are sweaty, you have toe jam."

"I do not! The grass was dewy, it's not me," Kayn said, looking at her foot. She sniffed it. *It was fine.* Tossing a handful of grass at his face, she stated, "I don't smell, you turd."

Crawling to the garden, he chuckled as he dug his hands into moist soil, got up and in an ominous voice, he declared, "I am the turd master. King of poo hands and you shall be my first sacrifice."

Her twin walked over with a scrunched nose, saying, "Gross, what are you doing?"

Kevin cackled, "Poo hands," chasing Chloe, who took off in a blur of blonde hair.

Happily watching Kevin chase her squealing twin around Grandma Winnie's buttercup strewn yard, she found a four-leaf clover and planned to secretly give it to him so Chloe wouldn't wreck his four-leaf victory.

"Eat your snacks in the yard poo hands and friends," Granny announced, placing a tray on the doorstep.

Kayn wandered over to Granny Winnie by herself and left them to their muddy games. Choosing a peanut butter sandwich, she said, "Thank you."

Sitting on the stoop with her, Granny questioned, "How come you're not playing?"

Holding out her balled hand, Kayn explained, "Can't. I'm saving this for Kevin, so he doesn't drop it again."

"Is it a spider?" Granny Winnie probed, grinning.

Grimacing, Kayn denounced, "I don't like those. No spider cooties on my hands."

Beaming, Granny urged, "Give whatever it is to me so you can go play poo hands. I'll make sure he gets it." Kayn opened her palm. Inspecting the coveted treasure,

Granny said, "I hope my grandson knows what a good friend he has in you."

Eating a chocolate chip oatmeal cookie, she watched as Kevin tackled Chloe in the grass laughing. With wisdom beyond her years, Kayn admitted, "Sometimes, he can't see me when she's here." Chloe kissed Kevin's nose. Red-faced, he ceased his poo hand white dress destruction plot and gave up, wiping his hands in the grass.

Grinning, Granny Winnie agreed, "It's true, sometimes he can't. Your sister is distracting." Passing another cookie off the plate, his grandmother, leaned closer and whispered, "He will." She got up and quietly closed the door as she went inside.

Trying to fit the entire cookie inside of her mouth, she had her cheeks stretched out, drooling as he walked up. With that exact timing, Granny came out to place another plate of cookies on the stoop. Kevin was standing there gawking as she tried to speak, just mumbling incoherently, drooling.

"She's so weird," Kevin muttered, shaking his head.

Granny poked Kayn's back and busted a gut laughing as Kayn turned with an entire cookie in her mouth, drooling. Messing up Kayn's wild blonde curls, she announced, "Your sense of humour is worth its weight in gold, child."

The cookie was stuck. Help, Granny.

Like she'd heard her inner plea, Kevin's Grandmother grabbed the middle of the slimy cookie in her mouth, and it broke. She passed her a glass of milk and whispered, "You don't help yourself out at all. I love you, sweet girl."

She knew it. She always just did whatever crossed her mind without thinking it out. Wiping milky cookie drool on the back of her hand, Kayn jumped up, declaring,

"Catch you on the flip side poo hands," wandering away as her duplicate delicately flounced over like a magical fairy princess. *Poo hands. That was funny.* Plucking a seeding dandelion from the grass, she danced around the yard twirling and giggling, setting tiny parachute people loose in the air with sunshine warm on her skin under a cerulean midsummer sky. *Drooling on herself or not, it was a perfect day.* A garden snake slithered over her feet. She chased it into the woods, stopping to watch squirrels on cedar branches. Listening to the trickling creek, she picked up a pinecone, pitched it into the forest, and waded into the cool calf-deep water. She sat on a smooth rock with her feet in the creek and smacked a mosquito feasting on her arm. There was a red splat. *Gross. It was drinking her blood. She wet her hand and wiped the red splotch off. She felt like getting wet.* Scooping water in her palms, she drank it and turned as she heard gentle padding of feet in soil.

Walking up alone, Kevin asked, "What are you doing?" Sitting on a log with feet submerged in the shallow moving water, he apologised, "I'm sorry I called you weird."

Peering over her cupped palms of water, Kayn teased, "Don't worry about it poo hands," giggling as he splashed her. "Want to watch TV inside with Chloe?"

"Why would I want to be inside watching TV when I can sit in this creek with those squirrels over there to hang out with?" Kayn taunted, smiling.

Dipping his head in the creek, he shook off like a puppy, spraying her with water until she retaliated. They drenched each other hysterically laughing, and as always, she didn't really think it out as she grabbed a handful of slimy mud and flung it at his face. Standing with wet dark curls, creek muck splattered on his face and his mouth open, feigning shock, he knit his brow, declaring, "It's on, Weirdo!" Wildly firing mud back.

Kayn blocked it, provoking, "Not the poo hands. Say no to feces, poo handed fiend!" Rifling mud back, neither one noticed as Granny walked up.

"Take that, creepy weirdo!" Kevin proclaimed, firing a handful of mud. Kayn ducked. Granny took it in the chest. "Uh oh," he whispered.

Kayn turned and saw Granny standing there covered in mud and commented, "Nice work, poo hands."

Her serious demeanour broke, Granny shook her head, laughing, "You kids will be the death of me." She froze like she'd said something she wasn't supposed to. Regaining her bearings, Granny instructed, "Wash yourselves off with the hose before you come in. I'll run you a bath."

Watching her walk away, Kayn whispered, "What was that about?"

Kevin shoved her into the water and chased after Granny yelling, "Bath shotgun!"

"You can't call bath shotgun, poo hands. It's not a front seat," Kayn mumbled, getting up.

Her memories flashed to Chloe's perspective. Kevin was chasing her with muddy hands, laughing. She was having fun as he tackled her. He was above her in the sunshine, instinct took over, and it was her first kiss. Kevin was embarrassed, but she had a crush. She'd been hurt when he didn't want to stay with her. She was jealous but too young to understand why. She was pouting on the couch watching soap operas with Granny while they were getting muddy at the creek. She travelled childhood from various vantage points, and in the end, she understood her twin always had feelings for Kevin. Their fragmented memories blended to create one intention. Kevin whispered her name; she opened her eyes. *They were on her bed in her childhood bedroom.*

Caressing her jaw, gazing into her eyes, he whispered, "I could stare into your green eyes forever."

A flood of emotions rushed back as though the last two years hadn't happened. With his loss aching in her soul, she whispered, "What is this?"

"It's just a dream," Kevin whispered, touching her hair.

There was a pizza menu on the nightstand. It felt like Jenkins was going to bust into the room. Entranced by first love, they tenderly kissed, pulling away as fireworks lit up in their souls. In a heartbeat, they were seventeen in love feverishly stripping off shirts with not a care in the world. The image flickered. Confused, she whispered, "Wait."

"Why?" Kevin asked, gazing into her eyes. He kissed her lips once more, seducing, "No harm, no foul. It's not real."

Melting into the past, Kayn forgot everything but how she felt before immortality was thrust upon her. Recklessly lost in first love never brought to fruition, feverishly making out, Stephanie's angry voice cut through their frenzied bliss, "Asshole!"

They dove away from each other with nowhere to go inside a bush, eyes wide. *Dear lord, they were really doing that.* Tossing Kevin's shirt at his face, Kayn decreed, "You tricked me."

"I didn't mean to," he backtracked. "I was hugging you trying to bring you back. I thought you were asleep. I was feeding you a dream, I would never."

Putting her shirt on, she shot him a dirty look, taunting, "Go fix things with your girlfriend, poo hands."

"She's not my girlfriend, weirdo," he countered, grinning.

Kayn brushed herself off, scolding, "As your friend, stop being a dick if you want to be with her."

Grinning, Kevin chuckled, "Maybe."

Clutching his arms, Kayn sighed, "If she storms out there and tells everyone we were making out, it's going to cause a lot of drama. I haven't even had a chance to make up with Frost."

Walking through bushes, Kevin apologised, "I'm sorry but..."

"Don't say it," She ribbed with a hip check.

Laughing, he toyed, "I want to finish that dream."

"I wouldn't hold my breath," she stated as they emerged from the bushes. *After years apart, the need to be near him was still so strong. She'd moved on. Focus. Concentrate on fixing this. Stephanie was nowhere in sight.* With a menacing finger, Kayn ordered, "Fix things with your girlfriend."

Walking away, he razzed, "She's not my girlfriend."

Snatching a rock off the ground, Kayn rifled it at his back as he jogged away, laughing. She wandered back, smiling. *The bodies were gone. She'd missed the cleanup. Sweet.* With a skip in her step, she went into the RV. Stephanie was standing there. Opting to just say it, Kayn said, "I was asleep, I didn't know it was really happening, but I told him to stop being a dick."

Smirking, Stephanie brushed past, provoking, "I'm here for Tiberius, not your help." She strutted out.

Well, that went as expected. Her attention turned to Grey. *He looked like someone just kicked a puppy.* She sat next to him, asking, "Are you alright?"

"Lexy and Tiberius took off together, I'm not fantastic," he admitted, drinking coffee like a shot of whisky.

Damage control. She whispered, "Did she tell you?"

"What?" Grey prompted, focused on Lexy's absence.

Messing his hair, Kayn switched subjects, "How was the delivery?"

Gazing into his empty mug, Grey mumbled, "Horrible. They're healing her."

"Don't you want to be there when she wakes up?" Kayn probed with a reassuring squeeze.

Meeting her eyes, Grey answered, "I cut her baby out, I'll wait here. I just hope she doesn't hate me."

She wanted to ask about it but didn't want to rock his mood swing. Instead, Kayn consoled, "You're a sweetheart, nobody could hate you. I'll see if I can help." Glancing back as she walked away, she knew her affirmation helped. Pausing at the bunks, she wanted to crawl beneath the covers and disappear. *She had to call Frost before they ran into Triad. What was she going to say? Stephanie caught us making out in the bushes, I thought it was a dream. He'd sworn to forgive her but hadn't factored in her doing everything wrong, all of the time. Kevin was a touchy subject. This was a phone call, not a text.* She felt for her phone, picked it up, saw a bunch of messages from Frost, and tossed it on her bunk. *She needed a minute. Why couldn't she be a normal girl for five seconds?* They were healing Emma's vacant abdomen as she walked in. The visual of the missing infant yanked her heart back to reality. *There was nothing normal about her anymore.* Without a word, Kayn placed her hands by Mel's. Feeling the heat build in the core of her being it flowed down her arms to help seal Emma's wound. Her chest rose and fell. Kayn took her hands away as the teen's eyes fluttered.

Gasping, grabbing her healed stomach. Emotion flooded Emma's eyes as she felt her childless womb, panicking, "I need Grey. Where's Grey?"

"I'll get him," Kayn offered, fleeing the room. Pausing to compose herself, she made her way to the table where Grey was staring into his mug, and announced, "Emma is asking for you." He took off. Curious, she followed, watching as Emma and Grey embraced by the washroom, sobbing. Mel joined their emotional reunion. Emery walked by, giving her a dirty look. *Why she was getting the stink eye?* Kayn enquired, "Problem?" Catching her off guard, Emery tackled her like a linebacker and bit her arm like a maniac as she flailed. The others came to her rescue, tugging the fierce immortal off.

Emery coldly decreed, "I bite back," strutting away.

Standing in the hall mortified, Kayn's eyes darted to Mel as she guessed, "I must have bitten her."

"You bit everybody," Mel revealed, following Emma into the bathroom.

Awkward. "Everyone?" Kayn asked, making eye contact with Grey.

"Everybody," Grey answered with a grin, walking over. "After what I had to do to Emma, my head wasn't in the game. I was killed right after Triad showed up. I didn't get a chance to see you in action. The last thing I saw before dying was Lexy no holds barred taking everyone out. I woke up in the in-between, made sandcastles, drank a Pina Colada, got a lecture from Azariah, you know how it goes."

"Wasn't Emma there?" Kayn enquired, curious.

Peeking at her vibrating phone, Grey replied, "I didn't see her. Mel showed up and told us how the rest of the fight went down. Emery was trying to put Lexy down when you took off into the bushes. Kevin went after you. Lexy got away. I was dead, so Tiberius was sent after her. Either he's been chasing her all day, or he had enough clout to bring her back himself."

"I'll go look for her with you," Kayn offered.

Shaking his head, Grey replied, "I had an enlightening chat with Azariah. I can't keep punching holes in walls and lighting shit on fire with my mind pressuring her to continue choosing me over everyone else, it's not right. When feelings surface, it's a pent-up explosion of everything suppressed. All I want to do is hold her and tell her how much I love her, but I've put her through decades of forgetting in the morning. I need to shift my focus so she can grow. If he was able to pull her out of a Dragon state, she has real feelings for Tiberius. It's time to stop being selfish and show her the same devotion, she's always shown me."

Smiling, Kayn toyed, "How long will you remember this revelation?"

Holding out his pinkie, Grey answered, "Pinkie swear you'll help me see this even when I can't?"

They shook pinkies. "I'll tell you when you're being an idiot if you promise not to light me on fire."

Laughing as they shook pinkies, Grey pledged, "I vow to never light you on fire unless duty requires it. Your turn Guardian half breed. Promise you won't pheromone drift, light me on fire or dose me with toxic nightmare-inducing hallucinogens?"

"I vow to never intentionally pheromone drift, light you on fire or dose you with nightmare-inducing hallucinogens unless duty requires it," Kayn mischievously sparred with a shove. Sitting on her bunk, she confessed, "I need to text Frost back, Kevin is a touchy subject."

Joining her on her bunk, Grey admitted, "Kevin's friend was choked. Trust me, half-truths always backfire. Stephanie is going to throw this at Frost the second she runs into him, it's better if he's prepared. If he knows it's coming, at least he'll have a comeback."

"What did Stephanie say happened?" Kayn questioned, curious as to how far she thought it went.

Taking her hand like a brother, he squeezed it, disclosing, "She says, she caught you guys naked in the bushes."

Liar! "We weren't naked, it was PG thirteen. Kevin was reminding me of the past to bring me back, we thought it was a dream," she admitted, looking into Grey's eyes so he'd see she was telling the truth. "She yelled asshole, we snapped out of it and jumped away from each other. I was mad, he was apologising. It wasn't like we snuck off together."

Grinning, Grey chuckled, "You don't need to convince me of your innocence."

Switching subjects, she asked, "Where's your shirt?"

Smiling, he answered, "Killian told me to take it off so I could hold the newborn against my skin. It was the most incredible thing."

"I'm glad it was you," Kayn whispered. Humanity stirring images of muddy grins and carefree joy flashed through her memory. For a heartbeat, the loss of mortality and those balmy summers of innocence ached within her as a reminder that a part of her would always long for who she used to be before violence and trauma gave her the ability to look away from the light.

"Even the darkest roads can lead to beautiful things, you just have to want to see it," Grey commented in response to the weight her soul was carrying.

He was an intuitive guy. There was no point in acting like it was easy to release the visions Kevin gave her to bring her back. Kayn mumbled, "I have no idea what I did or how I ended up with Kevin, but I know why. There was a time when he meant everything to me."

Caressing her face, Grey explained, "You grew up mortal together. I can't imagine what it would be like to have a reminder of mortality on the other team in my immortal bubble." Tucking a wild curl behind her ear, he lowered his voice, "Every time you can't eat, can't sleep, can't breathe, love, it leaves a scar on your soul that opens as they enter a room. Time dulls the ache, but don't ever forget they are one of the few capable of destroying you. They can make your day or wreck it just by showing up. That trigger is how he brought your emotions back."

The RV jolted, knocking her into him as they started moving. "Everyone isn't back yet, where are we going?"

"I'll go see what's happening," Grey announced, getting up. "Text Frost before he starts texting me, and I have to play dumb."

Grey walked away. Whoever was driving the RV, cranked an oldie. I Think We're Alone Now, by Tiffany, blared as she read Frost's detailed description of what he was going to do to his sexy Siren. She couldn't read it with a straight face. It was impressively naughty. Groaning, Kayn flopped on her bunk. Covering her face with her pillow, she screamed into it. *Her afterlife was confusing. She wasn't always a sexy Siren. Sometimes she was warrior, and on occasion, a serial murderer for the greater good. Whatever that meant. The greater good was a loosely used phrase in these parts. The scenarios she'd found herself in lately hadn't felt like noble causes. They'd been bailed out by other Clans far too many times. She'd spent most of her time killing people, trying not to, or having mind-blowing sex with her kryptonite under a full moon in the desert. It didn't feel like she had a well-balanced immortality. Her afterlife was a gong show. More kryptonite, less shitshow extravaganza would be nice.* Feeling pressure on her bunk, she thought it was Grey coming to tease her and mumbled, "Go away."

"Not a chance," Zach's voice answered.

Whipping off the pillow, Kayn dove into her Handler's arms. Hugging him with all her might, she muttered, "Don't ever leave me, I'm a train wreck without you."

Embracing her, stroking her hair, Zach whispered, "Time to accept your afterlife setting, Brighton." He let her go, laid next to her and said, "Spill it. What did you do?"

Putting the pillow over her face again, she mumbled, "I bit everyone and made out with Kevin. I didn't mean to. He was feeding me memories to subdue the Dragon."

Grinning, Zach shifted to face her, taunting, "Again?"

"It's been a long time since I made out with Kevin," she answered.

"I meant biting everyone. I'm here to bring you back now, no need for your ex to ply you with memories. Give me that cell. I need to see why you were screaming into a pillow," Zach harassed, snatching her phone. Reading for a minute, he teased, "Oh, my Siren. Wow." After brief a pause, he asked, "You haven't read all of these messages yet, have you?"

With her interest peaked, she replied, "No…why?"

Zach stole her phone and took off with it like a child. Kayn chased him, trying to snatch it back, bumping into Mel avoiding her clutches. "Don't be an ass, Zach! It's supposed to be private!"

He hollered, "Heads up, Greydon," tossing her cell. "We have to intercept a stolen newbie."

"What? I didn't see that one," Grey said, reading Kayn's texts, grinning until he reached the final message, where his expression altered. He loudly announced, "One of Trinity's newbies was taken. They've been incapacitated. They can't pursue them to stop Leonard from opening the portal. I thought you guys took him out in Vegas?" Handing her cell back, he pestered, "This is why you need to read messages, Brighton."

As she read his final text, her heart sunk. *The girl they took used to be Triad. It was the girl Kevin tried to get her to blow a job for.*

"I don't know about you guys, but if I'm going to be in the same vicinity as creepy pretty bird Leonard again, I need a drink," Mel declared, opening the fridge. "Anybody else?"

Might as well. Kayn held out her hand. Mel passed a beer as she questioned, "Where is this portal?"

Taking a beer, Grey explained, "Anywhere. Abaddon can summon Portals at certain times of the night with a large-scale sacrifice and a shell strong enough to house the demon. Who is this tool trying to bring back again?"

Sitting at the table with the newbies, Zach accepted a drink, sighing, "Jezebeth. He's already tortured and killed me once this week. Can I opt-out of taking this job?"

"Afraid?" Sami heckled.

Killian's voice piped in from the front, "I'll pull this rig over to come back there and smack you."

She wanted to ask where Lexy was but decided it was best to leave that subject alone.

Sitting beside Zach, Kayn offered, "Trade me places, I'll smack Samid."

"Way to be a team player," Sami taunted, rolling his eyes, being an asshole like it was his job.

She was going to enjoy killing this kid during training.

Dean asked, "Where is everyone else?"

"Good question," Grey responded, drinking his beer.

Emery's voice answered, "There was a side job, Lexy's renting a car, she'll catch up."

That was obviously a lie.

Shaking his head, smiling, Grey sighed, "Brighton, your inner commentary isn't helpful. Go call Frost."

My bad. Taking her phone, Kayn got up from the table, and highway surfed to the back. Getting comfy cross-legged on a pillow, she messaged Frost. *Drama had me sidetracked. We're on our way.*

He texted back. *We're almost there. Triad's on their way too. I'll see you in a few hours.*

Shit. There goes their sexy reunion. Blocked on what to say, she texted. *Bringing Bad Markus to a demon fight?*

Frost messaged her back. *Bad Markus doesn't know anything. Arrianna is keeping him occupied.*

Cool. Kayn texted, slapping her head.

He texted her. *How did Emery do as your proxy Handler?*

He already knew. Kayn texted him. *Everything went wrong. I only know what I was told. Grey and Killian had to cut the baby out of Emma, Haley and Astrid took off with her. Grey died right after they got to the fight while Lexy was killing everyone. I guess I started biting people. Emery was already trying to subdue Lexy when I took off. Triad was there, Kevin took off after me. Emery couldn't take down Lexy. Tiberius was sent to subdue her.* Her cell started vibrating. *Holy shit, he was calling. No, she wasn't ready to speak. She had to answer. Damn it.* Swiping the phone, Kayn said, "Hi."

"Hi," Frost replied. After an awkward silence, he stated, "You might as well just give it to me straight, I'm going to see the guy in half an hour."

Her stomach sunk as she unleashed the sordid details, "Kevin was feeding me memories of chasing us with mud. I was calling him poo hands. I'm guessing the teenage years were next. Stephanie yelled, asshole. We jumped away from each other. I was upset. He thought it was a dream too. It was PG thirteen, we didn't know we were going through the motions. I told him if he liked Stephanie, he had to stop being a dick. I knew I needed to call you, but there was lots of drama going on when I got back. I tried explaining things to Stephanie for Kevin. Grey cut Emma's baby out with her awake with Killian, he thought she was going to hate him. Emery bit me back, and honestly, I was nervous." Hearing his irritation as he exhaled, she resisted the inborn reflex to dull her response by submerging emotions into nothing and remained present, for him.

"Okay, I'm not going to sugar-coat it, that stung, but at least I'm prepared. Listen, Kevin was the first choice to be your Handler, we've used him to bring you back before. It makes sense he'd choose to go after you. I know who he was, and still is to you. I knew being with you while you were evolving was going to be tricky, but when I told you I'd forgive you for anything, I meant it. Do me a favour, define PG thirteen."

She knew he was going to call her on that. Kayn clarified, "We were making out in the bushes, neither one of us knew it was happening. We'd taken off our shirts, nothing else."

"Okay, we're past it. I'm Siren, I know it's in you too, see how easy that was." Changing the subject, Frost questioned, "Did Tiberius have enough pull to bring Lexy back?"

Peaceful relief washed over her as she answered, "He must have, she's not back yet. Triad took her to rent another vehicle. Grey had a talk with Azariah, he's in a surprisingly good place about it."

"She must have done something to calm him down," he commented. "He really seems fine with it?"

"Not fine, just accepting. He said, he needs to focus his attention elsewhere so it can run its course, whatever that means," Kayn explained.

Grey walked in, taunting, "My ears were burning."

"Sorry," Kayn whispered, getting up with a hand on the wall to steady herself.

Balancing against the door frame, Grey suggested, "Put your boyfriend on speakerphone so we can chat."

Holding it away from her lips, she offered, "I'll just give you the phone." They went over a surprise pothole, Kayn bailed on the floor, giggling.

Grey was laughing as she got up to say goodbye to Frost, "Sorry, bumpy road, I fell." With Frost laughing in her ear, she said, "I'm passing you to Grey. See you soon, hun. Hope Leonard doesn't have you all tied to poles when we show up." Tossing Grey her phone, she announced, "I need to use the washroom."

"Thanks for oversharing!" Grey called after her.

Of course, the washroom was occupied. She raised her hand to knock and heard Emma crying. *She needed to go pee. Sometimes, when she was recently brought back from a Dragon state, it was difficult to find the words to soothe someone else's woes. She liked Emma, but barely knew her, and right now, she was only capable of kiddie pool deep. It was in her mortal nature to be empathetic, but it was slowly rebooting. Right now, she knew how she needed to respond but didn't have the verbal ammo to back it up.* Ignoring the reflex to go get Zach, Kayn knocked.

After a momentary pause, Emma answered, "I'll be right out."

"I'd pee in a bottle if I could, I'll be quick," Kayn replied, wincing as her inner dialogue replayed in her mind. *I'd pee in a bottle.*

Unlocking the door, Emma tried to come out with her eyes swollen from weeping. *No, she couldn't let her go out there like this, she wasn't Satan.* Kayn whispered, "Forget about it. Stay in here. Take all the time you need."

"Are you sure?" Emma replied with a heaving chest.

She really had to go. "Don't worry, hun," she assured. "Take all the time you need." Emma closed the door. *She could have just had her stand in the hall for ten seconds. She wasn't capable of complex thoughts yet. This was a bumpy highway. If she peed herself in front of everyone, she was never going to live it down.* Holding it, she manoeuvred past the others to the front, clutched Killian's shoulder and pled, "Please, quick, pull over so I can pee."

Irritated, Emery asserted, "We're on our way to a time-sensitive job. Pee in a glass and toss it out a window."

"I can't," Kayn decreed. "All I need is ten seconds."

Dead eyed unsympathetic, Emery provoked, "Suck it up, you're immortal."

They went over a jarring pothole. Squeezing her thighs, Kayn threatened, "If you don't stop, I'm going to pee on your lap." The RV swerved to the side of the road.

"You have sixty seconds," Emery shouted, laughing.

She went outside the door, yanking up her underwear as the RV began rolling. She shuffled after it with shorts around her ankles yanking on the handle. *It was locked. Assholes.* They slowly drove away with her cursing, penguin waddling after the RV. It stopped. She tugged up her shorts, stormed up and yarded on the handle so hard the door came off the hinges. Enraged, Kayn tossed it. Everyone at the table had wide eyes as she stomped up to the front, shouting, "You'd better run!"

Killian scrambled out the driver's side door, hysterically laughing, "It was Emery, it wasn't me!"

Swatting at Emery as the immortal dove out, Kayn yelled, "We're dealing with this shit right now, you crazy bitch!"

Frost asked, "What was that?"

"I'd better get up there. Kayn stepped out to go to the washroom, someone thought it would be funny to take off. Your girlfriend was penguin waddling after the RV with her shorts down. They stopped, she tore off the door, now she's trying to kill people," Grey chuckled. "Just another day in paradise. See you in a few hours. Have fun with Leonard."

Grey dashed up to the front. Nobody at the table moved a muscle. He leaned out the missing door, laughing as he saw Kayn chasing Killian and Emery freaking out. Looking at the table of confused Ankh, Grey motioned to the missing door, prompting, "This is your job Zach, get out there. We need everyone alive."

Getting up, Zach chuckled, "I'm on it."

"Dean, the keys hanging by the sink. Get the toolbox out of the outside storage. You can help me fix this door," Grey instructed, grinning as everyone sprinted past the missing door again.

Still sitting, Sami mumbled, "So glad we have responsible adults in charge of us."

"If Kayn hears you, I'm not stepping in to stop her," Mel sternly declared, getting up to help. Manoeuvring past Zach in the doorway, she jabbed, "Go get her, Handler boy."

Chuckling, Zach revealed, "I have a plan."

Molly followed Mel out, leaving Amar's son at the table as Zach waited for the others to pass and tackled Kayn to the ground.

Squirming, Kayn threatened, "I swear if you don't let me go kick her ass, I'll…"

"You'll what?" Zach challenged, pinning her, grinning.

Standing in the doorway, observing it all, Sami taunted, "You are all certifiably insane."

Looking up, Kayn ceased trying to escape and stated, "I'll settle for smacking the kid."

Grinning, Zach let her go and said, "Go for it."

She leapt up as Sami clicked, she was really going to do it and took off down the hall.

Carrying the door, Grey shouted, "If you break another door, you're fixing it!"

Standing there watching, Mel yelled after her, "Don't kill Sami, I'm tired!"

When the coast was clear, Emery wandered over, saying, "Does she always overreact like this?"

Blocking the immortal from going inside, Zach declared, "Quit poking my Dragon."

Seductively close, Emery, queen of the pheromone drift drive-by, pressed intimately against Zach, baiting, "What are you going to do? Take your time, sweetheart. No need to use big words." Amar's continent's most powerful Ankh inched by, leaving him awkwardly standing there, weak as a kitten turned on.

Exhaling, Zach whispered, "She doesn't play fair."

Helping Grey fit the door in, Killian chuckled, "Rarely."

Clearing his throat, Zach said, "It's too quiet, I'll go check on Kayn." As Zach took off down the hall, everyone went back inside. Killian offered to continue driving, Grey went to check on Emma and once again they were on the road.

23

THE IRONY OF SOUL MATES

They were on a mission to intercept the Trinity girl Leonard kidnapped. Peering up from his cell, Orin instructed, "Turn here."

Obeying, Lily took a gravel road. They'd been travelling for twenty minutes feeling like they must be going the wrong way when they drove into an empty town with dust layered windows and cobblestone jostling their tires. Watching his long-time afterlife partner in crime, Frost's heart softened. When he let himself fall in love again, longing had shifted to relaxed friendship with Lily. Glancing back, Orin was texting like they were on their way to a barbeque, not a slaughter. His cell vibrated. Frost giggled, reading, *the penguin has chilled*.

"What's so funny?" Orin asked from the backseat.

Erasing the message so Kayn wouldn't beat Grey within an inch of his life, Frost answered, "Nothing."

"Chatting with your girlfriend? I like relationship you, but I miss my carousing buddy," Orin commented.

Gazing out the window, grinning, Frost taunted, "Lily will be your new wingman."

Musically laughing with silky onyx hair glistening in the sunshine, Lily teased, "You won't need my wingman services tonight, nothing's open. Orin, can you check to see if the location changed?"

"Keep your eyes open, we're meeting up with Triad here, it's hard to find," Orin disclosed.

Leaning against a building, Kevin waved. "Perfect, I was hoping to avoid this guy," Frost muttered.

Slowly cruising over with crackling tires, Lily teased, "It looks like your girlfriend's ex came to greet us alone." They pulled up with a window down. Leaning out, Lily harassed, "Did they leave you here, Kev?"

Confidently walking over, Kevin explained, "It's off the beaten path. Thought I'd save you guys the frustration of searching. Mind if I speak to Frost alone?"

Shrugging, Lily answered, "We're good listening to music and gossiping."

Humouring him, Frost got out. Kevin came over with his hand extended, diffusing tension by apologising, "It wasn't intentional. Just so you know."

Irritated by how likeable he was, Frost shook his hand and replied, "I'm not concerned. Just so you know."

Smiling, Kevin laughed, "Fair enough."

"Meeting me alone is a bold move after this morning," Frost sparred, walking alongside him.

"I volunteered," Kevin said, keeping pace as they strolled away from the purring engine. "I'll cut to the chase, having this girl changes nothing. With Amar's son in the mix, your group doesn't come out of the next Testing. I know, it caused drama when I came to Kayn with this proposal, so I'm coming to you. I followed through with the plot to help Ankh survive the last

Testing for this continent by killing the person I loved most, so she'd be traumatised enough to trigger a Dragon response. I had a front-row seat watching her move on. It's been hard, but I want to find a way to be her friend again, this is how it happens. This girl is nobody to you, but she's someone I could be happy with. Let us have her. Let me move on and fall in love with someone else."

Frost confessed, "I can't say the words, rules and all, but we don't intend to try hard to take this girl if that helps."

"Thank you," Kevin replied, turning back to the car.

Frost chuckled, "Don't thank me yet, kid. If you guys die and screw everything up, we might have to take her. I'm just letting you know we're ready to start training and not actively pursuing your girl." He opened the door for Kevin.

"Is this where I mention how many times, we've bailed you out this month?" Kevin harassed, sliding in beside Orin.

Grinning as he got in and closed the door, Frost stated, "You murder us more than you help us. I wasn't going to bring it up. I didn't want to make it awkward."

Openly laughing, Lily provoked, "Is this pissing contest going on all night or is it out of your system now?"

"You'll have to wait and see," Kevin flirted, winking at Lily's reflection as they turned up dust driving away.

Frost's phone hummed. Intrigued by the timing, smiling so hard his cheeks hurt, he read Kayn's text. *We're coming, I broke a door. I can't wait to see you.* He texted back. *You'll never guess who's in our car?*

It's Kevin, isn't it? Are you playing nice? Kayn messaged.

I'm not a nice guy, Brighton. Frost texted back, grinning.

With an endearing lack of experience, Kayn texted, *say hi.*

Grinning, Frost passed it on, "Kayn says hi."

"Hi back," Kevin replied, unphased. Catching Lily's gaze in the rear-view, he instructed, "Take a left at the fork in the road, it's not far. We're early enough to snoop around."

The fragrance of pineapple sage with a hint of salty air meant the ocean was nearby. "There's a full moon tonight, everything dark and twisty loves a celestial event," Lily said. Peering in the rear-view. "Is Tiberius with you?"

"As king of all things dark and twisty he should be, but no, they went to get a rental car," Kevin disclosed.

Grinning, Orin whispered, "I'd switch out that excuse before Grey gets here."

"You can tell him whatever you want, that's what I was instructed to say," Kevin admitted, shrugging. "I'm usually in charge of this group."

"If we kidnapped you, Triad would be in shambles," Orin taunted.

Kevin chuckled, "Blow another job this week you get a prize." A picturesque cottage and rustic barn came into view. Pointing to vehicles by the bushes, he suggested, "Park over there, this car is dusty enough to blend in."

They parked and got out. Inhaling sweet-scented air, Lily wandered towards the barn, sighing, "I've always loved these flowers." Floating in like queen of everything, she noticed their frenemies having a beer and teased, "It's frowned upon to get wasted before a demon fight."

Wandering over, Stephanie sparred, "It's never

stopped Ankh before." Passing Lily one, Kevin's attractive shifter friend, said, "It's hot. This is all we have. You're welcome."

Peeking into a claw marked stall, Lily smiled and replied, "Thank you." Taking in the ceremonial altar and scripture in blood on the ceiling, Lily reviewed it, "Cozy demon altar. Five stars on the creepy."

Passing one to Frost, Patrick appreciatively eyed him up, praising, "Your sexiness."

"Six of us, that's it?" Frost enquired, disregarding young Triad's flirtation, checking the place out. "Is it just me or is there an excessive number of sickles in here?"

Touching a blade, Patrick decreed, "Ambience."

"At least if we get chained up again, we have backup coming, that's handy," Lily stated, opening a cooler, thinking it was Triad's. A putrid odour wafted out. Quickly shutting it, she reminded, "Our demon blades are in the trunk."

"I'll go," Orin offered, holding out his hand.

"Thanks, Sugar," Lily replied, tossing him keys.

"Sneak attack or wait for brainwashed mortals to show up and blend in?" Steph asked, opening Triad's demon blade case, giving one to Kevin and Patrick.

Curious, Lily probed, "Have you met Leonard?"
"We have, I bet he called you pretty bird eighty times," Stephanie divulged, taking a practice swing with her blade.

Finishing his beer, Frost bantered, "Pump up those numbers."

They turned as Orin came in, asking, "I don't want to be the asshole pointing out the obvious, but did anyone check the house?"

"It's empty, I looked in the windows," Patrick answered, wiping sweat off his brow.

"The sun's going down. We should split up before we don't have the option," Orin suggested. A click drew his gaze. A black-eyed woman had a shotgun pointed at him. He rolled his eyes at Patrick.

Blankly, Lily responded, "We've come for the sacrifice."

Lowering the gun, the mortal, hailed, "Praise Jezebeth!"

They all repeated, "Praise Jezebeth." She didn't leave so they were stuck there as crackling tires announced the arrival of mindless mortals. Orin thought, *'When I had the instinct to double-check the house, I should have.'*

Frost telepathically instructed, *'We can't stand in the middle of the room if we're trying to be inconspicuous. We need to slowly back into the stalls. Can you hear us, Triad?'*

'I'll pass it on,' Kevin replied in his mind.

As others arrived, they inched away like they were making room until the crowd accumulated. Separated by a herd of vacant brainwashed mortals, as hidden as they were going to get, Lily was sparkling like a firefly in the dark. Frost thought, *'He'll see you the second he walks in Lily. Do you have this?'*

'Always,' Lily answered in her mind.

You could hear a pin drop as the hoard gathered until they were packed like sardines with the massive doors wide open. Floodlights turned on. Leaving his truck running, the painfully annoying immortal they'd come for, strutted into his barn of disciples with his hands raised, proclaiming, "I am Leonard, magical maker of mayhem, destroyer of souls, master of dark magic and sorcery. Tonight I shall bring forth Jezebeth to free you from mortal form. I welcome you to the next realm with the sacrifice of."

An engine revved as their host was ploughed down by a truck. Free of compulsion, followers crumpled to the floor. Lexy and Tiberius got out, cackling.

"Guess we'll clean this up," Lily commented.

Addressing his crimson-haired coconspirator, Tiberius proposed, "Shall we chop this guy up and spread him out?"

"Sounds good. We'll take half, you bring half with you?" Lexy decreed, grabbing a sickle with a skip in her step.

Frost thought, *'Quickly Kevin before someone stops you.'*

Smiling, Kevin sprinted to a girl with her wrists bound, urging, "I'll untie you in the car. We need to get out of here."

Nudging Frost, Lily whispered, "You softie, I saw what you did."

Torching the barn, they stood watching it burn. With half of Leonard in a potato sack over her shoulder, Lexy stated, "Let's get rid of this idiot somewhere creative."

24
YOU

*I*n Kayn's afterlife, there was always scenery monotonously whirling by windows, bursts of raucous laughter from the Ankh playing board games amidst off-key singing along to the driver's playlist. It was an endless road trip. *Sometimes, all her heart desired was to be still.* After texting with Frost, she'd buried her face in her pillow, pretending to be asleep on her bunk, longing for simpler days spent lounging in pyjamas in front of a TV with snacks, a tub of popcorn and nowhere to be because it was Saturday. *She didn't even know what day of the week it was anymore.* Even though she was still fuming about chasing the RV with her shorts at her ankles, she understood the need to throw a grenade at monotony. *Being accident-prone, she didn't need anyone going out of their way to point out the obvious. She made a fool of herself daily. She was supposed to be an authority figure to their newbie Ankh. If they didn't make it out of the Testing, it would be her fault, she was horrible at being immortal. She could trigger the Siren easily, but being a Conduit was Russian Roullette with powers. The Dragon was* *trauma-induced. It was becoming far to easy to shut off her emotions. The new gifts she'd discovered were too volatile to summon up just to see if she could.* There was a thump, thud, thumping, thud. They pulled over. *They hit something. Fantastic. They were going to be so late. At least they hadn't hit something large like a moose. That was silly, you can't hit a moose in Mexico. Can you?*

Everyone groaned as Killian yelled, "We have a flat, give us a minute!"

Laying next to her, Zach assured, "We all suck at being immortal, and I'm ninety percent sure there aren't moose in Mexico. If you continue overthinking everything like this, the hamster wheel between your ears will spin off the track."

Turning to face him, Kayn countered, "If I gave you even half of my abilities, yours would be too."

With a knowing grin, Zach whispered, "Go get a knife and meet me in the bathroom."

Intrigued, Kayn jumped off the bunk and took off into the kitchen area. Digging through the drawers, she grabbed a knife, held it up like a prize and ran away.

Grey shouted after her, "Where are you going with that knife, Brighton?"

Giggling, she ran to the bathroom and locked the door. "Who are we stabbing?" Kayn taunted, stoked.

"Do it, stab me, it's so cool," Zach egged her on.

Trying the handle, Grey asserted, "You can't stab anyone, Brighton. We're already running late."

Zack whipped off his shirt, urging, "Trust me! Do it!"

Wiggling the handle, Grey pounded on the door, saying, "Nobody is stabbing anyone!"

Kayn whispered, "We're going to get in trouble."

"From who?" Zach provoked, "Do it!"

Shrugging, Kayn stabbed her Handler in the stomach and yanked the blade out. It seeped for a second, he wiped away the blood with toilet paper. *It was healed.* Awestruck, Kayn praised, "You're a Healer, Zach!"

"It barely hurt," Zach giggled. The giddy duo, danced like dorky kids, laughing.

She didn't have to worry about him anymore! She took the knife from him, and stabbed herself to check, "You heal as fast as I do!"

Hammering on the door, Grey yelled, "Our symbols are going off. I'm breaking the door down in 3, 2..."

Kayn opened it and stepped out of the way, Grey ended up in the shower. Spinning, he scolded, "What in the hell?"

"Look! Zach's a Healer now," Kayn explained, shiving her Handler again to show Grey.

Wiping off the blood, Zach announced, "Good as new!"

Everyone's symbols went off, so they were gathered in the hall. Barging in, Mel, high-fived Zach, cheering, "You've got your powers!" The trio hugged as lookie-loos dispersed.

Grey walked out, muttering, "I need a drink."

That's a fantastic idea. "I'll be back," Kayn declared, beating Grey to the fridge. Grabbing celebratory drinks, she inched out of the way, making room as their tire saviours came in.

"Who set off our symbols?" Killian questioned, smiling.

Raising her hand, Kayn confessed, "It was me, Zach's a Healer now."

"Cool," Killian commented, going to the front.

Raising his beer, Grey saluted, "Yeah, frigging cool. Hey, let's all stab each other in the bathroom."

Leaning across the table with distracting cleavage, Emery stole Grey's drink, blatantly flirting, "I plan to hang out with you tonight. Don't take off." With a seductive sway of hips, the Siren vanished into the front with his beer.

The table of newbies was uncomfortably silent as Zach strutted in, toying, "Nobody ever makes their intentions that clear for me."

"Right?" Kayn taunted, passing his drink. *Good for him. He said nobody, instead of referring to girls. He was becoming more open about his flexible preferences. She'd read between the lines there. By the expression on Dean's face, so did he.* Drawn to Emma's fight to suppress emotion, a wave of guilt washed over her. *Did that happen today? So much happened in a short period of time. They were jerks. They'd been pushing Grey's buttons. After finding out everything he knew about his mortal life was a compelled lie, he'd been forced to cut a baby out of Emma, then Lexy took off with Tiberius.* Getting Grey another, Kayn scooted onto the bench and sheepishly slid a beer over, apologising, "You've had a shitty day. I was excited about Zach getting an ability. I should have stabbed him later."

Accepting the gesture, Grey raised his beer, "That was almost a deeply touching apology. You're right, you should have stabbed him later."

Clinking drinks with him, Kayn teased, "The end of your day may be great?"

"I can't take off. Lexy will be back, we need to talk things out," Grey answered peacefully.

After behaving himself for a good fifteen minutes, Sami commented, "Maybe she won't come back tonight, Tiberius is a sexy guy?"

Grey politely excused himself, saying he had to go to the washroom, Kayn got up to let him out and silently watched him walk away. *Getting angry was pointless, Sami enjoyed it.*

"Does intentionally hurting people make you feel

good?" Dean asked, going after Grey. Everyone else got up and left in solidarity.

After that bold show of unity, it was clear someone had to get through to Sami before his self-destructive tendencies destroyed them all. It was like he was trying to make it impossible for the others to like him. Getting up, Kayn said, "Do you want a drink, Sami?"

Shocked they were staying, Sami answered, "I guess."

Passing him a drink, Kayn enquired, "What was it like growing up knowing you were immortal?"

"Nobody likes me. You don't have to pretend you want to spend time with me," Sami bluntly stated, taking a drink.

Intrigued by how he read the situation, Kayn prompted, "Why do you think they don't like you?"

"They left the room," Sami deduced.

"I'm trying to see things from your perspective." With an idea, Kayn whispered, "Can I speak freely?"

"Why not." Samid replied, taking another sip.

"When I was younger I spent a lot of time, scrolling back to the beginning of conversations to figure out how it went wrong," Kayn confessed. "Do you ever do that?"

Smirking, Sami explained, "If I don't speak, I'm accused of being antisocial. When I do, it's the wrong thing at the worst time. My father was so sure I would fail, he sent me to another country so he wouldn't have to watch it happen. Imagine the shame my lack of interpersonal skills will cause when I kill a Testing group?"

He knew his father believed he would fail. He was just living up to his lack of expectations.

"You're a realist," her Handler conceded. Shrugging like it wasn't a big deal. "You can't survive. Why get attached or try? I get it. Your dad hurt your feelings." Zach tried putting things into perspective, "Mine burned down our house with my family in the basement and buried me alive."

Seeing what Zach was trying to do, Kayn interjected, "My twin triggered our Correction. My family was murdered by Abaddon. I was in a coma for a long time. My brother wasn't there when it happened. My dad's best friend moved in with us. They came back to finish the job."

Unimpressed, Sami stated, "I never left the compound. I was evidence of Amar's indiscretions. For one mortal day, I'd welcome the agony. I died without ever living."

Zach put his empty in the sink, grabbed a pen and paper out of the drawer and suggested, "Make a list of the things you've always wanted to do. If you're nice for twenty-four hours, I'll reward you with something from your list."

Intrigued, Sami agreed, "I can do that."

Watching over Sami's shoulder, as her Handler went to see where they were timewise. Kayn grinned. *Number one on his list was to kiss a boy. Awe, Sami wanted to kiss Zach. It was cute.* Leaving him writing his list, Kayn got up, saying, "I went to get Mel a drink and disappeared. Delivery time." Grabbing a beer, she found Mel chatting with Grey. "Better late than never?" Kayn giggled, passing it to her.

"We were eavesdropping, that was sweet," Mel praised, squeezing her arm. "Sit with us. Lily texted Grey. The job's over. We're meeting at a resort for a few days of downtime. It's been a busy month."

There was nothing she wanted more than a few nights in his arms. Kayn reached for her flashing phone, there was a message from Frost. *We have to dispose of Leonard. I can't wait to see you.* Smiling, she texted. *We're going to need so many boxes of Twinkies.* It started flashing. Grinning, she read his response. *That's it, I'm tossing our half of Leonard into a ditch, I'll race you there.* Giggling, she texted. *Half of Leonard? That was random. There has to be a story behind having half of pretty birdy guy.* She knew it was going to be good as her phone vibrated. Kayn read his explanation. *Each Clan took half, he won't stay dead.* Snickering, she toyed via text. *That outta do it. I'll be waiting in the shower.* Her phone rang. Holding it to her ear. *Everyone was arguing about Frost wanting to half-ass the body disposal. It was a pocket dial.* She hung up, giggling.

Elbowing her, Mel pestered, "Your cheeks will be sore from smiling by the time we get there."

She couldn't tap out yet, she'd be smiling for days. Ridiculously excited as the RV turned, Kayn grinned. *Knowing she was going to see him felt like running at full speed towards a cliff.* Her nerve endings were lit up livewires. Adrenaline pulsed as her spirit animal Siren cracked open its eyes. Giddy, she froze mid-torso wiggle, stopping short of bouncing like a sugar cranked child. Harnassing her excess energy, she leapt up as they coasted to a stop. *She needed to shower so she'd have less of a serial murderer vibe going on.* The trio rifled through bags, dying to get out of the RV to begin their mini-vacay.

Raising a bag like a trophy, Grey cha cha'd away, singing, "See you losers oceanside in twenty minutes."

Losers? It wasn't a contest.

Tucking chestnut, shoulder-length hair behind her ears, Mel mocked, "Wooo, I hip-checked my friends and got my bag first, somebody buy me a pony."

He, he. Grinning, Kayn baited, "If you gave him a pony for doing something, everyone would lose it." *Here's a pony Greydon Riley, get over yourself.*

Zipping up her bag, Mel admitted, "Easy to talk to ex playthings are tempting after a few drinks."

She should get a pony for having enough afterlife experience to understand that sentence. She'd wanted to tell the new Ankh, she'd never lived before she died, but it wouldn't be the truth. Parts of her had, the poet, athlete, and friend. Those parts of her were always there. She loved and was loved back. There was a roof over her head and simple issues, but she hadn't known it then. She'd been a fledgling envisioning a swan, wanting others to see it but never feeling it. She didn't see her destructive tendencies until her feathers had been plucked and her wings were broken.

"Your inner dialogue is truly epic," Mel teased, giving her shoulder a pat as she left.

Something was on the floor. Reaching for it, she picked up the plastic topaz ring. Slipping on the bubblegum machine prize, admiring it, Kayn recalled Frost giving it to her. *She thought she lost this.* She'd been confused back then, stuck between her old life and new. For a year he was always nearby, overtly a scoundrel, ignoring her. After sinning his way across the country, he began mercilessly revving her engine and walking away, making her want him back. Luring her in like a fish on a reel, he cast her out at a camp for a week to see who her heart wanted. His were the last eyes she gazed into as she dropped into Testing, and after she survived, they were inevitable. *Every cell ached until she admitted it.* Realising she'd gapped out, Kayn grabbed her bag and stepped out into bliss-inducing tropical sunshine. Wandering over to her friends, she paused to smell an exotic flower. *This place was incredible.*

Lexy yelled, "Heads up, Brighton!" Tossing her keys, she pointed to the beach.

Wooden signs directed her down a cobblestone path with fragrant flowering bushes to their cabana on the beach with a deck facing the sea. The scent of the flowers lingered as she unlocked the sliding door, stepping into the room with crisp white sheets and a spotless tile floor. There was a fancy fruit basket on the nightstand. She peeked into the ensuite with a tile shower. *It was disappointing when there wasn't a tub.* Stripping, she quickly showered. With damp ringlets, Kayn slipped on her barely-there pastel blue string bikini, grabbed her cell and stepped out onto the deck into the inviting salty breeze. Her friends were frolicking in the sea with music playing. *They'd needed this break. What else did this resort offer besides a spectacular view?* Seeing a restaurant and bar, she decided she was hungry. *She required something, burn your tongue off spicy. Did she have time?* Laying on her stomach on a lounger with sunshine caressing her back, she checked for messages. Bummed, there weren't any, she was about to make a run for the bar when she saw someone approaching with trays.

An attractive server delivered trays to the table beside her. Placing a fish bowel sized Pina Colada by her, he said, "Frost will be here soon."

"Gracias," she replied, smiling. The waiter left a bottle of tequila with bowls of salt and lime, shot glasses and a bottle of yellow liquor. Curious, Kayn sat up to snoop. Unscrewing the lid, she sniffed the banana liquor. *This was a sugary hangover waiting to happen. What was under this cover?* Peeking under the lid, it was enchiladas with a side of hot sauce. *He'd better be careful she might think he loved her.* Smiling, she devoured her spicy meal, covered her tray, and rushed to the washroom. Hearing footsteps, her heart leapt. Teeth brushed, feeling sexy ish, Kayn emerged, expecting Frost. Zach and Mel were pouring themselves shots. *Come on, you guys.* She walked over intending to shoo away her lusty escapade blocking friends.

Handing her a drink, Zach chuckled, "You've got half an hour. Do a shot with us before we don't see you for days."

Mel raised one, saluting, "May beautiful memories always outweigh the bad."

They did shots. *Banana liquor with toothpaste wasn't fantastic.*

"I need a bottle," Zach announced, checking the label.

Gazing at the gorgeous beach, Kayn commented, "I just brushed my teeth. I'll need another to know what it tastes like."

Grinning, Zach teased, "Twist my arm." Repouring their shots, he questioned, "I don't need to come up with a toast deeper than Mel's, do I?"

"To best friends!" Kayn cheered, holding her shot. They repeated her sentiment, downing theirs. *Now, it was tasty.* She declared, "These shots would be even better with whipping cream."

Leaning over the railing watching shirtless Grey running into the surf with a board, Mel sighed, "He always looks like he's having fun."

Nudging Mel, Kayn revealed, "When he was six his older sisters died protecting him. His memories were wiped. He had to cut a baby out of Emma, Lexy took off with Tiberius. If you're revisiting the idea out of boredom, let Guru Grey surf it out."

"Way to kill a mood, dead sisters, cutting babies out, love of your life sleeping with your nemesis. What's next, you going to roast that Gecko on the hot sand and eat him?" Mel ribbed, shoving her.

"What Gecko?" Zach panicked, scooting away like it was dangerous.

That was a peculiar thing to be afraid of? "It's just a lizard Zach," Kayn teased, touching it to prove it wasn't scary.

"That's just a spider," he taunted, pointing behind her.

She wasn't going to fall for it. There wasn't a spider there. He was messing with her.

Wincing, her Handler provoked, "You are going to lose your shit. That's a jumping spider." Zach warned, cautiously stepping away.

She didn't believe him. What were the odds of a giant gecko and a spider being on the deck at the same time?

Squirming, Zach prompted, "I'd move."

Busy ogling Grey, Mel turned to see what the fuss was about. Her eyes widened as she stepped back, soundlessly mouthing, "Holy shit."

That was convincing.

Darting off the deck into the sand, Mel urged, "You don't need to be a badass. Move!"

She had to look. As she turned, a fist-sized furry arachnid soared at her landing on her chest. Shrieking like a Vampire in the sunlight, Kayn did a gold medal backwards high jump, clearing the railing, she landed on her back on the beach, freaking out, "No, no, no! Get it off! Please! I can't! Help!"

Mel, their spider slaying superhero swatted it off into the sand.

Panicking, Kayn scurried backwards as it crawled away. Everyone was laughing. *She never got to look cool. It was a thing.*

Zach helped her up, consoling, "Don't sweat it, Brighton. Everyone has an irrational fear of something."

Surprised she hadn't lost her bikini top, Kayn adjusted it, laughing, "Did everyone see that?"

Using his hand as a visor, her Handler chuckled, "Grey's underwater, he missed it."

They went back onto the spider free deck for their drinks. Leaning over the railing observing Grey in the ocean, Kayn teased, "He'll be too exhausted to know you're alive." Their sun-worshipping friend caught a wave. *Grey looked majestic. It almost made her want to give surfing another try.*

"The energizer bunny has nothing on Grey Riley," Mel commented, as he vanished beneath a crashing wave. "Let's be honest, our dating pool is shallow."

Zach whispered, "He hasn't lit anything on fire yet, he's fine. Go for it, Mel."

Giggling, Mel sparred, "Who else is there?"

Checking out the beach, Zach declared, "Killian is a hot international guy with outstanding hair. Dean and Sami are into dudes. I'm stuck in the friend zone until the end of time. Orin is your dad. Okay, I get it. Killian and Grey, that's all you have to choose from. Now, if your preferences varied, your options would be wide open."

Meeting her Handler's eyes, Kayn dared, "If you could pick one person on this beach for a no complications one night stand, who would it be?"

"I have to choose Mel, she's standing beside me," Zach baited, watching Emery and Lily tanning on towels on the sand.

"Gee, thanks," Mel laughed, tossing an ice cube from her drink at the self-appointed king of her friend zone.

As Sami sprinted into the surf, Kayn asked, "Did you see his wish list?"

"I forgot about that," Zach answered.

"Number one on his unbucket list is, kiss a boy," Kayn harassed, poking his side.

Grinning, Zach jeered, "Sami can't be nice for twenty-four hours. I'll ask Dean to take one for the team if he does."

"You made the bet," Kayn pestered as a server wandered over, asking if there was anything they wanted.

Holding up the half-empty bottle of banana liquor,

Zach enquired, "Kind sir, can I get this room a new bottle with a spray can of whipping cream?"

"Right away, sir. I'll be here all night if there's anything else you need," the waiter flirted, eyeing up Zach.

"He's cute," Mel provoked.

Sipping melted Pina Colada listening to music hanging out with friends. It felt like they were ordinary people on a tropical destination vacation. Alcohol numbed inhibitions as they moved to the music, dancing on the deck overlooking the ocean.

Grabbing Mel, Zach steered her away, singing, "See you later, Brighton."

Her heart soared as she saw Frost carrying the bottle of banana liquor and whipped cream, Zach ordered, lugging his backpack. She jogged over to help.

Dropping everything as she ran into his arms, he nuzzled her neck, taunting, "When we get inside, I'm going to untie this ridiculously sexy bikini with my teeth and cover you in whipping cream."

With her arms around his neck, Kayn hovered her lips a breath from his, naughtily provoking, "Not if I cover you in it first."

With his body against hers, he said, "I missed you."

Deviously grinning, Kayn picked up what he'd dropped, shuffling backwards, seducing, "How much?"

"So much," he laughed, diving for her, tugging her bikini string. Her top fell off. Concealing her chest, she ran inside, cackling. Retrieving her bikini top, he followed her into the charming cabana, commenting, "This is nice." Dropping his backpack, he tugged the curtains closed, took off his shirt, tossed it on the bed and questioned, "How did you get a full canister of whipped cream?"

Pouring banana liquor into glasses, she explained,

"Zach ordered it, I wanted to try it on shots." Spraying cream into each glass.

Wrapping his arms around her from behind, Frost kissed her shoulder, sensually toying, "Remind me to thank Zach."

Handing him a drink, Kayn urged, "Try one." Sitting on the dresser, she toasted, "To memorable places."

Using large glasses, cream ended up on their noses. "I bet that's why people use shot glasses," she giggled, licking her lips.

"You missed a spot," he seduced, grazing her lip with his thumb.

He'd made her ache with a touch. Dipping a finger in her glass, Kayn brushed it on his nipple, flirting, "I'll get that," taking her time licking it off."

His eyes darkened as he warned, "I'm going to make you scream."

Daring him to lose control, she tugging the string on her bikini bottoms, provoking, "Your move."

Dropping to his knees, he buried his face between her thighs and shook her to her core until she was clutching his hair, whimpering as her pheromones released, triggering his. Lost in Siren euphoria, their lips met in frenzied lust as he took her with volatile desperation until she raked her nails down his back as they climaxed like hedonistic animals. He carried her to bed and kissed every inch of her flesh, taunting her with his tongue, vowing to love her as she did the same. Afterwards, she lay spent in his arms with her head on his chest, listening to his heartbeat, wishing the night could go on forever, loving him with all she was.

Kissing her hair, he pledged, "If we vow to always forgive each other, nothing can break us. I'm yours. I'm going to love you for as long as you'll let me. There's nothing we can't fight our way back from."

"Ditto," she responded, yanking his chain, giggling as he kissed her all over, whispering, I love you, each time his lips left her skin. Arching her back lost in tender kisses, caresses, and declarations, she felt their bond in the core of her being. With their unquenchable passionate union solidified by raw emotional confessions, they intimately made love, moving together as one with their gazes locked as devotion rose to a breathtaking crescendo and subsided with tears in their eyes.

With everyone gathered by a firepit and music blaring in the middle of the night, it was clear their Clan had the resort to themselves. They were players in an immortal game where Connections could be forced, and memories wiped, every moment had to count. Happiness wasn't part of the deal, so when you had the time you took it. They put on swimsuits and went for a stroll on the beach, holding hands with salty ocean air, floral fragrance and silken sand beneath their toes. Deliriously enamoured with each other, it felt like a beautiful dream as he tugged her into his arms. They swayed to music muffled by rhythmically crashing waves and kissed under a slivered moon. Lacing fingers, they shared unfiltered tales of first loves without flinching walking under a breathtaking display of glimmering stars. They waded out, splashing each other in the surf until heavy eyelids prompted the pair to wander back to their cabana where she passed out with her head on his chest, listening to the beat of his heart.

THE SLIDING DOOR OPENED, STRETCHING LIKE A BLISSFUL kitten in the sunshine, Kayn opened her eyes as Frost came in with a tray of fruit, pastries, and coffee. Beaming, she mumbled, "Best boyfriend ever."

Placing it on the dresser, Frost crawled on the bed

and kissed her, confessing, "I thought I'd soften you up before springing a change of plans."

Forcibly rolling him over to straddle him, Kayn taunted, "You better not be going anywhere. I'm not even close to done with you."

"I wouldn't dare, but we need to be out there before bad Markus arrives," he flirted, clutching her hips, biting his lip.

"Take your shorts off," she commanded, with a devious glint in her eyes.

"In twenty minutes," he finished the sentence.

"Nooo," Kayn pouted, gyrating her hips.

"Need help?" Frost toyed as his palms heated her hips.

Passion sparkled in her eyes, she moaned as goosebumps prickled and waves of knee-buckling intense pleasure surged through nerve endings. Raspily crying out, she collapsed on him, whimpering.

Beneath her, Frost chuckled, "Raincheck on the foreplay, come on, time to eat." Clutching her ass, giggling, he said, "I need to change now."

Her senses were humming with gratification, she couldn't even move. Forcing herself to get up, she clued in. "I'll be back," Kayn goofily quoted, leaving him on the bed, laughing. Tugging the string halfway to the washroom, she strutting away bare assed, swinging her string bikini bottoms.

"Brighton, you're the sexiest woman alive!" Frost called after her.

Her rosy-cheeked reflection was adorable. You'd think she'd be far past blushing. Smiling, she cleaned the garment, hung it in the shower and brushed her teeth, thinking of the first time she saw Frost. *He was a surprise shirtless immortal guy on her bed. She'd let a stranger brand her, it still made her grin. Her best friend Kevin had the bad timing to be crawling in her window. With psychic lineage, he came along for the ride. That life of mortal innocence felt like the fairytale now. She'd hit a point where nothing surprised her. Perhaps, it was all part of evolving. If someone told her she was going to fall in love with Frost a few years ago, she would have laughed.* Feeling his presence, she saw him behind her in the mirror and said, "I'll be right out."

Handing her a new bikini, Frost warned, "Lexy is having breakfast with us, avoiding discussing recent choices with Grey." Grinning, he collected half from the shower.

"He let her avoid him?" Kayn enquired. *That was strange?*

"I haven't talked to him," Frost whispered. Kissing her cheek, he tugged the string on her top and took off with it, chuckling, "I'll hang this on the deck."

Quickly fixing herself up, she came out, smiling at her sister. Trying to choose a pastry, Kayn questioned, "Fruit or meat?"

"No idea," Lexy admitted. Choosing one, she bit into it, saying, "Fruit," pointing one out for her.

Devouring every delectable morsel, Kayn probed, "Are you okay?"

Smiling, Lexy nodded, admitting, "I was sure Grey was going to burst in and light something on fire or throw a temper tantrum, but he hasn't even come looking for me. We have separate rooms, maybe he requested it. I suntanned on the deck and went to sleep early."

She wanted to tell her everything but wasn't sure if she should. Maybe Grey was the one who needed a minute with everything? Lexy started laughing. "What?"Kayn asked.

"Your inner commentary has no filter, you might as well just tell me now," Lexy teased, snatching a melon.

She might as well just say it. She'd want to know what

she was up against if she hurt Zach. Kayn shared the complicated tale, "He found out he had two older sisters and an aunt who died trying to save him when he was six. His life in Scotland was erased, the memories of his father were planted. He cut a baby out of Emma and died in the fight. Tiberius went after you. Instead of killing him, you took off together. Azariah made him understand you needed these experiences, he's handling it well."

"He didn't light anything on fire?" Lexy asked.

Shaking her head, Kayn replied, "Nothing. I'm curious though, how did you take off with Tiberius?"

"I have no idea how but I know why," Lexy confessed, pensively. "It doesn't matter. It can't go anywhere. It was a stupid rebellious move, but I don't regret it."

Pouring shots, Kayn handed one to her sister. Raising hers, she saluted, "No regrets." Repeating her words, Lexy drank hers as Frost came in with Grey by his side.

Giving Frost a dirty look, Grey sighed, "Cute, parent trap move." His eyes met Lexy's. Neither spoke.

Grinning, Frost suggested, "Come on, Brighton. Let's grab food at the buffet. They need to talk it out. We all have to be on the same page to keep up with Bad Markus."

Saying nothing, Kayn followed him. Taking Frost's hand as they walked the beach to the restaurant, she gushed, "You got a crazy amount of brownie points this morning."

Chuckling, he baited, "Remember that when I screw up."

Swinging their arms, she saw everyone on the restaurant patio. *Emery was eating with Zach. Plot twist.* Emery gave her an unimpressed look. Kayn sighed, "I'd better rack up points myself, apparently the Dragon bites."

With an arm around her, as they went in, Frost kissed her hair, saying, "I know. Ignore Emery, top of the food chain immortals like to be the most powerful one in the room. They get pissy if someone gives them a run for their money."

Filling her plate at the buffet, slyly observing the intimate breakfast with her Handler. *Go, Zach. She was impressed.* Kayn whispered, "What can't she do?"

"She's lots of fun once you get to know her," Frost said.

"Ugh, don't remind me," Kayn baited, elbowing him.

Grabbing fruit, Frost taunted, "If you start counting up my past indiscretions, you'll always be pissed."

"Maybe, don't refer to ex booty calls as lots of fun?" She toyed, stealing fruit off his plate.

Swatting her away, Frost chuckled, "You are standing in front of the buffet."

"You were standing next to me," Kayn jousted, grinning, as they sat at an empty table.

Realising she was joking, he stole back his fruit, took a bite, and seduced, "We should bring a plate of fruit to our room. I'll feed it to you later."

The newbies wandered in, hungover. Emma's body was restored to its factory settings with no hint of pregnancy. *She wanted to talk to her but didn't know what to say. What could anyone say?*

Taking her hand across the table, Frost responded to her thoughts, "Wait for the right time, it'll come to you."

Her eyes darted to her Handler, chatting with Emery in Spanish. *His sexy went up ten notches using his native tongue. Well done, Zach.* Frost's phone buzzed, drawing her attention away from her Handler's conversation. Her boyfriend read it and chuckled. *What was he up to?*

Standing up, clapping to catch everyone's attention, Frost pointed to the beach and ordered, "Eat up. Everyone needs to be by the firepit on the beach. Get drunk, act natural."

Get drunk, act natural. Seems legit. Getting up, Kayn probed, "I know that laugh, what are you up to?"

With an arm around her, as they left the restaurant, Frost explained, "I didn't want to wreck our perfect night, talking about it." He stopped, tugged her closer, kissed her lips and whispered in her ear, "After we've dealt with this, I'll make it up to you."

Running her hands through his hair, Kayn taunted, "Quit stalling and spill. Why do we have to be at the same place on the beach?"

"I can't disclose the details. We can't risk spooking the idiot inhabiting Markus. We've lured him into a controlled environment. Everyone working here is affiliated with the Aries Group. That's all I'm allowed to say," Frost replied.

It was her inner dialogue, wasn't it?

Laughing, as they continued walking, Frost answered her thought, teasing, "It's not just you. There are others."

It was true. She had no filter.

Racing, Lexy shoved Grey, he face-planted in the sand. With arms raised like a champion crossing a finish line, she stole the chair, shouting, "Eat my dust, Greydon!"

They'd made up.

Finding chairs by the firepit unused in daylight hours, she leaned back, closed her eyes and pretended they were just on vacation. A tray of slushy drinks came by. Recognizing the person serving cocktails, Kayn smiled as she took one. Some were sprawled on towels sunbathing, others were standing talking. Everyone was, go hard or go home drinking. Molly and Zach were chatting in Spanish now. *It was cute. They had something in common. She really liked three of the newbie Ankh. Sami was still growing on her. They were starting to remind her of her own Testing group.*

Blissfully enjoying the sunshine, Emery commented on her inner dialogue, "If you let yourself get attached, it'll hurt more."

"We made it out," Kayn replied, looking her way.

Passing her a shot of tequila, Emery changed subjects. She raised a shot, cheering, "To frenemies."

Cute. Someone cranked the volume on the music as Kayn raised her own, repeating, "To frienemies."

"Your Handler's a nice guy, intelligent, kind, he was a good choice for the job," Emery stated. As her eyes darted to the conversation Zach was having with Molly, she smiled.

Looking her way, Kayn agreed, "He's the best." They drank, she listened as everyone talked, enjoying the warmth of the sun on her skin. *She was beginning to see what Frost meant, Emery was alright.*

Frost reached for her hand, she took it, smiling. *Yes, she had no filter at all.* Emery had the newbies playing never have I ever. Tiny Molly was packing shots back like a two hundred pound linebacker. *This should be entertaining.* Sami was chilling in the sun on his best behaviour. *That was hilarious. Zach was going to have to kiss him.* Out of nowhere, Grey started asking everyone to arm wrestle. *Was that his inner Scotsman or Aussie? Either way, it was hilarious. Her inner Canadian always made her apologise for random things. Oh, no. Big Sexy let Grey win.*

With his accent, growing thicker with every shot,

Grey lost it, "Try Asshole! I demand a rematch!" Laughing so hard he tipped over, Killian sprawled in the sand, giggling.

They were endearing idiots. They were all so amazing. Staring at Emery, until she noticed her eye stalking her, Kayn praised, "You're amazing." *She loved everyone.*

Giggling, Emery replied, "You're wasted."

Standing, waving, Frost shouted, "Welcome to paradise!"

They were at the bar. Frost, Lily and Killian took off to greet the others. Her pulse raced, she heard the echoing thudding of her heart. The beach distorted like a funhouse mirror. *No! Shit! Not now! She couldn't have an Enlightening.* She tried sipping her Pina Colada, missed the straw and looked. It had melted and shrivelled into her boiling slushy. *Oh, no. It was going to blow up. Damn it! Shit! She couldn't think! There was nowhere to put it! Zach!* She felt Zach's hands on her shoulders, her darkened veins vanished as her palpitating heart slowed. Kayn glanced back and whispered, "Thank you."

"Dump the drink in the sand," her Handler instructed.

Impressed it didn't explode, she dumped it.

With his hands on her shoulders, Zach soothed, "Deep breath in, deep breath out."

Closing her eyes, breathing until she was calm, unaware of anything but their bond. As he took his hands off, she looked back. Smiling, Kayn said, "Thank you. That came out of nowhere." Getting up, they embraced.

With his chin on her shoulder, Zach teased, "You good now? Any murderous impulses?" She started giggling in his embrace. He scolded, "Don't laugh at that question, I'll be nervous all day."

She pulled away, met her Handler's gaze and baited,

"I should get them to put my slushy drinks in a coffee mug just in case."

Taking her hands, Zach declared, "Normal temp, I think you're good to go. Maybe, you should let everyone else deal with this situation today?" Passing her his slushy, he urged, "I haven't even taken a sip yet. Have mine, I'll send someone to get a coffee mug."

Everyone was watching. Embarrassed, Kayn mouthed, "I'm okay." *It felt weak when she couldn't control herself.* Needing her escape, she looked for Frost, forgetting he took off. *He was at the bar with everyone, unaware of what happened.*

Sami got up and offered, "I'll go get a coffee mug. Does anybody else need a drink?" A bunch of hands raised. Sami laughed as he took off.

Sami was doing better.

Looking her way, Emery explained, "You'll get used to those surges. The first year of Enlightening is the hardest. When we have time, I can teach you how to direct energy elsewhere."

Softening, Kayn nodded and replied, "I'd be into that."

Smiling, Grey admitted, "Pyrokinesis is hard to control."

Nodding behind Grey's back, Lexy brushed herself off, suggesting, "Brighton needs a distraction. Surprise training time. Come on, try to take me, newbies."

Molly leapt up like a badass, declaring, "It's on!"

Grinning, Zach commented, "She's great."

The rest of Ankh arrived. Holding Markus' hand in a floral dress, Arrianna laughed, "Some things never change."

Void of polite pretence, Markus turned a chair, sat and brutishly yanked Arrianna onto his lap.

Everyone watched as tiny framed Molly screamed

like a maniac, attacking Lexy, who used the girl's motion to launch her through the air. Molly landed with an explosion of sand. Leaving her lost in a cloud, their crimson-haired warrior, laughed, "Next!"

Shrugging, Dean strolled over, enquiring, "Do I hit you first?"

"Try it," Lexy egged him on. Dean swung a few times as she manoeuvred out of his way like he wasn't even trying, laughing, swept his leg and motioned like she had a weapon. "Dean's dead, who's next?"

"I'll go," Kayn declared, grinning at her sister.

Practically tackling her, Zach scolded, "Absolutely not!"

Laughing, Kayn mumbled, "Spoilsport."

Putting an arm around her, Frost whispered, "Have you been misbehaving?"

"Just boiling Pina Coladas with my mind," Kayn replied, grinning as Frost started laughing.

"I'll do it," Emma volunteered, coming over, crouching with fists raised.

Knowing how protective Grey felt after what he'd been forced to do, Lexy vetoed her turn, "Maybe you should give yourself more time."

"I'm a blackbelt. I won silver in my weight division last year boxing, and I was on the wrestling team, don't wussy out," Emma challenged, smirking.

"We have a dark horse," Emery announced, impressed.

Intrigued, Lexy declared, "Bring it."

Like a dance, they were darting and weaving, avoiding leg sweeps. Emma landed a right hook, everyone was blown away. As they cheered the newbie with the pixie cut on, their body napped leader's facade unravelled. Enraged, Markus tossed Arrianna off his lap. *Here we go.*

He rifled a chair at Lexy who dodged out of the way. "Do you think me a fool?" Markus bellowed.

Yes, one hundred percent. Grinning, Frost smacked her butt. *Oh, yes, inner dialogue. My bad.*

Storming over to the no longer pregnant girl, Markus grilled, "Where is it?"

"Where is what?" Emma, with a flat tummy, responded, innocently.

Zeroing in on Frost, Markus commanded, "Give me the location of the child."

Boldly, Frost provoked, "She gave birth days ago. Did I forget to tell you?"

"The LOCATION!" Markus bellowed.

Casually, Frost answered, "Africa."

"No, the last baby is there. This one went to Australia," Lexy corrected, sauntering over.

"I will have you all entombed for this," Markus menaced under his breath, pacing back and forth, cursing.

Oh, he wasn't even trying to pretend he was Markus anymore.

Arrianna needled, "Is something wrong, Honey?"

Caressing her face, Markus whispered, "As punishment for believing you could outsmart me, I'm keeping you as my pet." Tossing a coin, a spinning black portal opened midair. The imposter launched Arrianna into the swirling vortex ominously declaring, "Foolish halfbreed spawn! Enjoy your last twenty-four hours!"

Waving, Frost grinned, and sang, "Enjoy yours."

Bad Markus stepped into the vortex, his body was spat out into the sand. Orin and Grey picked up Markus' soulless body and carried it away. *Arrianna was just tossed into a black hole, and nobody seemed concerned.*

"We're fairly certain we've got this handled, carry on

with your day," Lily announced, sprawling on a towel in the sand like nothing happened.

Fairly certain? Grey was luring traumatised Newbies away with snacks and beer. Immortal or not, they were teenagers.

Hugging her Frost flirted, "Where were we?"

Her shiny thing was trying to distract her. Kayn laughed, "You don't seriously believe I'm going to just carry on with my day without an explaination."

Grinning, Frost seduced, "It would be easier if you did. I'm not allowed to say anything yet."

Her afterlife felt like endless sacrifices with reprehensible behaviour, partying and snacks. Honestly, she wasn't even sure what warranted a reaction anymore.

Taking her hand, Frost telepathically answered, *'Kind of. Do you want a snack?'*

Yes, she did. She didn't give a shit if it was a cliche, she deserved a snack after seeing that crazy shit.

25
OVERTHROWING THE KING

*S*ometimes, *when power changes hands, there are no trumpets playing, no wars to be won, just a backroom deal and willing parties. This was one of those occasions.* Spat out of the vortex onto marble tile before crown council of the Third-Tier Realm disorientated, Arrianna looked up.

Holding out his hand, crown Prince Amadeus explained, "Second-Tier aren't built to travel between the realms, it may take you a minute to regain your bearings."

Amar wasn't here. What if they didn't believe him?

Smiling, the Prince helped Arrianna up, assuring, "Power has changed hands. My older sister has taken the throne. The King has been exiled. When he reveals your leader's location, the Guardians will decide the length of his entombment."

Taking in the luxurious, jewel-toned velvet curtains and ornate tapestries, Arrianna clarified, "Are you telling me the King of this realm stole my boyfriend's body?"

Motioning for her to come, Prince Amadeus, admitted, "For five hundred years we've been awaiting the Daughters Of Seth Prophecy. My brother believed Second-Tier fearing us would hold off the inevitable. The council refused to take preemptive measures to stop all possible Second-Tier births, knowing Earth's Guardians would never allow it. Only pure-blooded Third-Tier can use portals without detection. Our King entered your realm with every intention of violating the Correction treaty with your Guardians, he cloned himself so he wouldn't be missed. This gave us the means to dethrone him. Hopefully, our reaction to this act will shift the tides."

Stunned by who she'd been spending time with, strolling a dimly lit corridor with the Prince, Arrianna replied, "Good to hear."

Standing before a mural depicting a what appeared to be a galaxy with a golden sheen encompassing certain planets. Amadeus explained, "The glowing ones have atmospheres and resources capable of supporting intelligent life. First-Tier aren't self-aware. Their varying belief systems hinge on symbolism altered to suit a primitive need to cast judgement and seek power. First-Tier souls have a long way to evolve, your galaxy is relatively new. All civilisations have the ability to mature into the paradise envisioned during creation."

Trying to find home in the golden-hued planets, Arrianna gave up, and asked, "Which one is Earth?" Amadeus pointed to a tiny one off to the left. Assuming the planet they were on would be prominently displayed, she probed, "Where are we?"

Motioning at nothing, Amadeus teased, "Interdimension Portals didn't come up in science class. Distance and time are irrelevant. There are multiple versions of reality."

"Now, you've lost me," Arrianna laughed, impressed by his patience. Watching the Prince, she admitted, "You don't seem anything like your brother."

"I'm not," the royal responded. "I'm surprised you've been kind after what you were forced to endure to keep up the pretence. I can offer you something to lift your spirits."

Intrigued, Arrianna followed as he started walking away, saying, "I hope it's not wine. I've had a lifetime's worth to stomach your brother."

Chuckling, Amadeus disclosed, "When you see where we sent my corrupt sibling, you may want a celebratory glass." Eloquently waving his hand, revealing an invisible corridor, he prompted, "His punishment will be sent via Oracle to your Guardian as proof of intent. Moving forward, royalty shall be held accountable."

He vanished through a wall at the end of the hall. Closing her eyes, Arrianna stepped through into a darkened stable and wandered over to Amadeus, lovingly stroking a black stallion, asking, "Is that your horse?"

"Come closer, you'll figure it out," he urged, smiling.

Her eyes widened with delight as midnight angelic wings unfolded. Astonished, Arrianna confessed, "The child in me is freaking out. I didn't think these were real?"

Caressing the mystical creature of folklore and fairy tales, Amadeus disclosed, "They're immortal like us, but can only bond with a singular being, the attachment is eternal. We had to bring them with us."

Watching his connection with the being of her fantasy's, Arrianna noted, "Lexy refers to you as a friend, she doesn't make those easily."

Grinning, the Prince, confessed, "She's a force of nature. Being near her is an addictive rush of every emotion, all at once. Rationally, you know you're standing in the path of a tornado, and it might kill you, but it's so awe-inspiring you can't even make yourself move."

"You're into her," Arrianna taunted, seeing the truth in his eyes.

Grinning, Amadeus sparred, "She's in a confusing place romantically with three guys, putting my hat in the ring right now, wouldn't be good for my ego."

"Do First-Tier on other planets look like us?" Arrianna questioned, stroking the glorious winged being.

Smiling at her, Amadeus said, "No, inhabitants evolve to suit their environment. Planets are colder, hotter with more gravity or less. To put your mind at ease, Earth has the worst reputation in interplanetary travel. I've heard horror stories about the dark shit that happens if you crash. Earth is like a haunted house, you're curious enough to do a drive by but you wouldn't want to live there."

Laughing as they continued their stroll, she commented, "Why didn't you take the throne?"

Leading the way, Amadeus answered, "My sister is older. Honestly, I've never wanted it. I'd leave all of this behind to go hang out in your haunted house." Stopping, he passed her a small Ankh pendant, explaining, "You have Guardian offspring in Ankh, and we haven't hadn't had enough time to weed out the Third-Tier working my brother. There's no way he pulled this off by himself. It would be unwise to rock the boat with your Guardians. Keep that in your right hand, and we'll have a private telepathic connection. Helping her put on a tan cloak, Prince Amadeus whispered, "Not a word when we enter the viewing chamber. Our seats will be the only ones left." He scaled uneven cobblestone stairs.

Concealing the pendant, she caught up and followed

the Prince as he walked through a wall into a jade room. Oracles in teal robes with golden ties at their waist and gold bands on their heads with dangling glowing stones were kneeling by a pool. Royalty sat in plush feather topped chairs with their Queen in a crimson gown wearing a crown adorned in jewels. Amadeus sat with his sister. Amar waved in the last row. *The chair beside his was the last empty one.* She made her way to the back and sat by Amar. He raised a finger, hinting for her to be quiet as the water began swirling. Mesmerised by glowing pools, her eyelids grew heavy as she slipped into a dreamlike state.

A swirling black orb opened in the jungle and the ousted royal was spat out into the dirt. Scrambling to his feet, the King bellowed, "What is the meaning of this?" Enormous jaws descended, he was graphically devoured by a T-rex. The spinning vortex reopened, the overthrown royal was spat out once again. Leaping up, he felt for injuries, threatening, "I will kill every last one of you!" Raptors jumped out of the jungle. The King slowly backed away, commanding, "I am your master, prehistoric fiends!" Calculated as a pack of wolves, they attacked, grabbing limbs.

Haunting pitchy shrieking brought Arrianna back to her Immortal Testing as prehistoric carnivores savagely tore the defeated leader apart. With a graphic spray of blood, they took off with his limbs in jagged jaws. *Drawn and quartered by raptors, fitting punishment. She hadn't thought of herself as vengeful, but after what she'd endured to get to the truth, this was uncomfortably satisfying. Amadeus was right, she could use a drink.* A minute later, she was passed a goblet of wine. Smiling, Arrianna took it. *The Prince was right, she did need a filter.*

Amadeus' voice piped into her mind, *'Most Second-Tier do. Don't worry, there's no love lost for my sociopath* sibling. Your Oracle explained how his mistreatment of you, clued your Clan in that it wasn't Markus. Your love for Markus is admirable. I know what my brother put you through, morally. No need to filter on my account.'

Sipping her wine, Arrianna responded, *can everyone hear my thoughts or just you?*

Amadeus answered, 'What you're holding is an Ankh filter, it blocks your thoughts from anyone who isn't Ankh. I have a receptor. There's only one. My sister agreed we owed you privacy. Not even our Oracles can read your thoughts. Amar can hear you and any Ankh staff. Clan loyalty runs deep, you have nothing to fear.'

After being spat out of the void, the King got up cursing. Searching for a focal point, he whispered, "This is enough. You've made your point. Let me out of here."

They watched as he was killed in countless macabre ways by dinosaurs until he refused to get up. A clear encasement appeared, offering the King momentary reprieve. The newly crowned Queen spoke into the feed, "On the off chance you aren't intelligent enough to figure it out brother, you've been exiled for violating our treaty with the Guardians of Earth. It is now my reign. Tell me where the leader of Clan Ankh is?"

Smirking, the forcibly retired ruler, bartered, "I need out, you require answers, we can come to an agreement."

"There will be no deal, we can ride this out for months if need be," the Queen firmly decreed.

Sighing, the King confessed, "The host I placed Markus in has a blinking check engine light. He'll show up in the in-between soon enough. I certainly hope Markus' remarkably talented girlfriend is here for the show. I planned to keep her chained up as my pet. Don't punish her harshly, for aiding and bedding me."

The Queen's voice, stated, "Abetting you twat waffle."

Street cred for the Queen. Twat waffle, that was awesome.

Amadeus' voice was projected into the jungle, "Brother, tell us where Markus is so we can settle this conflict."

"Give me ten minutes with Arrianna, she'll get it out of me," he provoked, creepy grinning.

Asshole.

"We sent the poor girl back, you've wasted enough of her time," the Queen needled, breaking protocol by turning to wink at Arrianna.

Grasping at straws, the King declared, "If they don't hear from me, my associates have intructions. I'd tell you, but I'd hate to ruin the surprise."

Shit. Arrianna and Amar's eyes met. *When I left, they were all on the beach. They needed to be warned.*

'The Guardians are connected to our Oracles, they'll send backup. Get comfortable, you two are witnesses for Clan Ankh,' Amadeus rationalised, staring directly ahead.

"You'll tell us everything when you grow weary of this," the Queen taunted. "There are clone winners in the jungle. If you can find one willing to help you survive in dinosaur laden jungle for seven days, you may opt for entombment." The shield protecting him vanished.

Defiantly, the King stated, "Agreed," sprinting into the jungle. Running with all his might past greenery and tropical flowers until he found a cave, he strolled in smiling like he'd won. A dozen starving clones of Seth Hogan and James Tanko stepped out of the darkness into flickering campfire light wielding rustic weapons. Insolently, the banished royal solicited, "Which of you shall be rewarded with riches for helping the King?"

Eyeing up the ruler a James Tanko clone inched

closer, taunting, "Funny story, a guy showed up at our hotel room in Vegas, asking if we'd be willing to do a private comedy show. We were drugged, kidnapped and taken to another world, where we were cloned and eaten by dinosaurs for entertainment. We made it out eventually, and instead of being returned to Earth, we were granted jobs as janitors cleaning up after pompous immortal assholes."

This wasn't the alien abduction scenario she'd envisioned.

"Stop backing away, wait for the punchline, King dipshit of pretentious asshole land," a Seth Hogan clone harassed. "We've been deprived of nutrients in a machine that speeds up starvation, brainwashed into craving human meat, and dropped back into this jungle of dinosaurs. Side note, you look delicious. I know, I'm having cannibal feelings. How about you, James?"

Eyeing up the King like a snack, James confessed, "Deep, intense carnivorous emotions."

Insolently, the King proclaimed, "I am ruler of this realm! You will not threaten me, clones!"

Grinning in unison, they charged with weapons raised as the King booked it out into the jungle right into a T-rex's jaws. The pack of clones stepped into the safety of the cave. James menacingly pointed, scolding, "We get the next one, you asshole, that was bullshit."

Hundreds of times, the overthrown ruler dropped from a swirling vortex into the jungle and ran the gauntlet into either cannibal comedians or ferocious dinosaurs until they were summoned into an adjoining room behind a red velvet curtain to dine with royalty, leaving their Oracles projecting the feed. After the new Queen sat at the elaborate table, they silently sat down. *The shock was wearing off. She'd been with that abusive King for days knowing it wasn't Markus. She'd never been asked to push her boundaries like a Siren.* A plate was placed in front of her. *The face she adored was now attached to vile deeds and self-disgust. What if they couldn't get past it?*

Concerned, Prince Amadeus whispered, "Pretending an imposter was the man you love was a lot to ask. You aren't accustomed to deciet."

Arrianna confessed, "I've been unfaithful, it hurts."

Trying to lighten her spirits, Amadeus rationalised, "Not technically."

Placing mystery meat in a thick tortilla with no utensils, tears clouded her eyes, Arrianna laughed. *It was true.*

Snapping fingers, the Queen announced, "Second-Tier, do you have questions?"

It felt like she should err on the side of caution, but this was her one chance to get away with it. Arrianna asked, "I understand the reason for the Correction at sixteen. I know you use energy as a power source but the technology is well within your means. Can't we just turn in bad Tri-Clan for Testing?"

"Would you do it?" Amadeus probed, smiling.

No, they wouldn't. She knew it.

Intrigued by her reply, the Queen responded, "I used to feel the same way until the weight of the galaxy was placed on my shoulders. In taking on this throne, I checked to see if the future has been altered. It hasn't."

Amar rationed, "Each choice alters a scenario, nothing is set in stone."

The Queen decreed, "Earth's volatile population must prove itself capable of understanding that having opposable thumbs and the ability to stand upright doesn't make them more worthy of life. Even with clauses to help humanity grasp their planet's frailty, they refuse to see. Until you've evolved past self-destruction during trials and comprehend, you are but a species in a vast foodchain supporting all life, we must continue testing so only those intellectually capable of immortality return to Earth. The trials start during your sixteenth year. Only souls Guardian's deem worthy are granted a second chance as sacrificial lambs for the greater good. Tri-Clan trains your partially mortal brains to reboot without a shock response after injury or death. Through this trauma, you attach to your Clan to make sure your fight or flight response comprehends greater good in a worst-case scenario. This is why you can't get out of Immortal Testing without your Clan. This process began over a millenium ago with our sacrifice. We killed our offspring, prohibited breeding with First-Tier, and left our home planet, knowing emotional ignorance was only going to gain momentum."

"You have us there" Arrianna commented.

The Queen responded, "My brother didn't see you as anything but half breed locusts. I know Tri-Clan is prepared to maintain order by whatever means necessary on Earth. I value your service and hope we can work together as allies."

Raising his goblet, Amar toasted, "To saving the world."

26
IRRESPONSIBLE ALLIES

Meanwhile back on Earth, Ankh had thrown caution to the wind with no idea they'd just dethroned a Third-Tier King. Blissfully unaware of the payback en route, some snuggled by a firepit as others danced to music hushed by interludes of thunderous crashing waves.

Witnessing the sun's breathtaking descent into the sea, mesmerised by shimmering light on the surface extending to shore with Frost's arms encircling her waist as water lapped at her thighs, a final hint of radiance glinted, dulled, and vanished leaving only the soft luminescence of a slivered moon. "Where do you think Markus is?" Kayn asked in near darkness.

He's alive somewhere. If he were dead, he'd show up in the in-between," Frost replied, swaying to music. Tenderly kissing her shoulder, he baited, "Race you to our room."

Pushing him into the water, Kayn dashed to shore. He caught up, passing friends by the fire, grabbed her, and she tumbled into the sand, taking him with her.

Giggling on their backs as night lit up with stars, Kayn enquired, "Where are we off to next?"

"Haley and Astrid should be here by dawn, then we're headed to the Ankh Crypt. We'll train newbies in the in-between while we're waiting for Arrianna and Amar to show up. Hopefully, they'll know where Markus is."

They'd been ordered to do insane things in recent weeks. It helped to know it wasn't Markus setting them up for failure. A wave of nausea, cramp her stomach. *Shit.* Looking his way flat on her back in the sand, Kayn whispered, "Did you feel that?"

"What?" Frost probed, peacefully watching stars.

Maybe she drank too much?

Frost sat up, asserting, "I felt that. I'll warn everyone. Get the demon blades from the trunk."

Yelling was muffled by crashing waves as she sprinted to Ankh's vehicles and commenced yanking on locked doors. *No keys, damn it.* An incapacitating pitch dropped Kayn to her knees. Covering her ears as windows exploded impaled her with projectiles, her senses shrieked until torture ceased. Confused, she opened her eyes. Headlights were flashing in eerie silence. *She couldn't hear anything. All she smelled was copper. She was bleeding.* Struggling to get up, she stumbled, plucking visible glass out of herself. *What happened?* Heat signatures were battling on the beach with trailing streaks of orange and yellow. Her Ankh symbol heated. *They were being taken out. Wait... why was she in the parking lot?* Dizzy and broiling hot, she yanked out shards so she could heal. There was a hunk in her neck. *Oh, darn.* Plucking it out of her artery, a thick gush of blood considerably slimmed her odds. *Why couldn't she think?* She felt her head. *Not cool.* A chunk of glass was embedded in her brain. *Good times.* Well, this was a *no chance scenario.* She tugged it out, blood poured into her eyes. *She'd lost too much blood. She was going down.* Staggering, Kayn's ears buzzed and popped. Shots echoed in flashing light. *She needed energy to heal.* Mortal auras barking orders in another language had guns pointed at her. *This wasn't the Aries Group. She wasn't allowed to eat people. She was going to pass out.* During her abilities last-ditch effort, Kayn noticed way too many bullet wounds in her torso with shards of glass sticking out of everywhere like she was an immortal pin cushion. *When did they shoot her?* She plucked glass out, saucily slurring, "What kind of asshole brings a gun to an immortal fight?" Another shot rang out, the lights went out.

FEELING SAFE, TWITCHING FINGERS IN SAND, KAYN PEERED up. *That sucked.* Most of Ankh was sitting there chatting. Looked for her Handler, she got up. *Zach wasn't here yet, neither was Lexy, Orin, Emery or Mel. Ugh, she was the first Healer down. This was embarrassing.*

Strolling over, Frost teased, "Problem finding the demon blades?"

That pitch took me down in the parking lot, the windows exploded, I had so much glass in me, I didn't notice I'd been shredded by bullets," Kayn disclosed, stepping into his arms.

"It took me down too, I was shot five seconds in," Frost admitted, kissing her sweetly.

Crosslegged in the sand, tuned into the fight, their Oracle interjected, "Assassins were hired to take us out if Markus didn't check in. My orders were to evacuate the Aries Group employees without alerting anyone."

Irritated they were taken out by gun-toting mortals,

Frost stated, "You need to find a way to counteract the effects of that device."

"If the Aries Group remotely set it off, it was to help us. Get comfortable, most of us won't be healed until backup shows up. Our Healers are severely injured but not deceased. Lexy and Emery are the only two still fighting."

"Of course," Grey said, grinning.

Smiling, Jenna pressed, "Seriously, go have fun. I need to concentrate."

Grey cursed, "Damn it, kid." Everyone turned to look.

Dean was holding a seashell. "Awesome," Kayn cackled.

Confused, Dean said, "I wanted to hear the ocean."

"Oh, you will," Frost commented as tremors underfoot, and a thunderous whoosh drew everyone's attention to the towering wall of approaching water. Frost shouted, "Run! We jump, you jump!"

They took off like a stampede of mustangs in the desert pursued until they reached the sand's end and leapt into the air. Water rushed over the edge like a waterfall, through the woods below. Familiar with the agony of thrashing through branches in an otherworldy tsunami, Kayn resigned to let go, knowing it would be over soon. Vanishing beneath churning water, bodies flailed by as torturous trees thrashed flesh, the relentless current bubbled crimson as she succumbed to the freedom of having nothing within her control. As no more than flopping, tumbling flesh and broken bones, she thought of happy things until harsh reality subsided, leaving her on a peaceful shore. Only ever offered a momentary reprieve, she raised her eyes to bravely face what came next. *Seriously?* Two traumatised newbies were huddled together on a beach with no idea a truck-sized arachnid was poised to leap from a rock bluff above. *She remembered this place, shit.* Grabbing driftwood for a weapon, Kayn got up, saying, "Behind you." Shrieking, they ran into the cave as it leapt, creating an explosion of sand. *It didn't matter how much of a badass she wanted to be when faced with a spider. It could be the size of a Buick or teeny-tiny as a thumbtack, adrenaline didn't care, she was going to irrationally lose her shit.*

Screaming in the caves drew the spider's attention away. *There was no escaping what fate had in store. If you didn't face the giant one you were covered in tiny spiders, shimmying through a narrow passage between rocks. This was the lesson they needed to learn to have a chance in the Testing.* Distant pitchy shrieks of terror carried over the back noise of crashing waves. *The other newbies were dealing with flesh-eating wasps on the other side of the island if the trials were the same.* As more massive spine-chilling spiders crawled over the bluff, Kayn saw a shell on the beach. *It was tempting. She could pick it up and wash the spiders out to sea. With her luck, she'd end up riding one. Here we go.* A spider reared, spraying webbing, spinning her into a cocoon. *She didn't have to be here. She could think of anywhere and go there. Terrified, her mind couldn't settle on a destination. Safety. Rose Quartz.*

In a flash of blinding light, Kayn was barefoot in snow. Giggling, she bounced to the steaming rose quartz pool. *This was a great memory. She'd wanted Frost but wasn't ready to admit it. Now that she was, their time together always went by too quickly. She healed fast, there wasn't going to be time to look for him. About now, she'd settle for a slushy drink before waking in the land of the living.* One appeared with a yellow umbrella. *Nice.* Lounging in the glowing pool with Ankh's healing stone, sipping from a curly straw, Kayn gave relaxation a shot. *Had the newbies chosen to leap into a frozen pool or brave the flesh-eating hornets? Looking back, choosing their fate together was monumental in joining her Testing group. She'd woken up in a rose quartz healing tomb with a Clan of immortals she barely knew. Zach was left by Triad, and due to a selfless act, Mel was taken from Trinity. Just like that, they were a team of players in an immortal game with slim odds of survival. As their journey began, Grey gave the mismatched trio peach cider in plastic pink flamingo wine glasses. Instant friends, they toasted sharing stories. With Sami's defiance issues, it might be about attaching him to anyone.* She heard someone. *Frost found her.* She didn't need to look.

"Grey and I woke up in the forest," Frost announced, wading in bare-chested. Sexier than anyone had a right to be, he submerged himself in the glowing seductive pool. Rising out of the steam like a fantasy, he sat beside her, lacing their fingers, he intimately kissing her hand, whispering, "I'm glad I found you before you healed."

Resting her head on his shoulder smiling, Kayn disclosed, "I washed up on spider island beach a second before one jumped on the newbies."

"That's awesome," Frost chuckled. "They are training ass backwards. Who went into the cave?"

"Dean and Molly," she replied, enjoying their seclusion.

Jiggling laughing, Frost commented, "Poor Emma."

He hadn't mentioned Sami. "How are we going to fix the Sami situation?" Kayn sighed in the euphoria of the pool.

Snuggling her, he confessed, "All we can do is hope they attach during the trauma of training for Testing. I'm not sure what you said, but Amar's kid was much nicer on the beach." Beaming, Frost probed, "What did you do?"

"Zach got him to write a list of things he wanted to experience, we vowed to make it happen. A reward for every twenty-four hours he was nice," Kayn confessed, straddling his lap.

Gazing into her eyes, Frost caressed her face, provoking, "The infamous unbucket list. What's missing from yours?"

"Just making out with you in this pool," Kayn seduced, with her lips hovering a breath from his, toying with control. The intensity of their Sirenesque attraction called her bluff as their lips met in gratuitous freedom. Struggling to remove sparse ivory in-between attire as the all too familiar tingling travelling her being, she giggled, "Not now. No…" Turning to sand, her essence dissipated into the air.

"Raincheck," Frost chuckled. Smiling, sipping her drink.

SHE'D COME TO IN WILD SITUATIONS BEFORE, BUT THIS ONE *was a seedy romance memoir.* Restrained by her wrists, dangling from the ceiling with the sensation of motion and vibration of tires. *What in the hell?* Squirming in a bloody bikini, tugging at chained hands in a see-through box with Emery hanging beside her. *The lights were so hot. Were they in a giant terrarium?* Kayn commented, "You'd think, I'd be used to waking up in strange places."

Chillest captive ever, Emery pointed out, "No point in struggling, look at the symbol above us. You'll never guess what that guy's name is?"

What guy? Squinting in intense light, Kayn saw someone sleeping in a backwards-facing seat.

"His name is Clarice," Emery giggled.

They were in a glass box with Clarice holding them captive. It was hilarious. Poking Emery with a foot, Kayn whispered, "Why aren't we trying to escape?"

"You died, I let myself be captured," Emery confessed, dangling like an amazonian goddess in her bikini. "They're trying to keep us weak with low oxygen, intense heat and UV lighting. Clearly, Clarice has no idea what he's dealing with. The symbol on the ceiling and spelt chains mean someone in their circle does. I didn't want to miss an opportunity to cut the snake's head off." Swinging to boot the side of their encasement, Emery harassed, "Hope you're not religious Clarice! Kidnapping me is a hefty soul fine!" When he didn't react, Emery explained, "He's listening to music, napping."

It was stifling. She was so thirsty. "So, we're just letting them take us?" Kayn mumbled, lightheaded. *The brutal headache was subsiding. That was never good.* As her eyelids grew heavier, she slurred, "Oxygen deprivation or brain melting?"

"Could be either. Pretend to struggle, when he uncorks the hole, I'll keep him entertained. Maybe he'll forget to plug it long enough to revive you? There's airconditioning, it'll be easier to escape later if you're conscious," Emery instructed, kicking the glass, squirming, feigning distress.

Their unwitting captor leapt up and uncorked an orange-sized hole. Oxygen rushed in. *Oh, thank God.*

"Sorry, I fell asleep," Clarice apologised. "I'll sit closer." Towing his seat over, he said, "You're alive."

He was referring to her. Kayn's sense of humour reared its head as she deepened her voice, "Do you know who we are, Clarice?"

"Brujas," the boy answered matter of factly.

Leaning in, Emery translated, "Witches."

She knew what Bruja meant. Usually, they went with aliens. They may not know what they were doing, but the heat was rather effective at taking her out. She couldn't even think.

As Emery kept the hole unplugged by overshared naughty exploits, she tuned it out. *Kevin, can you hear me? I'm trapped in a giant lizard terrarium in the back of a truck somewhere in Mexico. She was too weak. He wasn't going to hear her.* Regaling spicy telenovela worthy tales of her exploits, unfazed by the heat, Emery's sizzling stories took a personal turn as she gave naughty details about hookups with Kevin, Zach and Grey. "I don't want to hear this shit," Kayn said, sweating to death, literally. As Emery carried on describing intimate encounters with Frost, her intentions were clear. *She was trying to piss her off.*

Kevin's voice piped into her internal dialogue, *'Did I hear that right? You are in a lizard terrarium in the back of a truck in Mexico?'*

Tell me you guys are still in Mexico, Kayn replied via thought.

'Part of Trinity is already at the resort healing your Clan. I'm with Patrick and Steph, we're almost there. You've been taken. Who else do they have?' Kevin questioned via their connection.

We're in chained to a roof of a sweltering see-through box in bikinis.

'Who is with you?' Kevin grilled, to get a clear picture.

I'm sorry, it's so hot in here. I'm with Emery. Their connection went silent. *Damn it, Kevin. Don't make it weird. She's entertaining our guard with the details of her sex life, so he doesn't recork the hole, we'll suffocate.*

Kevin's voice piped into her mind, *'Sorry, I wasn't trying to make it weird, I was just wrapping my mind around the scenario you're in. Are we talking about the same drop-dead gorgeous black goddess? Unnervingly sexy, hottest woman I've ever seen, Siren Emery?'*

Ouch, that stung a little, I guess so.

Kevin probed, *'She remembers me then? Man, that was one of the hottest nights I've ever had. Say hi.'*

Earth to Kevin, I'm half-naked in a stifling box with hoodoo on the ceiling can we focus on getting me out?

'I have to pull over, I'm driving,' Kevin explained. After an extended silence, he returned, *'Okay, now I can focus. I want to see what's going on. Look up at the symbol on the roof.'*

Kayn looked up, holding her gaze.

He prompted, *'Let me see the entire scenario. The glass, how everything is set up.'*

She slowly moved her eyes around where she was being contained, and at Emery tied to the ceiling.

He questioned, *'Are your feet solidly on the floor?'*

She couldn't see anything past her chest. *They are.*

'You're part Guardian. I know it's hot and confusing. Focus on one thing at a time, not the entire picture. What annoys you the most? If it's heat, blow the lights. If the symbol is bothering you, tug yourself up there and wipe it off. You may need to think outside the box to get outside of this. Be the all-powerful being you're destined to be and bust out,' Kevin urged in her head.

The speech reminded her of her teenage years when he was her track and field cheering section. His voice was still a trigger in her heart to keep going. Even with the hole unplugged, her brain was frying like an egg on a skillet. She needed to kill the glaring terrarium lighting. One thing at a time. With her arms restrained, she raised her head, willing the light to explode, nothing happened. *She was too weak.*

'One way didn't work. Switch plans and keep trying. You are a badass, wipe off that symbol,' Kevin instructed.

You're overestimating my energy level. Mesmerized by sordid tales, their captor was hanging on every word. *If*

I take too much of her energy, he'll plug the hole. I'll have a time limit.

'What are your options?' Kevin rationalised.

Stretching a leg, her foot contacted Emery's skin, heating as it siphoned, a rush of euphoric energy flooded her senses.

'Stop Kayn,' Kevin prompted.

Glaring at sweltering lighting, willing anything to surface, they exploded. Clarice thought a bulb blew. *Now, to get rid of the symbol.* Grabbing hold of the chain securing her wrists, Kayn lifted herself and flipped upsidedown. Smudging the symbol with her feet, she dropped. *Now, the chains.* Releasing a primal scream, Kayn snapped her restraints. The vehicle swerved. *Whoops.* Clarice was yelling at the driver, banging on the wall.

Breaking her restraints like it was no big deal, Emery laughed as vibrating wheels on pavement ceased. Tires spun, followed by the unmistakable sensation of falling.

Emery shouted, "Heads up, Clarice!" A flash of light shot from her hand, creating a protective orb around their young panicking captor.

That was cool. She'd accidentally done something like this before. Emery encased Kayn in a womblike bubble, they bounced off each other in the terrarium during decent, the orbs burst on impact. Unharmed, Clarice ran to the back, yanking on the door, screaming. *Shit, they were floating.* Water rushed in.

Emery shouted, "Let us out, Clarice! The choices you make in your final moments matter!"

With water up to his waist, the mortal heroically fought to open their enclosure, sobbing, "I'm not this person. It was quick money. It's a smooth box with no locks or seams. You were in here when I showed up, we're going to die. We're locked in from the outside."

Meeting Clarice's eyes, Emery reached out of the hole, offering, "Take my hand, you don't have to be alone." As his hand touched hers, she affirmed, "You tried to help. You've proven yourself worthy." Clarice slumped into the water as a tiny white orb shot through the top of the truck.

Drowning wasn't the worst way to go. She'd already been shot, stabbed and broiled today. You still there, Kevin?

"First order of business, let's protect these bodies from sea critters and decay. This is one of my favourites," Emery stated, encasing them in a womblike bubble together. As water began coming through the hole, Emery declared, "I want to find out who wrecked our vacation. Are you in?"

Yeah, if they find our bodies. "Sure, why not," Kayn laughed. In a blinding flash, everything tickled as she shot up through bubbling water towards kicking feet. With another burst of light, she gasped treading water at the surface. Confused but happy to be alive, she swam with all her might. Washed onto shore by a wave, Kayn crawled until she felt dry sand.

A deep voice, complained, "No fair, you get to be the hot one. Want to trade?"

Scrambling to her feet, Kayn spun, searching for Emery, trying to grasp the situation. *What was this?* "Who are you?" She grilled, fists balled ready to deck a middle-aged man.

Laughing, the stranger taunted, "Look at your hands, you'll figure it out."

Holy shit. There was black hair all over her arms. *What the? How did it happen?* She was wearing men's shorts. Her legs were hairy. *What was that? Holy crap, was she a man?* Freaking out, she saw a familiar twinkle in the middle-aged guy's eyes. *No frigging way. It wasn't. No.* "Emery?"

Beaming, Emery in a man suit, checked out her bodies wallet, revealing, "I can own Juan. That's a sexy name. Check out yours before our ride gets here, so you don't blow our cover."

Removing the wallet from her pocket to see who she was, Kayn looked at the DMV picture and mumbled, "Andre." Stunned, she climbed up the embankment after Emery in a Juan suit. As they reached the road, Kayn enquired, "How did you do this?" *She'd better put her back.*

Laughing, Juan provoked, "I know where our bodies are. Don't you worry about a thing, Daddy's got this."

Daddy? Dumfounded, she heard a choppy noise in the sky and looked up. *Was that a helicopter? Wait… if Juan was Emery, and this was Seth. Ugh, that meant every-one…Gross…Nooo.*

As the helicopter landed on the road, Seth in a Juan suit, patted her shoulder, declaring, "A father, son road trip, how exciting. Remember, you are Andre, I'm Juan."

Fuck, guess this was happening.

The Beginning

THE CHILDREN OF ANKH SERIES UNIVERSE

There are many books in this universe to keep you occupied while you await the next one. Read on Dragon lovers.

CHILDREN OF ANKH SERIES

Sweet Sleep
Enlightenment
Let There Be Dragons
Handlers Of Dragons
Tragic Fools

COA SERIES (FULL LENGTH BOOKS IN THE SAME UNIVERSE)

Wild Thing
Wicked Thing
Deplorable Me

COA NOVELLA SERIES

Bring Out Your Dead (A short novella)

THE CHILDREN OF ANKH SERIES UNIVERSE

Subscribe to The Children of Ankh Universe website and be the first to get updates, contests, and series release info. Hope to hear from you on social media.
"She's a batshit feral hitwoman for a Clan of immortals, and sometimes just a girl in love with a boy destined to be her Handler. The only thing standing in their way is cannibalism and intimacy induced amnesia.

Jump into Lexy's part of the universe. BUY IT HERE:
www.childrenofankh.com

BIOGRAPHY

Kim Cormack is the always comedic author of the darkly twisted epic paranormal romance series, "The Children of Ankh." She worked for over 16 years as an Early Childhood educator in preschool, daycare, and as an aid. She has M.S and has lived most of her life on Vancouver Island in beautiful British Columbia, Canada. She currently lives in the gorgeous little town of Port Alberni. She's a single mom with two sons, one in high school and another in University at VIU. If you see her, back away slowly, and toss packages of hot sauce at her until you escape.

Subscribe for welcome to the children of ankh series universe freebies.
www.childrenofankh.com

A PERSONAL NOTE FROM THE AUTHOR

I began writing this series shortly after my M.S diagnosis. I had many reasons to fight. I had incredible children, a wonderful family, and amazing friends, but this series gave me a purpose. Whenever things become dark, I use my imagination to find the light within myself. No matter what life throws your way, you are stronger than you believe. My hope is that the character's strength becomes an inner voice for the readers that need it. Stand back up and if you can't stand... Rise within yourself. We are all beautiful just as we are. We are all immortal.

All heroes are born from the embers that linger after the fire of great tragedy.

She slept a dreamless sleep free of dragons for she had slain them once again.

Dragon doodle page. Who is your dream ship? Send your series fan art to the website, it will be posted in a place of honour.

www.ingramcontent.com/pod-product-compliance
Lightning Source LLC
Chambersburg PA
CBHW071426070526
44578CB00001B/12